MW01534448

Coal Dust
And
Cave Mud

The Memoir of A

Coal Miner's Son

Hubert Clark Crowell

TO: CHRIS & JACK

Hubert C. Crowell

Published by Hubert C. Crowell

Marietta, Georgia

ISBN: 978-0-9894572-0-0

LCCN: 2012919051

1 2 3 4 5 6 7 8 9 10

"Without a dream we have nothing. What is life but a dream and being able to put a little bit of it to work." Hubert H. Crowell.

DEDICATED TO
MY MOTHER

Who put up with so much and who showed me how to have a good time
enjoying the great things that life has to offer.

Ola Nellie Clark

CONTENTS

PREFACE

Growing up just seems to happen, there is no stopping it. We get older each day. Along the way we have experiences that keep coming back and replaying in our minds over and over again. At some point in life a lot of us will have the urge to write about them. I don't know if my life is much different than all the other men who grew up in the 50's and 60's, but I would like to share it with you anyway.

Some people say that we are who we are because of our environment and genes, but things have happened to me that lead me to believe that there is a something more directing our lives on this small planet. There are connections that are hard to explain. Connections with the people we meet and the places we live and visit. When I paused and looked back on my life I found lots of things that seemed divinely directed. A lot of them were not necessary about me, but about others and I only played a small part in it. For example, when writing this book I knew that I needed someone to proof read it. As I neared completion of the book a new co–worker told me of her previous employment with a publisher and that she had done a lot of proof reading. You could just take this as good fortune, but I take as a God thing. He not only met her need for a new job, but at the same time provided a friend to proof my books!

ACKNOWLEDGMENTS

To Kathleen for the love and patience she has shown me through the years. For my daughter, Deanna, for the joy she has brought me. I would also like to thank my sister, Pat, for the stories of my past and for keeping the pictures. A special thanks to Jenny, who spent time proofing my work and giving me suggestions.

CHAPTER 1 MILLSTONE

I was born in Seco, Kentucky, near the Virginia state line. I was told that the doctor was drunk at the time, which may explain a few strange scars I have. We lived in the mining community of Millstone. The house was a cap board shack on the side of Millstone creek, which was prone to flash floods. My crib was under an old stove pipe in the ceiling that had been plugged up with papers. During a storm the paper got wet and fell out, covering me from head to toe with black soot. They laughed at me and said that I was the blackest baby they had ever seen.

Mom and Patsy at Millstone Creek

Aunt Pauline and Patsy

And that is how I started out in this life of adventure. The Clark family was mostly fun–loving, easy–going farmers. The Crowell family was mostly serious and hard–working coal miners. My dad worked for his father in the coal mines before the depression, and during the depression Dad went back to school in Providence, Kentucky, picking up in the eight grade at the age of eighteen. He played football until he was too old to play high school football, and then he graduated at the top of his class. Mom was the most beautiful girl in school, and Dad was the most popular. When they were married on June 14, 1936, at the Pleasant Valley Baptist church in Webster County, the church was full, and people were standing on anything they could find to look through the windows of the church.

The coal town of Millstone is at the junction of Millstone Creek and the North Fork of the Kentucky River, 4 ½ miles northeast of Whitesburg. A post office was established there on December 17, 1878, and the town was named Craftsville for the family of Enoch Craft, a Confederate Army veteran. It was renamed Millstone on June 19, 1918, and the Southeast Coal Company built a camp there that year.

Nicknames

When I look back on all the names of our friends and family, we all seemed to have nicknames and were not called by our real names. My middle name was changed from Clark to Clarkie. My sister's name, Patricia, was changed to Patsy, and Catherine was called Cathy. But my first cousin was called Bobby–and that may be his real name! I guess it sounded good to have a "y" or "ie" on the end.

Nightmare

I must have some attachment to the coal miners of the Appalachian mountains. I was born in a small coal mining community in the eastern Kentucky coal fields. Dad was a supervisor in charge of one of the mining crews. He started mining in western Kentucky and had taken a job near Seco, Kentucky in 1941, the year I was born, only three months after being certified to qualify for the position of Foreman of Coal Mines by the Commonwealth of Kentucky Department of Mines and Minerals.

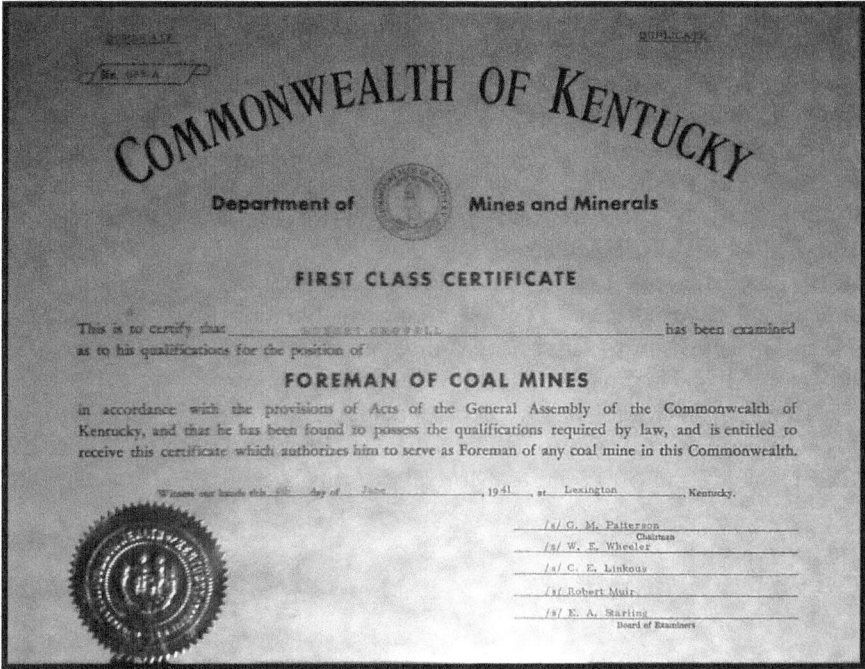

June 4th, 1941, Dad's foreman papers

I had never thought much about East Kentucky and had never had dreams about coal mining until twenty–nine years later when I had an experience that changed my whole outlook on life and the things that affect us. I would not call it supernatural, but I do know that when tragic events occur, it is felt by more than the ones that are directly involved.

On December 30, 1970, I awoke after having a nightmare about a coal mine disaster, and I shared the vivid dream with my wife. I had never dreamed about mines or disasters before and was quite surprised. Later that day we heard on the news about the Finley Coal Co. explosion in which thirty–eight people were killed. The location of the mine was given as eastern Kentucky near Hyden, Kentucky, only a few miles from Seco, where I was born. The explosion was caused by excessive coal dust and other combustible materials, insufficient rock dust, and other violations. The coal dust explosion was so extensive that dust and other materials were expelled from all eight openings of the mine.

Thirty–four widows and 103 children were left to mourn the loss. I do not know what possible connection other than being born so close to the disaster could cause me to have that dream. I only lived there a short time and had no relatives in the area.

3

Sleepwalking

Another strange event that was connected with that region occurred while I was very young.

Several years after moving back to Providence, we made a visit back to east Kentucky to see Uncle James Crowell and Aunt Christine. Their son Bobby was a year older than I. My uncle was working in the mines at the time. Bobby was a sleep walker. The house they lived in was a two story with a banister overlooking the downstairs. Bobby was walking the banister rail in his sleep. They were afraid to wake him for fear of scaring him and causing him to fall. I never understood how someone asleep could balance so well. The image of him is still clear in my mind.

After they moved back to Providence, Bobby and I remained very close, sharing and playing together. When he broke up with his girlfriend in his teens, we ran off together. More about this later!

CHAPTER 2 PROVIDENCE

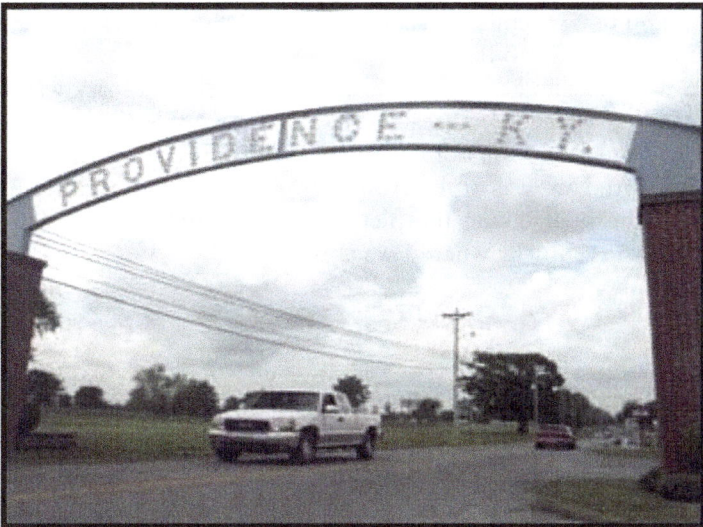

Providence, Kentucky arch

In Providence, Kentucky, population 4,400, the sign never seems to change—and there may be fewer people living there now. Located in Webster County and in the center of the West Kentucky coal field, farming and mining were the main source of employment. At one time Providence was the third largest tobacco stemming location in the country. We even had a tobacco barn behind our house.

I grew up in Providence, and though we moved a lot during my school years, we seemed to return to Providence at least for short periods. I was born in the East Kentucky coal fields where dad worked at the time, however I have no memories of that, only stories told to me.

Providence had sinkholes all around from all the underground mining. Strip mining was visible all over the county; the cuts were not filled in and most were filled with water. Some were used for dumps and others made great swimming holes.

Dad operated a small independent coal mine until he received his draft notice in 1944. After the war he returned to operating the mine near Providence. He was given a medical discharge on July 12, 1945 with a Purple Heart and Oak Leaf Cluster. He never talked about the war until he was much older, too much pain. Dad's biography is at the end of this book. [1]

My earliest memory, strange as it may seem, was standing in a latrine with Dad at Camp Fannin, Texas in 1944. I was three, and the metal urinal that reached the floor must have impressed me. I have no other memories of the visit there. We must not have stayed long as dad was finishing up boot camp and getting ready to be shipped off to the war. My sister says that Mom and us two children stayed in the small town off base, and Dad would slip out at night to be with us.

There was actually an earlier memory, although the story was told so many times that I may have dreamed it. But I have this image of my baby bottle slowly sinking to the bottom of a lake. My sister Patsy kept me from going in after it! Dad was at the front of the boat fishing and Mom was at the back of the boat taking the picture. I think that we had just moved back from East Kentucky where I was born.

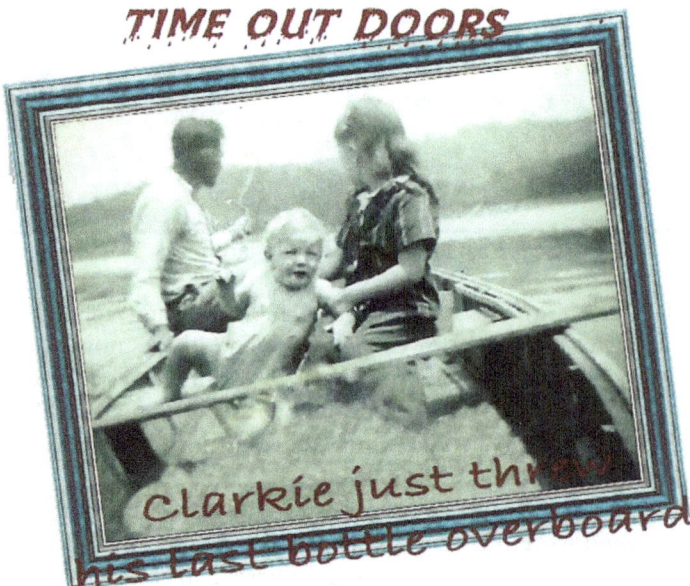

TIME OUT DOORS

clarkie just threw his last bottle overboard

Me during my second year, 1943

I also have a vivid memory of riding in the boat along the shore of an island in the lake and seeing a big cave. We pulled up and spent the night in it. Patsy has memories of a big rat in the cave. They kept telling me that I was too young to remember the trip, so here is my sister's version of the story:

Fishing with daddy was always an adventure. It may not have been a good adventure always, but it sure always made a memory. The day this picture was taken, we {Mama, Daddy, Clarkie and Me(Patsy)} were out for a day of fishing on Kentucky Lake. Everything was going fine until Clarkie pitched a hissey and threw his only bottle over the side of the boat into the lake. As I was trying to keep him from going over the side after his bottle, Mama decided it would make a good picture, and she was right.

The day got longer and longer We were tired, so Daddy decided it was too late to go home. He had caught one fish, and he saw a cave upon the hillside that looked (to him) like a good place to spend the night. I don't know about anyone else, but as soon as I looked into that cave and saw the BIG red eyes of a monster rat I was not a happy camper.

Mama had quieted Clarkie, and he was asleep on a pallet in the cave (with the rat). Daddy had made a fire and packed the fish in mud to cook all night for our breakfast in the morning (yuk!).

They wanted me to lay down by Clarkie and go to sleep, but no way with that rat looking at me, even though they told me it would not hurt me. They only got me to lie down when they promised me I could sleep between them. I didn't know a thing until I woke up the next morning on the outside next to the hole where I saw the rat. I never did quite trust Daddy on camping or fishing trips after that.

This was my first caving trip. I guess you could say that I was destined to be a caver from the start! I can still picture that cave though, not up on a hill as my sister described, but almost level with the lake. It was a large opening with lots of small holes in the rock. The floor was level and smooth, and the room was quite large.

As I Remember Providence

As I remember, Providence can be best expressed in a poem written for my poetry class. We were required to pick a place and write a description of it. I was 68 years old when I took the online class.

Providence, Ky., Coal Town, USA

Welcome to Providence, as you drive under the arch to my home town.
There is no town square, only a single traffic light to mark uptown,
where on Saturday nights we would all collect and hang out
looking for something to do, take in a movie or shoot some pool.
Like a village lost in time, nothing seems to change.
Streets are quiet by ten at night as if everyone had gone to bed.

Theater, restaurant, department stores and two pool halls,
police and fire department make up the main business section of town;
live stock auction and stockyard, just a block away.
Let's take a tour to my home from the center of town.
On my bike I can coast to within two blocks of home,
like a roller coaster ride down the long hill.

South down the hill for four blocks, past Coopers clothing store,
Plymouth dealership, Methodist church, Piggly Wiggly store and barber shop,
strong smell of coal dust as we cross the railroad tracks that skirts the town.
My grammar school is there on the hill to the right with dirty dark bricks,
like a prison waiting to hold us hostage most of the day,
swings moving in the breeze as if children were still at play.

Next door to the school stands Victory Baptist Church were we attended.
My favorite teacher, Mrs. Nickels, lived two houses ahead on the right,
The first home I remember is next door on the corner with white shingles.
A cinder block wall around the yard along the sidewalk was great for climbing.
Here I learned to first ride a bicycle down the alley and to the church,
shot a hole in my thumb with my first BB gun.

We moved across the street, second house on the left.
It looked huge when I was a child, imitation stone and two story,
now that I am older it looks like a small New England cottage.
Business have now closed, a statue of a miner stands were Coopers store
once stood, theater, restaurants, stores and pool halls all have gone.
Providence, a coal mining town, slowly drying up and dying.

Don't Shoot the Birds

The small house on Barbour street had a large yard for a city lot. Dad
built a garage, and we had a small garden. We had sidewalks and a paved
street. The yard was about two feet above the sidewalk with a cinder block
retaining wall on two sides. I had been given a BB gun for Christmas and
was looking for anything to shoot at. Mom was always saying, "Don't
shoot the birds," so I found other things to shoot at. For some curious
reason, I wondered if I could shoot the tobacco out of a cigarette butt. I
held the butt over the end of the BB gun and pulled the trigger. I missed
the butt but got my thumb. What a mess.

Dad was working for the West Kentucky Coal Company in 1950 and
was in charge of the underground operations at the large mine south of
Providence, Kentucky. He was making good money, and Mom was always
remodeling the house. One of the projects was to dig a basement under

the existing house. During the last stages of construction there were quite a few cinder blocks in the unfinished basement. Several of my friends and I took the blocks and built two forts, one in each corner of the basement. We then got our BB guns and had a battle. I kept getting hit in the back until I discovered that the other side was shooting at the wall behind me and the BB's were ricocheting around that basement like crazy. No one was hurt, but that ended the BB gun duels in the basement.

Dad would take me out to the mines quite often and give me small jobs to keep me busy. Before he took the job with the West Kentucky Coal Company, Dad owned a small mine south of town on Hwy. 109. This was a shallow mine in the side of a hill, and they used a small pony to pull the coal car out of the mine. I remember dad giving me a hacksaw and a pipe to saw through. I worked all day on that pipe but never made much progress. The mine went under Hwy. 109 on a hill. Later the mine settled in and a large bump developed across the road. Dad told me that it was due to the mine below.

When Dad went to work for the West Kentucky Coal Company in 1949, he opened the underground operation of the Stony Point Mine. This larger mine was quite an operation. They would strip–mine the coal until the overburden would become too thick, and then dad would come in with the underground equipment. Then they would just start the tunnels in the side of the strip cuts, avoiding the need for digging slopes to get to the coal. Modern equipment was used in the new mine, and I was interested in the front end loader. It had large arms in the front that scooped the coal up and onto a conveyor that reached out the back. Electric coal cars would back under the conveyor to be loaded. One day while barefoot, I jumped upon the front of the loader, felt the DC current and bounced right back off again. If I had stepped on it with one foot still on the ground, I am sure it would have killed me.

Dad let me splice the broken electrical cables that ran into the mine for the equipment. We would stagger the two cut wires and tie them into a square knot a few inches apart, then take a roll of rubber electrical tape and wrap the splice with the sticky side of the tape facing outward. We did this so you could quickly flip the roll of tape around the splice until the complete roll of tape was used up. This would stand the stress of pulling through the wet mine.

School Days, 1946 - 1952

My first and second school years were the best years of my school experience. I loved my first grade teacher, Mrs. Nickels, who lived next door to us. I was able to walk the few blocks to school from the first day. The floors in the schoolhouse were oiled wood and the stairs were worn from all the kids of Providence that ran up and down those halls. It was a brick two story building on a hill. In the basement was the lunch room and cafeteria. We would take our lunch money in each week or carry a lunch if we liked. Mom always gave me lunch money.

Holding Hands

My mind swims with thoughts of a pretty brunette,
In her hair she wore a small barrette.
As I walked her to school, I did not have the nerve,
to hold her hand or sit with her on the curb.
Day by day we would walk a little closer,
but if we touched I would lose my composure.
My hand would not leave my pocket,
and my mind would race like a rocket.
I remember the day and did not understand,
why she reached in my pocket and took my hand.
It felt wonderful, as we continued our walk,
secretly hoping, my buddies would not see us and talk.
Days in the second grade are gone forever,
but I will never forget that bold endeavor.

Third grade, third from left top row, second from right bottom row

In 1950 we lived on the corner of Barbour Street and S. Broadway Street. I was nine and in the third grade. The third grade was a rough year for me as I had a hard time learning to multiply and doing the other memory work, plus I seemed to get into a lot of fights. I can remember standing with my nose in a circle on the blackboard and having to hold books at arms length till they dropped as punishment for fighting in class.

When I Broke My Neck

Technically, I did not break my neck, but it sure seemed like it. The neck bones are interlocked, and I had one of them twisted out of the lock position and could not move my head. It was 1950 and I was in the third grade. One of the other boys and I were wrestling in the class room before class started, and he had a neck hold on me and was squeezing hard when something snapped. The teacher broke us up, and I knew that something bad was wrong because I could not straighten my head or move it.

Mom rushed to the school and took me to a chiropractor. The doctor checked me out, and then with both hands firmly grasped my head and snapped it back into place. He explained how the bones were interlocked and what had happened. He then explained that now that the damage was done, it would be very easy for the same thing to happen again. There was to be no more wrestling for me. I had to start learning how to avoid fights, at least the hand–to–hand type. It was hard for years afterward to walk away from bullies and to be called names. I guess in some ways the experiences helped me to become a loner–or at least not a follower. I chose my friends carefully and avoided rough groups and gangs. I sure disappointed my cousin Bobby when several years later he wanted me to take on a bully and I just walked away from him! It was just not worth it.

Rock fights were common on the school playground, and I seemed to always be the one that threw the rock that hurt someone. The playground was on the side of a steep hill, and we would throw rocks over the hill at each other without being able to see where the rocks landed. As fate would have it, I hit someone in the head.

I almost lost an eye about that time. We were breaking off old dried weeds and throwing them like spears. I was running and jumping over ditches when I fell and landed on the stump of one of the broken weeds. The dried stalk went in just above my eyeball below my eyebrow. I had a scar there for a long time. All this did not slow me down. It is a miracle that I survived my childhood days.

Another close call came that winter. We were sledding and always looking for the steepest hills. We would run and jump on the sled to get more speed. I was going fast and did not have much control when a stump got in my way. I stopped cold with my head right in the middle of that stump. It knocked me out cold for several minutes. I think that this is when I learned that my head was the toughest part of me, I also seemed to be top heavy. Any time I took a fall, I seemed to always land on my head. A few years later when we were living in Uniontown, Kentucky, they were clearing the school grounds and had a large pile of timber stacked up. We were climbing on it, and I fell from one of the large limbs sticking out of the pile and landed right on my head.

I also stepped on my share of rusty nails. I soon learned that if there were old boards laying around with nails, I would find them. Tetanus shots were common for me. I was twelve when I accepted Jesus as my Lord, and it was not a minute too soon. Without His protection I am sure that I would have not made it to age twenty. Although I have taken many falls, I have never had a broken bone. The out of place neck bone was the closest that I came.

Victory Baptist Church was only two blocks from where we lived in Providence. Like most kids I spent most of my time in church on the back pew. I was not even aware that I was listening to the sermon that Sunday, but when the invitation came at the end of the service, I almost ran down the isle. I knew from that day forward that God would be with me whatever I would be facing in the future.

School was just down the street a few blocks next to the railroad tracks. Across the tracks were the barber shop, gas station and the hill up to the center of town with one lone traffic light. Providence, Kentucky was a great place to grow up. My father's parents lived only a short distance in the other direction on Leeper Lane, which ran along the side of an abandoned railroad bed. My mother's father and her sister lived only two miles out of town to the west. I could ride my bike or walk to visit my grandparents on ether side anytime I wanted. As a matter of fact I was free to explore the whole town if I liked.

The Big Move

Mother had her eye on a larger home just a half of a block up the hill on Barbour Street. It was a three–story home with a complete apartment on each floor. One of the better ones in town at the time. In 1951 it came available and we moved in. It was great, we all had our own rooms. The upstairs was once a three–room apartment, and the kitchen was just to the right at the top of the stairs. The master bedroom was directly in front of the stairs overreaching the front porch. A second bedroom was on the left at the top of the stairs. My sisters got the bedroom on the left, our parents got the large bedroom, and the kitchen was converted into a small bedroom for me.

The kitchen bedroom was great. My bed was just under a window that overlooked the sun porch on the side of the house. The roof on the sun porch was flat, and I could step out of my window and onto the roof for a great view of the night sky. The kitchen sink remained, so I had running water in my bedroom. Under the sink there was a loose board that I removed for my secret hiding place. The fireplace chimney came up through the middle of my bedroom, creating a walk–in closet next to the sink and a great hiding place.

The house was heated with coal. In the basement corner room was the furnace and coal room. A chute on the side of the house allowed unloading the coal. You could slide down the chute to get into the house. Dad installed a stoker feeder to feed the small stoker coal into the bottom of the furnace, and occasionally we had to take out the clinkers that would build up from burning the coal. A boiler above the furnace supplied the steam to the radiators in each room of the house. Mom remodeled the house, creating an arch between the dinning room and the modern kitchen on the middle floor. She also added on a large back porch and had it screened in. We had perm–a–stone installed over the siding of the house so that it looked like a rock house.

There was a garage near the right side of the house. A driveway around the left side to the back led to the daylight side of the basement. The area under the back porch was a patio. A basement door with only one step down into the full basement that had a kitchen for a complete apartment. The back yard was large and had a drainage ditch in the middle. There was space for a garden on the other side of the ditch. I built a nine–by–nine–foot square fort there with a flat roof, and I sometimes had a second floor made of tobacco sticks.

Just up the hill on Barbour St. was the sawmill, which was a great source for building materials. The slabs or sides of the logs that were cut for lumber were free, and I hauled many of them home. The sawmill was also a great place to play with that mountain of sawdust to slide down. I still recall the heat from the sawdust when you would bury your feet deep.

The pavement ended at the mill, and the dirt road continued down to a field of sugar cane. There was a grinding mill in the middle of the field where a mule would walk around with a long pole attached to the mill. At the bottom of the hill Barbour Street ended. To the left was several strip cuts and the county dump. One of the strip cuts was full of clear water and made a great swimming hole with high banks to jump from. To the right the road followed the coal mine railroad to the road that lead out to the Clark farm and Pleasant Valley Road.

The field behind the house had an old tobacco barn and shallow pond that was a great place to play. Tobacco sticks are about one–and–a–half–inch square and about five feet long. They used them to place across the many rafters in the tall barn and hang tobacco on. The barn was no longer used and was full of tobacco sticks. We would climb the rafters and stack the sticks on them for flooring. We also used them to make rafts for the pond and building forts. At one time my next door neighbor Tommy and I dug a long ditch and, using the sticks, cardboard and scrap boards, placed a roof over the ditch and covered it with dirt. It made a great tunnel and hide out.

Dad knew about all the old coal mines that were under the town, and when our septic tank failed, he brought in a drill rig and drilled down into an old abandoned mine tunnel. When the drill hit the coal seam, dad knew that he was in the center of a pillar left to support the roof. He lowered a few sticks of dynamite down the hole and blasted out the side of the pillar into the mine. After that we never had trouble with the septic tank again.

Toby

Quite often on Saturdays I would ride down past the school and along the access road that ran along the tracks to the ice house and then out Hwy. 293 to the Clark Farm. The old farm house was on a hill overlooking the rolling farm land of west Kentucky. Grandpa Clark loved the house because of the breeze that always blew across the large front porch where he had his favorite chair. My uncle Paul and aunt Pauline lived with Grandpa and took care of him. Uncle Paul had a bird dog named Toby who was trained very well. Whenever anyone would come up to the house, Toby would run out to greet them and stick out his paw. He would continue to stick out his paw until you shook it, then leave you alone.

Toby was my best friend. We ran through the fields and played all day. Aunt Pauline had told me that Toby was not allowed to come into the house, but one day I was determined to bring Toby inside. I struggled with him and finally managed to get him through the back screen door. When I let go, he crashed through the screen to get out. He had been trained well and knew that he was not allowed in the house.

Aunt Pauline loved to make work into play, and she always had some project that we could work on. She sold Stanley products around the county, and we would unpack the boxes and stock the shelves in the small house that was down near the road in front of the main house. They always had a hammock or two in the yard to play in and a barn to climb through. My uncle Paul let me drive the tractor and help him build a new barn.

They loved to swim, and each year they would find a new spot for a pond and build a dock for swimming at each new pond. I can remember at least four ponds in which we swam and hunted frogs in, and each had a dock. I loved to watch aunt Pauline cook the frog legs, and when she put salt on them in the frying pan they would jump. Aunt Pauline was the oldest girl in the family of four girls and one boy, and their mother died at an early age, so she raised the younger girls. They had horses, a couple of cows, goats and chickens. Cherry trees lined one side of the house, and the large lawn had two tapioca trees with plenty of caterpillars on the large leaves for fishing. I loved to climb up into the cherry trees and eat the cherries with the birds. On the other side of the house was a large garden which always provided more fun work, like riding on the wood slide that uncle Paul would pull around with the tractor to level the garden. I think he used aunt Pauline and me for weights to hold down the sled.

Grandpa Clark taught me to play Crazy Eights and we would play for hours. He would sit on his porch and smoke his pipe, throwing the spent matches over the side. We would pick up the matches and build forts in the dirt with them. Each year during vacation time the families would return to Providence to visit, and we would have a great time with all the cousins.

I would go for long walks with Grandpa Clark in the woods, and he would show me how to make all kinds of things from the branches and bark. He could take a green stick about the size of your thumb and make a whistle by cutting the bark so that it would slide off, then cutting a flat side on the stick followed by a notch. Then slide the bark back on the stick and you had a great whistle. He also showed me how to braid strips of bark or binding cords used for bailing hay, into a whip. If you tied a strip of leather on the end, you could make the whip pop with a loud crack.

When Toby died a few years later, it was just not quite the same. When you visited the farm there was no longer a bird dog that came out to shake your hand.

Childhood Memories

I remember building forts with matches discarded at the end of the porch,
the sweet smell of that pipe packed with tobacco for your afternoon smoke,
playing Crazy Eights on the porch and having to go to the bone yard,
your favorite recliner on the corner of the porch, you could see for miles.

I remember long walks through the woods to the lake behind the farm
where you cut a young sapling, slid the bark off and made a whistle.
You showed me how to braid the bailing twine stored in the barn,
four strands would make a round rope, and three strands a flat one.

I remember the whips we would make tying the rope to a stick
and adding a single strand at the end to give a loud crack in the air,
the sparkle in your eyes when you saw us coming for a visit,
your bird dog Toby always there to greet us with a paw in the air.

I remember the catalpa tree you planted in the front yard for fish bait,
the yellow and black, fat juicy worms were great, and the fish loved them,
the heavy barrel .22 rifle you used to kill hogs, that you gave to me,
and the smoke house were the hams hung, right were you could see it.

I remember the old clock on the mantle and the chimes it made,
A story about a passing Indian who gave you a clay pipe
with a large carving of a deer stepping over a log with large antlers.

You gave me the pipe along with a leather case with purple padding.

I remember stories of a loving father from your four lovely daughters,
A newspaper article mentioning a visit of Mr. Clark from the country.
You were always happy and laughed a lot, loved your chair on the porch
and said you always had a good breeze and could see your friends drive by.

Benjamin Luther Clark, 1881-1955

The Ledger

The nineteenth century country store was more like a trading post than just a store. Farmers swapped all kinds of products and crops for supplies, and they seldom paid cash except when they took their harvest to markets. Outstanding bills were often paid once a year.

The Yarbro store was a typical western Kentucky farm store. It was located between Providence and Princeton near the Tradewater River to serve the local farmers in the community of Yarbro, Kentucky.

There was this old book that laid around the Clark farm for years. My aunt Marie even drew pictures in the back of it. No one wanted to discard it. It was retrieved by my cousin Jerry Ziegler, and he keep it safe for years, then passed it on to me.

The nine–inch–by–fourteen–inch–by–two–inch thick book is dark from years of use, with red corners and a black design on the cloth cover. The edges are torn, and the cardboard backing under the cloth is showing. The binder has five sections divided by ¾ inch ribs. Each section is two inches high.

The top section is plain and had been eaten through to the edges of the pages inside, leaving a one–by–two–inch hole.

The second section from the top is black with a border design across the top and bottom in gold. The word "LEDGER" is printed in ¼ inch high gold letters across the middle.

The next section down is also plain and had two black border lines across the top and two across the bottom.

The next section down is red with the same gold border design as the black section. There is no printing, but there may have been an index number, but it ss worn and hard to tell.

On the front is the name "**H. D. Yarbrough, Yarbro, Ky**." Huston D. Yarbrough was born in February 1880 and married V. E. Wood on April 19, 1898 in Webster County, Kentucky

Inside the back cover is a drawing of a lady with a hat, gloves and a wide collar dress. One hand is on the back of the hat, and the other is holding a small handbag. The dress has a belt with eight buttons, a note states that it was drawn by Marie, August, 17, 1938. Twelve pages have been cut out of the back of the ledger. Pages 384 through 522 are blank. Pages 523 through 544 are missing, and 545 is blank. Page 546 has the drawing.

Page 391 list expenses for the hospital stay at Vanderbilt Hospital and funeral expenses for Luther Clark..

The ledger was used by the store during two periods, 1911-1912 and 1922. The first pages of the ledger contains an alphabet index of the store customers and the pages for transactions.

The earliest entry is December 31, 1909, where a transfer was made from an older book. Balances still on the book by September 29, 1922 were transferred to an account slip. I am not sure if the store closed then or what happened.

Most of the last names are very familiar, and a lot of my relatives are listed in the ledger.

I could not find any record of Yarbro, Ky. The road that I believe it was located on is now called Barnes Store Road, State Route 293.

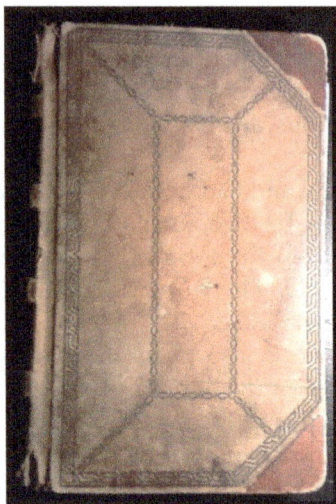

Yarbro Store Ledger

LEDGER INDEX

	NAME	PAGE	TIME FRAME & NOTES
A:	Jas Adkins	29	7/14/1910 – 1/18/1911
	Sam Armstrong	125	4/1/1911 – 2/20/1912
	Frank Armstrong	108	4/3/1911 – 8/26/1911
(Sugg)	J. J. Armstrong	6	7/30/1911 – 9/12/1911
B:	Bassett Brown	1,2,3	3/11/1910 – 2/12/1911
	Amberis Brown	5	12/31/1909 – 11/30/1911
	Anderson Brown	7	1/19/1910 – 7/19/1911
	Bill B. Browm	9	4/4/1910 – 4/29/1910
	Morgan Brown	11	4/1/1910 – 10/16/1911
	John W. Brown	13	5/13/1910 – 10/23/911
	Greenie Brown	15	10/6/1910 – 1/13/1911
	J. H. Beard	17	2/21/1910 – 2/11/1911
	Sarah Bruce	19	3/19/1910 – 9/13/1912 [1]
	J. N. Bruce	21	3/19/1910 – 11/30/1910 [2]

[1] Last purchase was on 11/20/1911, and the balance of $1.00 was paid off with one bushel of pears.

[2] Last purchase was on 11/30/1910, $10.00 was paid by Lillie on 1/31/1911, $5.00 on 9/2/1911 and $4.05 on 12/20/1912.

	Johnie R. Bruce	23	2/16/1910 – 12/23/1911 [3]
	Annie Bruce	27	3/28/1910 – 9/30/1911
	Jas Bassett	29	6/14/1910 – 1/18/1911
	W. H. Barnes	31	9/10/1910 – 5/31/1912
	Ellis Bright	33	5/14/1910 – 12/21/1911
	W. B. Barker	35	3/19/1910 – no other entry
	Ann Brown	77	4/16/1910 – 1/30/1912
	Mance Brown	195	7/7/1910 – 3/6/1911
	Bill Burchfield	26	7/16/1911 – 10/30/1911
C:	W. W. Clark	37,38, 39,40	1/1/1910 – 2/15/1912 [4]
	Luther Clark	41,219, 220	5/13/1910 – 1/10/1912
	Geo Cullen	43	3/14/1910 – 12/19/1911
	W. E Curry	45	4/9/1910 – 1/20/1912
	Jas Crowell	47	3/14/1910 – 12/7/1911
	Jay Coffman	87	4/2/1910 – 10/24/1910
	Clarence Crittenden	42	4/14/1910 – 1/23/1911
	Love Crenshaw	183	4/15/1910 – 1/30/1912
	Frank Crenshaw	185	6/6/1910 – 12/7/1911
	Mrs. Annie Crowell	78	10/7/1911 – 1/1/1912
	Marshal Cullen	34	6/11910 – 1/8/1912
	Enach Curry	58	6/6/1910 – 2/6/1911
	William Crenshaw	161	1/10/1910 – 2/1/1911
	Ben Curry	46	9/29/1910 – 7/31/1911
	Geo Curry	56	1/18/1911 – 1/20/1912
	Joe Carpenter	40	4/18/1911 – 5/3/1911
	Vernon Crowder	10	5/22/1911 – 9/15/1912
	Roy Childress	10	6/8/1911 – 7/6/1911 [5]
	Dan Clark	4	7/22/1911 – 1/20/1912
	Vira Crowell	4	8/7/1911 – 12/1/1911
	J. Ed Cullen	367,368	7/22/1922 – 9/29/1922
	Will Conley	389	9/5/1922 – 9/29/1922
	B. l. Clark	273	Family Birth records

---

[3] Paid $75 by check on 1/25/1912, $2.00 by hauling on 11/20/1914, and $10 by cash on 2/15/1915.

[4] Note at bottom of page, "March 30, 1920 Paid in full."

[5] Account was paid off by Crarder Bursk.

Brooms		299,300	Family broom business
Broom corn on shares		301	
Days worked in brooms		302	
Cows bred		128	1933 thru 1949 entries
Sows bred		57 & 165	1943 thru 1950 entries
Old Nell mare bred		165	1942 & 1943 entries
D:	Burnel Doris	51	2/17/1910 – 2/12/1912
	John Doris	55	1/1/1910 – 4/1/1912
	Josep Doris	57	1/1/1910 – 4/1/1912
	J. F. Doris	59	5/31/1910 – 12/9/1911
	G. B. Doris	61	3/24/1910 – 12/18/1911
	P. J. Devers	65	3/11/1910 – 1/15/1912
	Joseph Devers	67	9/27/1910 – 1/1/1912
	Nel Devers	68	12/3/1910 – 12/21/1911
	Chester Dunbar	171,200, 221,222	1/1/1910 – 12/1/1911
	Hume Doris	68	4/9/1910 – 1/19/1911
	Lee Devers	193	6/14/1910 – 6\10/1911
	John L. Doris	199,212	7/23/1910 – 1/5/1912
	Geo Devers	68	9/3/1910 – 11/10/1911
	Polk Devers	194	9/20/1910 – 12/31/1911
	Clone Devers	68	12/3/1910 – 12/21/1911
	Walter Devers	68	1/10/1911 – 12/22/1911
	Dan Doris	206	2/28/1911 – 4/25/1911
	John H. Devers	9	9/16/1911 – 10/9/1911
	W. E. Dilender	305,306, 307	5/5/1922 – 9/29/1922
E:	Henry Evans	69	1/1/1910 to balance old book
	Mary Edward	21	1/2/1911 – 9/19/1911 [6]
F:	W. L. Fox	70	1/1/1910 – 11/11/1911
	Brownlaw Felker	73	1/1/1910 – 4/23/1912
	Barker Felker	74	1/1/1910 to balance old book
	Nel Felker	75,225	2/19/1910 – 7/17/1912
	Will Fox	181,182	4/13/1910 – 6/12/1911
	Zalman Fox	189,190, 213	5/4/1910 – 1/11/1912
	Henry Felker	72	5/10/1910 – 1/16/1912

---

[6] Account was paid off by Jas Williams on 3/23/1912.

	Billy Felker	74	7/23/1910 – 11/14/1911
	Mrs. Hattie Tike	150	7/28/1910 – 12/2/1911
	Fox Brothers	182,184	9/27/1910 – 11/1/1912
	Jas Felker	72,126	11/7/1910 – 12/21/191911
	Ed Lee Felker	72	11/12/1910 – 12/6/1911
	Jack Felker	73	12/2/1910 – 2/4/1911
	Charles R. Farmer	383	8/25/1922 – 9/29/1922
G:	J. G. Givens	76	4/8/1910 – 8/24/1911
	M. A. Givens	79	3/28/1910 – 1/15/1912
	Thamk B. Givens	81,94	4/8/1910 – 2/19/1912
	R. G. Givens	82	1/1/1910 to balance old book
	Evert Givens	83	6/9/1910 – 1/20/1912
	John B. Givens	85	4/28/1910 – 4/20/1912
	Jas Gobin	87	1/1/1910 to balance old book
	Mrs. Gobin	87	12/12/1910 – 9/2/1911 [7]
	Jas Givens	88	4/6/1910 – 2/23/1912
	Bill D. Gunther	91	3/19/1910 – 2/23/1912
	Miss. Sallie Givens	93	10/24/1910 – 12/27/1911
	Demmie Givens	90	1/26/1911 – 7/15/1911
	Thamk & Everett Givens	36	5/3/1911 – 12/9/1911
	Luther Glover	249,250, 251	3/11/1922 – 9/29/1922
	Charles H Gold	295,296, 297,298	4/27/1922 – 9/29/1922
H:	R. L. Hall	97	9/13/1910 – 2/11/1911
	John Hall	99	3/20/1910 – 1/10/1912
	Tom H. Hall	101	3/18/1910 – 1/10/1912
	Neely Holloman	105	1/1/1910 – 11/15/1910
	Joseph Harrington	106	1/1/1910 to balance old book
	Dan Holowell	107	1/1/1910 to balance old book
	Wm. N. Hubbard	108	1/1/1910 to balance old book
	Elizabeth H. Hutton	109	1/1/1910 – 2/13/1911
	John Hayden	69	4/9/1910 – 12/4/1911
	John D. Hunt	71	5/11/1910 – 6/6/1910
	Dan'l Hunt	71	5/11/1910 – 12/20/1911
	Allen Hart	202	12/5/1910 – 3/18/1911
	Dick Holowell	107	1/25/1911 – 5/9/1911

[7] Account was paid on by John Gobin on 9/2/1911.

	R. W. Hunter	26	8/30/1911 – 2/20/1912
	James O. Holloman	269,270	3/27/1922 – 9/29/1922
	John Hall	275,276, 277	4/3/1922 – 9/29/1922
	Lucien Hammond	335,336, 337	5/20/1922 – 9/29/1922
I:	Chas Ipock	110	
	James Ivy	110	10/12/1910 – 9/16/1911 [8]
J:	Mrs. Annie Jayce	13	8/11/1911 – 9/30/1911 [9]
K:	Jas Kemp	111	1/1/1910 – 11/1/1911
	Joseph Kain	143	1/1/1910 to balance old book
	B. B. Kelley	325,326	5/5/1922 – 9/29/1922
L:	Noah Ligett	113	1/1/1910 to balance old book
	Henry Lovan	113	1/1/1910 to balance old book[10]
	Walter E. Larkins	110,231	3/31/1910 – 3/15/1912
	Geo Larnson	112	4/11/1910 – 9/8/1911
	W. A. Lane	112	12/19/1911 – 1/11/1912
	Majars & Ledbetter	261	3/13/1922 – 4/22/1922
	Lanie Ledbitter	265	3/25/1922 – 9/29/1922
M:	John R. Melton	114,217	3/12/1910 – 12/30/1911
	Willie Marrs	116	
	Robert Miller	118	1/1/1910 – 2/13/1911
	Wm H. Mason	119	1/1/1910 to balance old book
	Mrs. Fanny Montgomery	118	5/12/1910 – 2/20/1912
	Bunard Massey	111	8/24/1910 – 4/24/1912
	Joe Montgomery	117	12/19/1910 – 2/4/1911
	John Montgomery	117	12/22/1910 – 11/7/1911
	Sam Montgomery	123	1/28/1911 – 2/15/1912
	Dollie Morse	118	3/11/1911 only entry
	Majars & Ledbetter	261	1/1/1910 – 9/30/1910

---

[8] Balance was paid off in 1922.

[9] 50 Lbs of sugar in 1911 cost $3.40.

[10] Balance was paid by Pete Ruark with produce and melons.

Mc:	Auther McVey	113	1/1/1910 to balance old book
	Edward McGregar	170	11/15/1910 – 12/29/1911
N:	Dan Neeley	120	1/1/1910 to balance old book
	Smith Neal	120	1/24/1911 – 3/26/1911
O:	M. T. Oakley	121	1/1/1910 to balance old book
	Herman Oakley	121	10/29/1910 – 10/28/1911
P:	Sam Perdue	122	
	Dillard Perdue	123	1/1/1910 to balance old book
	J. Breck Patts	124	6/19/1910 – 2/15/1912
	Joseph Paris	84	4/29/1910 – 6/17/1910
	Gus Poole	84	11/19/1910 – 4/17/1911
	John Parker	241,242, 243,244, 245	3/10/1922 – 9/29/1922
R:	J. W. Ramsey	127	1/31/1910 – 4/25/1912
	Sammel Ramsey	129	1/1/1910 – 6/30/1913
	Joseph Ramsey	131	3/11/1910 – 5/31/1912
	John Ruark	119	2/16/1910 – 12/25/1911
	(Dock) J. D. Ramsey	120	11/9/1910 – 4/16\1912
	H. Robinson	14	9/25/1911 – 11/13/1911
	Jas A. Ralph	4	10/13/1911 – 11/26/1911 [11]
	Bob Ramsey	16	12/21/1911 – 1/26/1912
	Ed Reynols	233,234	3/2/1922 – 9/29/1922
	Frank Ringo	331,332	5/12/1922 – 9/29/1922
S:	R. T. Skninner	133,134 135,136 137,138	1/1/1910 – 1/20/1912
	Benj Skinner	139,140, 141,142, 208,209, 210,227, 228	3/12/1910 – 5/11/1912
	Marian Skinner	143	1/1/1910 to balance old book
	Strother Stevens	144	1/1/1910 to balance old book
	Sam Stevens	145	

---

[11] Account was paid off with cash by Luther Clark on 1/20/1912 and 2/20/1912.

	Tamy Skinner	146	1/1/1910 to balance old book
	Greg Stevens	150	1/1/1910 to balance old book
	Will C. Stanley	149,186, 187	1/1/1910 – 12/18/1912
	Tom Seymore	145	9/24/1910 – 11/19/1910
	Lawrence Smith	211	5/13/1911 – 1/25/1912
	John Stevens	215	5/19/1911 – 3/8/1913
	Reese Stevens	78	11/13/1911 – 12/9/1911
	Lorame Syms	15	12/9/1911 only one entry
	Richard Smith	315,316	5/5/1922 –9/29/1922
	Nathan W. Scott	359,360	6/26/0922 – 9/29/1922
	Francis Smith	373	8/2/1922 – 9/29/1922
	Blain Sevens	379	8/21/1922 – 9\29/1922
	Chas. Spock	110	1/1/1910 to balance old book
T:	Mack Thompson	147	6/24/1910 – 1/20/1912
	Marian Trail	149	1/1/1910 to balance old book
	Sherman Trayler	150	1/1/1910 to balance old book
	Mrs. Hattie Tike	150	7/28/1910 – 12/2/1911
U:	Chas Utterback	151	2/4/1910 – 1/10/1912
	Oscar Utley	153	1/1/1910 to balance old book[12]
V:	Joseph Vinson	154	1/1/1910 to balance old book
	Elmer Vaughn	155	1/1/1910 to balance old book
W:	R. B. Wood	156,157	2/18/1910 – 1/20/1912
	John Wood	159,160	1/1/1910 – 1/30/1912
	Edward Wood	163	6/19/1910 – 12/21/1911
	Tom Warhook	165	1/1/1910 to balance old book
	Thas Wyatt	166	1/1/1910 to balance old book
	John Wilson	167,168	1/15/1910 – 12/26/1911
	Walter Wilson	169	6/9/1911 – 12/20/1911
	Pricie Wood	179	2/28/1910 – 2/7/1912
	Lee Wood	180	4/1/1910 – 2/8/1911
	Cary Wood	187	5/4/1910 – 12/13/1910
	James Williams	191,192, 203,204, 205	6/7/1910 – 3/23/1912
	May Wood	179	8/2/1910 – 1/15/1911

---

[12] Paid 4/22/1911 By acct to J. W. Brown $4.00, on a balance of $6.45.

	Iley Wood	180	8/17/1910 – 4/2/1911
	Rasco Wood	158	9/9/1910 – 12/29/1911
	Lee Wilson	119	12/8/1910 – 6/28/1910
	Calvin Wilson	169	1/16/1911 – 10/10/1911
	Lynn Wood	180	8/10/1911 – 9/25/1911
	Goldie Wade	20	10/17/1911
	Bert Wood	179	11/15/1911 – 12/30/1911
	Bert B. Wood	281	3/1/1922 – 9/29/1922
	Ed Webb	341,342	6/4/1922 – 9/29/1922
	Thomas F. Wyatt	349,350	6/15/1922 – 9/29/1922
Y:	W. M. Yarbrough	171,172, 173	3/7/1910 – 2/16/1912
	Will Yarbrough	175,176, 202	1/1/1910 – 12/27/1911 [13]
	Charley Yarbrough	197	7/18/1910 – 2/29/1912
	Jas C. Yarbrough	207	2/27/1911 – 1/21/1912
	James C. Yarbrough	283,284, 285,286	4/19/1922 – 9/29/1922

One of the more interesting patrons of the Yarbro Store was one Ellis Bright. The following entries were made on page 33.

1910					
May	14	To 5 gal oil	.70		
May	28	By cash	____	.70	
June	18	To healing oil	.50		
June	22	To 9 yds bed tick	1.80		
July	5	By chickens	____	2.30	
July	25	To 1 bobbin pearl	6.00		
Aug	2	To 1 sack	.10		
Aug	27	By cash	____	6.10	
Oct	15	To flour, meat & coffee	9.40		
Oct	27	By corn	____	9.40	
Dec	26	To shoes	5.00		
1911					
Jan	16	To 1 sweater	1.00		
Jan	31	By cash	____	6.00	

[13] The last transaction on 12/27/1911 says, "To Mrs W. A. Diver $4.50," followed by a Mar 15, 1913 entry, "By Note evendate. $106.32."

May	29	To shoes & ect.	5.75	
June	20	By hens	_____	.98
Dec	21	By cash	_____	4.77

This is a good example of the trading that took place and also the trust in giving credit with no interest.

Most of the trading in this book ended December 31, 1911. A few entries were made in 1922, when the current book must have filled up and they pulled out this old one to use until September 29, 1922, When a new book must have been started. Any transactions made after 1911 were only payments until the 1922 entries.

The Coal Mine Wars

Dad always ran a non–union coal mine, and when he took over the underground operations at Stony Point, it was also non–union. I first became aware that there were problems when the railway bridge that crossed HWY 293 at the edge of town was burned. The railroad was used to haul coal from the Stony Point coal mine. After that I can recall dad getting up in the middle of the night, grabbing his pistol and heading to the mine.

We were told to avoid the back roads that led to the mine as they were mined. The company hired the local police to guard the roads, and land mines were laid in front of a heavy log guard post with machine gun holes on each side. Union organizers were always trying to disrupt the operations by placing dynamite under the railroad cars. Once they dropped dynamite from an airplane over a nearby town. Dad knew most of the trouble makers and kept a close eye on them.

Stony Point Coal Mine

Stony Point was not far from us on the same side of town, so when I would walk or ride my bike out to Leaper Lane to visit Grandma, I could cross the lot behind her house and climb up the strip mine hills of the mine.

I would collect the dynamite wire buried in the dirt and use it to wire lights in my playhouse or build electric motors that would spin like crazy. It was around this time that the telephone company removed the old telephones and installed the new dial models. I would follow them around, collecting the batteries, which had nice clips on top for the wires. With all the copper wire and batteries I had, I was always looking for something to make. I made a motor using four nails and a board that would support the armature with a center nail resting on the wire between the vertical nails on each end. A couple of more nails wrapped with wire provided the magnet field. A couple of more wires for brushes touching a couple of pieces of tin foil, on the turning nail. Then I connected a battery to watch it spin. We made telegraph sets as well. It took more than a year to use up all those batteries.

Dad would take me out to the mine, and I loved to watch the men at work. Claude Cain was one of Dad's best employees. He maintained all the electrical equipment and ran the shop. One son, Larry Cain, was the same age as I and we played together a lot. Claude developed the wooden roof pins that were used in the mine when the roof conditions were wet. The wood would swell and hold the rock above in place.

In 1952 the Bureau of Mines published a circular on the successful use of wooden roof bolts in Stony Point Mine.[2]

Claude also loved to build racing boats. They lived just up the street from us, and I would watch him work on the boats.

When the strip mining operation reached a point that there was too much rock to move, they would leave one big cut down to the coal, and dad would take over driving tunnels into the coal.

This was before Continuous Miners, or Long Walls were invented. It was called conventional mining with room and pillar type of mining.

Stony Point, Moving Coal

Tradewater river flowing above
through the rock to tunnels below,
men digging coal a labor of love,
except for being so wet and low.

The more coal they removed,
allowed more water to creep in,
what they were doing had to be improved,
time was against them, no way to win.

There it lay black and waiting,
to be removed from below the river,
waiting for one with skill and planning,
it would be my dad who could deliver.

Holes drilled for metal roof bolts,
allowed for more water to flow,
wooden roof pins replaced the bolts,
first successful use and would not let go.

As wooden roof pins swell and hold,

the miners dug fast, never stopping,
moving coal from the deep wet hole,
needing motivation to keep digging.

Only one way, remove it swift,
before the river could overtake,
one new car a month to the shift,
digging the most without a break.

Miners won and retrieved the coal,
in the race against the mine flood,
diving new cars for meeting the goal,
after a year of sweat and blood.

The miners from their toil gave in return,
a new high school gym to the city,
Providence High students should learn
from these great men about giving freely.

Rosin Prank

I did not need to wait till Halloween to pull a prank, but it did bring to
mind a lot of them. One of my best was the rosin–and–string prank. I
pulled this off many times and never told anyone, even friends. It was just
my private secret. I would look for a nail or screen window hook on a
neighbor's house and tie a length of heavy string to it. I would then run
the string back a good ways to some bushes in which I could hide. Pulling
the string tight and rubbing the rosin up and down the string in long
strokes created a vibration up the string and into the house. I never knew
just how it sounded, since you couldn't hear the sound from outside, but it
sure must have sounded weird. I would watch the lights come on, doors
open, and they would come out on the porch looking for the source of the
noise. I would chuckle to my myself and wait until the house quieted back
down, then start rubbing the string again.

Lighting Strike

I loved to walk or ride my bike out to Leeper Lane and visit Grandma.
This was the same house that Dad and his brothers grew up in. The house
had four large rooms on the main floor and a fireplace in each room. Coal
was used in them to keep the house warm in winter, and a coal–burning
cook stove was in the kitchen. The upstairs was one large room, I imagine
that was where the boys slept. There were four boys and one girl. There
was a large back porch and a cistern the caught the water off the roof for

drinking. The front porch went completely across the front of the house. The front yard had two large oak climbing trees. I remember clearly standing at the end of that porch one evening as a thunderstorm approached. Lightning hit the ground not more that a few feet in front of me. I have never had a fear of lighting, but I do have a lot of respect for it.

Dad's brother lived further out on Leeper Lane. Uncle Ben and Aunt Evelyn had four girls and one boy. James was eleven years older than I, so I played with the girls. They were all tom girls, and when Bobby and I would visit, they would show us how to swing from tree to tree through the crab orchard. It was hard to keep up with them.

Their house burned down, and while they were building a new one, they lived with us in the house on Barbour Street. I recall seeing a jar of melted pennies from the house and a rifle with the barrel bent.

Uncle Ben worked at the mines also, and he died in 1960 in a mine accident, crushed between a loader and the mine wall.

Dixie was a year–and–half younger than I. She caught up with me in the eighth grade and helped me with my homework, and then she went ahead of me in school. I had a hard time keeping up!

Ball field

On the east side of town near where Bobby lived, there was a large field near the railroad tracks. Boys from all over town would gather there, choose up sides and play ball. Nearby was an old overgrown pond that my grandpa Crowell would fly fish in. I remember watching how smooth he would throw the line out to just the right spot in the pond. He ran a small – and I mean really small – gas station across town, and he would walk about two miles back and forth every day. The station was about ten–by–ten feet square, and flats were repaired outside. He died in 1951, so I have very few other memories of him. He was a very hard worker and never stopped. Grandma died in 1957. I remember her funeral well. I was even allowed to touch her cold hand.

Grandma Pat and Grandpa Crowell at his gas station

After a game of baseball, if there were coal cars on the tracks, we would run the cars. This was a very dangerous game. You would run down the inside of the empty car, up and over the middle, then back up again with enough speed to jump to the next car. Closer to the center of town the tracks passed below the school. We would also run the cars there. One day an air hose broke loose, making a very loud noise, and scarred the daylights out of me. I think that that may have ended my running of the railroad cars.

Paper Route

After getting my bicycle I took on a paper route for about a year. You would have to get up each morning before dawn and ride up town to the back of a store where the papers were dropped off. We would gather and fold the papers into a square for throwing, except on Sundays, when the paper was too thick, then we would roll it up. We were given a canvas saddlebag to place over the luggage carrier for the papers. My route went up through the north side of town, then down through the black section where about half of my customers lived. We were always given a few extra papers that we could sell or give away to new customers. The route continued across town to the tracks near were Bobby lived, then I would have a short ride back home and get ready for school. Once a week on a Saturday we would leave later, when everyone was up, and make our collections, turning the money over to the paper and getting our pay. Can't remember how much it was, I believe that it was a percentage of what we took in. The winter time was rough and cold on that bike, and we always went no matter what the weather was like. I never had any trouble collecting for the paper, and everyone was very nice.

I again delivered papers for a short time in Spring City. One of my customers, for some reason I can't remember why, I had to go through the house to collect. It was packed from floor to ceiling with books and papers. There was only a narrow path through the middle. I will never forget that especially – when my desk or work area at home starts to pile up!

Hunting and Fishing

Dad went hunting or fishing almost every weekend, and we ate plenty of wild game. Dad bought me a .410 shotgun, and I learned how to climb fences and walk through the woods without shooting someone or myself. When it came time to clean the game, I always had the job of holding the legs while Dad skinned the rabbits and squirrels.

Hunting was all serious stuff, with no playing around, but fishing was another story. If I got tired of fishing, I could just play along the bank, as long as I stayed far enough away and did not scare the fish away from where Dad was fishing. A lot of the time we fished late in the night or even spent the night. One spot Dad went to a lot was called Three Ponds. It was on the way to Kentucky Lake.

Dad built a small six–foot long plywood boat to place on top of the car for fishing trips. He took my cousin Bobby and I to Kentucky Lake once with the boat, and we crossed the lake just above the dam to a small island to spend the night. The next day a huge storm came up, and Dad did not think that the boat would stay afloat with all of us in it. He took us over to the dam and let us walk across while he took the boat across. We would stop and watch him disappear behind the waves as he ran the motor wide open, up one wave after another.

Other times we fished below the dam where the spillway was located. We snagged the fish in the swift water with large, four–pronged hooks. You did not need any bait.

We also spent a lot of time on the Ohio River fishing. Dad caught a river catfish once that was longer than I was. They hung it on a tree to skin it, and I remember standing next to it. After the floods we crossed over to the islands where the corn fields were flooded. The water had gone down and left large shallow pools with carp trapped. You could see the fins all over the muddy water. We wadded in and grab them in the mouth and tail, throwing them into large sacks. We tied the sacks to the sides of the boat and crossed the river to the car. We placed the boat on top of the car, and added water to keep the fish alive then headed for home. What we could not clean over the weekend we let loose in Uncle Paul's new pond for later.

Uncle Dan Clark

When I was eleven, my uncle, Dan Clark, lived with us for a while. He not only showed me how to be unbeaten in checkers, but also how to play chess. Uncle Dan was a very interesting person. He logged virgin timber in the Tennessee mountains, managed the grounds for Vanderbilt hospital in Nashville, Tennessee, repaired watches and played a lot of chess and checkers.

He told me about the time that he could not get grass to grow on the hospital grounds because of all the rocks. He had six inches of top soil spread over all the grounds to solve the problem.

Checkers is a game played by two persons, each with twelve pieces, on a checkerboard. You can only move forward on the black squares until you reach the king row, and then you can move that piece forward and backward. You must take jumps when offered, even if it means you lose two or more pieces in the process.

If at all possible you want to gain the advantage by taking two for one or position your piece between two opposing pieces where your opponent has no choice but to give up one or the other.

I have gotten rusty over the years and not played much checkers, so I make mistakes now. But I will never forget the basic strategy for the start of the game of checkers. Keep a pyramid of your pieces in front of you. With this pyramid you can block your opponent from reaching the king row and may gain the advantage by swapping one piece for two. Hold on to the pyramid for as long as possible and work your plays around it. With a little practice you will be able to become the master of the game of checkers.

Start out with the pieces on the sides. Move the three pieces on the left all forward one square, keeping the pyramid intact. Try to maintain this strong defensive formation, and look for the chance to swap one for two.

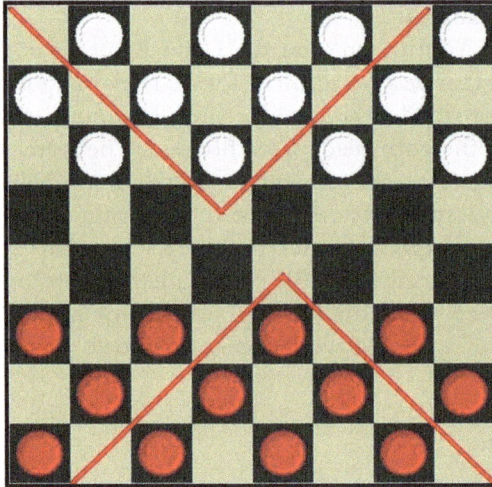

Keep a pyramid of your pieces in front of you

CHAPTER 3 MOVING AROUND THE SOUTHEAST

Uniontown

In 1952 we moved to Uniontown, Kentucky. I was 11 at the time and looked forward to the new experience. The company provided houses for the key personnel, and as dad was in charge, mom had first pick. She chose an old farmhouse, and mom got to remodel it totally at company expense. My bedroom was upstairs on the left side, and my sisters shared the bedroom in the back center upstairs with a bath. Mom and Dad had the bedroom upstairs on the right side. The stairway to the first floor was in the center going down to the back door with the kitchen on the right, utility room and garage on the left. Living and dining rooms were at the front.

Uniontown was on the Ohio River and had a levy built all the way around the riverside to the hill on the east side of town. The mine was on the south side of town just across the levy. The Uniontown coal mine was owned by Justin Potter, head of the Nashville Coal Company. It is estimated that it cost $6.5 million to open and was at the time the largest river coal mine in the United States, employing nearly seven hundred men. The road went under the long beltline that carried the coal to the river for loading onto barges. Dad arranged for the family to take a ride on the barge tugboat on the river. I was amazed at the way they could push the barges along the river in a long line.

Nashville Coal Company

Stony Point was owned by the Nashville Coal Company, and the Nashville Coal Company was owned by Justin Potter.

Justin K. Potter, generally known as Jet, was in the 1950's Tennessee's richest man, with a fortune estimated at $200 million. Justin (Jet) Potter never recognized John L. Lewis and the United Mine Workers of America

(UMWA). He was among the last of the big holdouts, refusing to fall into step even when the UMWA brought the industry's other giants into line. Hating all unions, he welded his fourteen–hundred miners into one of the most belligerently anti–union work forces in or out of the coal industry. If Lewis got nasty, Jet hired guns and threw up barricades around his mines. The barricades held. Of all the tough nuts in a tough–nut trade, Jet was the one Lewis could never crack. [3]

In 1953 the Nashville Coal Company opened a huge new Uniontown coal mine on the south edge of the town across the levy and within a quarter–mile of the Ohio River. Dad transferred from Stony Point and was placed in charge of the operation.

I remember how impressed I was when Mr. Potter, came and spent the night with us, in our new home in Uniontown, Kentucky.

Salty Well Water

The old farmhouse did not have running water before Mom had it remodeled. The well drillers came out and drilled down to the water table, looking for good water. All they got was the saltiest water I every tasted. If they drilled much deeper they would have struck oil, but we did not own the oil rights. There were several oil wells near by. I used to stop at them when riding my bike to town. The rubber washers used on the pumps made great cleaners for my bike. We would split them and slip them over the center part of the wheel between the spokes. They would spin and make the metal shine like new.

Under the back porch there was a cistern that was used to catch rainwater off the tin roof. It had not been used for years, so it had to be cleaned out. Dead rats, boards and all kinds of trash came up out of that hole. After it was cleaned we had water hauled in to keep it full. A pump supplied water to the new plumbing.

My room was upstairs, overlooking the driveway alongside the house and the alfalfa field. The ceiling sloped down on each side of the room. Mom had a sheet of plywood installed along one of the low walls that I could let down for my electric train set. My bed was under the window, and I could see the stars at night. We got our first television set while living here, a large B/W with only a few channels. Howdy Dowdy Time was my favorite. My sisters shared a room in the middle with a small bath, and Mom and Dad had their bedroom on the other end.

We had a gym set in the front yard that was my sister Cathy's, and we both spent many hours there. It had bars across the top for hand walking, swings and a slide.

The crossbars on the side were just the right height for climbing up and getting on top of my Shetland pony.

Shetland Pony

Dad was making good money at the mine, and for Christmas that year I got a pony. Some of the older small mines were still using ponies to haul coal out of the mines, and Dad bought one of them. The pony still had calluses on his back from the harness. I loved that pony, but he had a mind of his own. When I would get on him for a ride, he would not move.

A friend of mine from the farm next door would ride down, and then the Shetland pony would follow the horses wherever they went. When we turned to head back home, he would run at top speed to get back to his pasture.

The pasture belonged to my friend's family and they planted alfalfa in it. My pony loved it and got so round that I could not get my legs around him; I could however lay down on his back. I spent a good many hours just stretched out on his bare back while he grazed in the alfalfa field.

Crows, Tragedies and Prank

The farm across the road and a little closer to town had a large family, and I played with them on occasion. Just off their back porch was a large tree that the crows liked. Sometimes it would be so full of crows the limbs would bend and almost break. That's when they would bring out the shotgun and see how many crows they could kill with one shot! One of the boys died that year when they were cleaning a loaded gun. I think about that each time I pick up a gun.

My uncle William W. Clark was accidentally killed by his older brother when he was only nine years old. He was jumping on a brush pile to flush out a rabbit in 1921. Uncle Harley was only twelve at the time. He later became an electrician, and even as a teenager loved to play with electric.

The farm house had a swing on the front porch. Uncle Harley would attach a phone cranked magneto to each side chain and the girls would have a visitor sitting between them, they would grab their hands and Harley would turn the crank! Often the visitor would have to make a trip to the outhouse afterward.

Uncle Harley would think nothing of touching live electrical wires and would seldom turn the power off when connecting lights. He laid down on a pew in a church he was working on and passed away. I often wondered if all those shocks may have caused his heart to fail, or if it was the sorrow, over the loss of his brother.

Mountain Oysters

Most of the farmland around us belonged to a large farm next door heading away from Uniontown. They had a son that was just a little older than I was. We would ride the farm jeep all over the farm and go horseback riding. I would go with him on occasion when he would do his chores. One day there was a lot of activity up at the barn. They were castrating the steers. I was invited to a special breakfast the next day, but decided against it.

Log Cabin Hideout

Across the pasture behind the house there was a stream with water year around. Across the stream was the mine property with a service road that ran up the hill through the woods to the mine. I often walked to the mine to watch all the construction. Another friend whose father also worked at the mine would meet me half way. He was bigger and stronger than I was. We found a lot of evenly cut logs in the woods and decided to build a log cabin with them. We kept it a secret. Dad found it and let me know that we were using his mine props, but decided to let us have them with a warning not to take any more.

When my 12th birthday came around that year, Mom gave me a big surprise. When I arrived at my hideout, all my school friends were there singing Happy Birthday! I was so hurt that our secret hideout was a secret no more that I ran all the way back to the house and locked myself in the bathroom, crying my eyes out. I hoped that they enjoyed my party!

One secret that was not exposed was the time capsule I buried along the creek bank. I placed several things in it, but I cannot remember now what they were. I think that when we moved I dug it up.

Swimming Pool

Digging was fun for me, and I was always looking for an excuse to dig a hole. My little sister wanted a swimming pool, so we asked Mom if I could dig one for her. Mom was great at letting us do just about anything we wanted to do. So we picked a spot in the backyard and I started digging. Mom then ordered a small load of concrete, and I spread it out over the bottom and sides.

The Swimming Pool

As a kid I loved to dig again and again.
Holes and dirt fascinated me, I would dig like a pig,
or like a groundhog making a den.
I would look for any excuse to dig.

I offered to dig a swimming pool
for my sister complete with concrete lining.

Cathy was excited to wade and float in the cool
swimming pool built by her brother for reclining.

Mom consented and gave me a spot.
Shovel in hand and thoughts of digging to China,
I began to dig deeper and deeper until it got hot.
A challenge it was, and I knew it would be fine.

I mixed the concrete and spread it on thick,
like making icing for a cake, smooth then hard.
It sure felt good to dig such a nice pool so quick.
How proud I was of my hole in the yard.

When my sister got in she could only stand
and float, almost without touching the side.
There with her tube and the sides close at hand,
you see the swimming pool was deeper than it was wide!

Later in the fall Dad returned from a turkey shoot. They called it that, but they shot at targets, not turkeys, and then the winners would bring home prizes. Dad was a very good shot, and he hunted a lot. His prize this time was two geese. As it turned out, one was male and the other female. We would not let Mom kill them for Thanksgiving dinner. I found goose eggs all over the place, in the fields and even in the yard. They were huge and one egg would almost fill a frying pan. They were good though. Soon we had goslings following the mother goose all around the yard and they loved to swim in our swimming pool. [4]

After they were grown I found several of them dead along the stream, that ran between us and the mine property, with a patch of feathers missing from their underside. We believe that it was turtles that pulled them under and drowned them.

The swimming pool turned green, but winter was coming anyway.

Fireworks

I loved fireworks and could shoot them off all day long. In the back of comic books there were always ads for boxes of fireworks for twenty or thirty dollars. I saved up my allowance and placed an order for a big box.

When they came in the mail, I had a blast blowing up everything I could find. I would blow holes in the ground, make the toys fly in the air and at night set off Roman candles and rockets. They must have lasted for at least a week. Mom said she sure was glad when they were all gone!

Nails

That year I stepped on several nails, and of course they were all rusty. I had to get several tetanus shots. After school we played around an old woodpile, and there were a lot of nails left in the boards. To this day I remove every nail from any old board that I replace.

It was also a rough year at school in Uniontown. In the middle of the playground there was a large pile of brush and logs that made a great place to climb. There was one large limb sticking out of the brush pile about five feet off the ground. I was walking out on the limb when I slipped off and landed right on my head. I guess that was a good thing because Dad was always saying that I had a hard head. No damage was done, except being out for a little while. It was the second time in my life that I took a hard hit to the head, and I would have a few more in the years to come.

Hail Storm

It was the strangest thing I had ever seen. It was still warm weather when one morning we had a freak hail storm. The ice was piled up about two feet high on the side of the schoolhouse where it had blown.

By lunch time it was mostly gone, not even enough for a good snowball fight.

Time of Sorrow

Mother was expecting her fourth child, however he was stillborn. I felt guilty for a long time, thinking that I may have caused Mom to be stressed out. Cathy and I fought a lot and upset Mom. He is buried in the Fox Cemetery and was never given a name.

My Brother

The longer my mother cried, the tighter I held her.
A stillborn child, a lost brother, it still seems a blur.

Buried without a name in the cemetery on the hill,
never to feel the wind or to have that thrill,

of riding a bike with me through the countryside,
never to see the ocean, the waves or moon at high tide.

I longed for a bother to share life and all it has to offer,
but then again I know where he's at, and he did not suffer.

38

I blamed myself and thought I might have been the cause
by my actions, until I had time to think and pause.

There were more factors involved than I could perceive.
When things go wrong, how nearsighted we can be,

thinking we are always the ones at fault.
One day I will ask God about things that are difficult,

and sit down with my mother and brother to share
experiences, like caving and a close call with a bear,

and all the other experiences that life gave to me,
There must be a reason he died and not me.

My Dad's Friend Steve

Steve Steff worked with Dad in the mine. He was the General Superintendent and Dad was the Superintendent. Steve had a bulldog that was well trained. He would tell that dog to sit, and he would stay in the sitting position forever, or until he was released.

Steve must have liked me because he gave me a surplus 1884 Springfield trap door rifle. I proudly display it on my office wall. He told us that they were cleaning out an old Army depot and the government was selling off the old rifles still packed in grease from the Indian wars. I never fired it, but one time I did cut open a .410 shotgun shell to remove the buckshot, and then inserted the shell and fired the blank shell. The shotgun shell was a little tight, but it did fit. I did not want to ruin the rifle groves in the barrel by firing the buckshot through it.

Someone had carved a big H on the stock. It was there when I got it. maybe Steve thought it was for me as it had my initial already on it. Dad kept it for me, and later when I was settled down, I found it stored in the attic of Dad's Florida home.

Rescue Shaft

Dad would talk about the mine and the operations, but He did not take me into the Uniontown mine, though I did visit the showers and all the work clothes hanging from chains on pulleys. Each worker had a small cage attached to a chain that was tied to the wall. You could lower it and place your belongings in the cage and hang you street clothes on hooks attached to the cage. Then at the end of the shift the workers would swap clothes and raise the cage. The room look really weird with all those things hanging just above your head.

While the mine was digging the slope, I got caught in one of the blasts. Rock came raining down through the trees all around me, some of them quite large. I was glad when the slope was finished.

After the close call with the flying rocks, I stayed clear of the work that was going on. My friend and I dug some tunnels in the dirt banks that were left from some grading. Later, I was not involved, but one of the tunnels caved in on my friend. They got him out OK.

One problem the mine had was a bad roof. Dad was very concerned for the safety of the men, so he had a rescue shaft drilled upon the hill behind the house that reached down to the mine. As far as I know there was only one person that ever went through the hole. A worker was lowered down to punch out the last bit of coal at the bottom and decided it was easer to go out through the mine and ride out instead of going back up the hole.

Every time I hear about miners being trapped underground, I think about how wise Dad was to drill that hole. I hope that the practice was kept up after we left.

Being young I never quite understood exactly why Dad left Uniontown, but I did know that there was some disagreement at the management level.

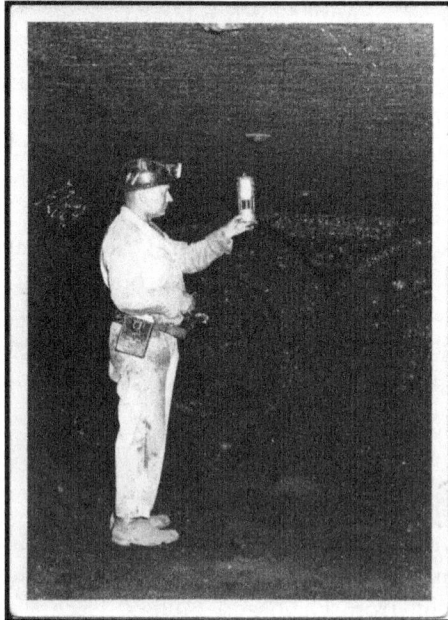

Dad checking for gas in Fies Mine, Madisonville, Ky.

In November, 1953 we moved back to Providence for a short time. We still owned the house there, and Dad worked at one of the local mines. In the summer of '54 we bought a house trailer and moved to Tennessee where Dad opened the first of two Tennessee coal mines.

Haletown

Haletown is not really a town. It is referred to as a populated place in Marion County, Tennessee. The marker at the I–24 rest area just before crossing the Tennessee River reads, "NICKAJACK CAVE, 5¼ miles southeast was the town of Nickajack or Anikusatiyi, destroyed by Ore's force. Sept. 14, 1974. The town occupied a space between the river and the cave in which was a storehouse for plunder. It was also used by the Confederacy during the War Between the States as a source of Saltpeter." Hales Bar Dam 5, built in 1913, was located on the Tennessee River below Chattanooga, Tennessee. I said "was" because it is now covered by the large Nickajack Lake. The dam was leaking so bad due to the caves in the limestone that a larger, more stable, dam had to be built in the 1960's down river.

Haletown, at Hales Bar Dam, is on the east side of the Tennessee river near the Alabama, Georgia and Tennessee state lines. Nickajack Cave is six miles down the river, and parts of that cave crosses under all three states, Georgia, Alabama and Tennessee. Haletown was no more than a post office and a trailer park found up Hicks Hollow Road. A few miles north, where Aetna Mountain Road winds up Aetna Mountain, Dad leased coal on the side of the mountain. Claude Cain, a close friend and mining partner, built the tipple and assembled the beltline that ran from the mine to the hill side for loading the coal onto trucks. There was a small stream that ran down the mountain and through the trailer park, and a shower house where Dad would clean up after working in the mine. The movie "Long, Long Trailer" had just come out, and Mom was excited about living in a trailer, so Dad bought one when we left Uniontown. We still owned the house in Providence and rented it out.

There were few boys to play with. There was a black boy that I made friends with during the short time we lived there. Before school started, we moved across the river to the Alabama line. This was a larger town with a theater and a few other things to do.

Nickajack Cave

Musician Johnny Cash visited the cave in early October 1967, intending to commit suicide inside it. But he had a spiritual experience there that caused him to stop his habit of drug abuse. Country singer Gary Allan recorded a song about this experience on his 2005 album, "Tough All Over".

Johnny Cash in his book, "CASH", said that he first visited the cave with friends, Bob Johnston once, and Hank Williams Jr. another time looking for Civil War and Indian artifacts. During his suicide attempt, he crawled for two or three hours until the batteries in his flashlight went dead, and he laid down to die! In the darkness he starting focusing on God, and there in Nickajack Cave became conscious of a very clear, simple idea: he was not in charge of his destiny. he was not in charge of his death. he was going to die at God's time, not his.

Nickajack Lake was filled up by December 16, 1967. The entrance to the cave was originally 140 feet wide and 50 feet high. The entrance is now half flooded. It is not possible to enter the cave as the TVA has installed a gate in the flooded entrance.

When I visited the cave I had to climb around the fence at the viewing area and around the cliff to get to the entrance.

South Pittsburg

South Pittsburg is between the mountains and the Tennessee River, and five miles down river from Nickajack Cave. We moved the trailer to a small lot on a road that continued from town, up the narrow valley and a short way up the mountain. The center of town was about a quarter–mile down the road. Claude Cain worked the mine with Dad and rented a large house about halfway to town. His son, Larry, was the same age as I, and we were great friends. His younger brother Randy often played with us also.

The summer break before school started, Larry and I went to the mine with our dads. We did the outside chores and picked the rock out of the coal on the beltline as it was going to the tipple. Dad always said that one boy was half a boy and two boys was no boy at all. I think that he was referring to the work that he could get out of us.

Aetna Mountain Mines

It was about a thirty minute drive up Aetna Mountain to the mine. The mine on Aetna Mountain was created by cutting the side of the hill away to expose the coal seam and then just tunneling into the side of the mountain. The lease that dad had was between two other mines, and no one knew where the mine operators would go once they got underground. Dad soon found out that each time they would move to the right or left, they would break into the old workings of the other mines.

The older mines used ponies or donkeys to move the coal out on tracks for the coal cars. The coal seams were too low for the animals, so the rock had to be cut out of the ceiling for head room. This slowed the forward progress of the mines. Dad and Claude used electric mining cars and cutting equipment, with a beltline following along to quickly move the coal. They pushed ahead of the other two mines by driving straight back into the mountain to get ahead of the competition.

I recall one evening when I decided to go into the mine and meet Dad as he was coming out. All I had was a flashlight, but I knew that all I had to do was follow the beltline and the electric car tracks until I reached them. On the way I noticed one of the openings into the adjacent mine and had to take a look. I was shocked as I stepped over into the other mine. I could see the main haul line with the cut out roof and then row upon row of props for as far as I could see. I saw a wall of coal along one side. As I peered around the side, it turned out to be a very thin wall with more rows of props and no pillars. The wedges at the tops of the props were pushing out from the weight of the mountain. I sure was glad when I got out of there. A common practice in taking out coal in the mountains is to tunnel through the mountain, leaving pillars as you go to support the mountain. When you reach the far side, you then start retreating, removing the pillars as you go. The mountain then drops down closing off the mine. I had never seen props left in the mine to hold it up. Dad and Claude used roof pins along the main route to support the roof. Claude had even invented a wooden roof pin that worked great in areas were there was water seeping in through the ceiling.

Swimming Hole

At the end of the day we would all gather below the tipple and bathe in the pool created to hold water for washing the coal. When Larry was with me we would quit early and go swimming. As we were in the mountains and the road was hardly ever used, we did not bother with swimsuits. Larry and I were taking our usual swim one evening when two girls and a boy showed up. They must have lived somewhere on the mountain, and they looked very rough. They started making fun of us and throwing rocks. We would not come out of the water as we were nude. Then one of them hit Larry in the head with a rock. Before I knew it I was all alone. Larry was out of sight, chasing them down the road, naked as a jaybird. He did not catch them, and I am glad he did not because he sure was mad and I had seen him in fights before.

Coal mining in the mountains is quite different from level country. You never know how high the coal seam will be. Dad told me of one mine he visited that the seam was so high that they had to use telephone poles for props. However, it did not last for long and closed back down to only inches. As long as the coal remains four to five–foot high, the equipment can clear and you can make a profit. However if it gets lower and you have to take out rock to move ahead, it gets very expensive. Walking in five–foot–high coal can be quite interesting. Coal miners walk bent over with their hands grasped behind their backs. This saves the back from strain. I have found this to be helpful in caving also.

Loose Rock

I sat there in the dark alone listening to the drip of water in the distance. Dad was ahead at the face of the mine setting the black powder charges before leaving the mine for the night. I heard a creaking sound above my head, and I moved to another waiting position a few feet away. Suddenly a huge bolder about twice my size fell on the spot where I had been sitting just a moment before. Dad had told me to listen to the rocks, and that they would warn you before something happened.

The miners hated the round boulders that stuck to the roof between the coal seam and the sandstone ceiling. You were always bumping your head on them or, when you least expected it they would fall, blocking the road way or tracks in the mine. These boulders consisted of a very heavy rock unlike the sandstone or the fossils found in the border area of the ceiling. They are black like the coal and smooth like something left over from the past when the coal was still exposed to the surface. They could be fossils like the thousands of bamboo looking rocks that have to be picked out of the coal.

One of my jobs was to lean over the moving belt line and pick out the rocks and fossils as the coal passed by. I was about thirteen when dad starting taking me to the mine during the summer months. He said it was to give me something to keep me busy and out of trouble while school was out. On Friday he would give me ten dollars for the week, and I would spend it on the Saturday movies. Once he gave me a hundred–dollar bill by mistake and I did not realize it until I paid for my movie ticket. Of course I brought him the change back.

Being a boy, I played around the mine more than I worked. As long as I made up a good pile of dummies, paper bags about a foot long and the size of the dynamite sticks, and was around when the belt started running, I was free to roam and play on the tipple or explore the mountainside.

School was rough on me in South Pittsburg. I seem to get a whipping at school almost every day, and sometimes twice a day. Our spelling teacher would send us to the Principal for one lick for each mis spelled word. And if we were sent to the office for any other reason, you would get at least three licks. I was glad that we were there for only half a school year!

Mirror on the Mountain

The town was very close to a large mountain with bluffs overlooking the main road through town. While we lived there, some kids placed a large mirror on the bluff to reflect the sun down on the town. It almost caused several accidents until the police were able to remove the mirror. I never knew who was responsible, and they never arrested anyone.

Larry and I played a lot together and also got into a lot of trouble at times. He lived just down the road on the way to town, and we had a small lot with the trailer on it. Larry had a smaller brother and several sisters, so there was always plenty to do. There was a shed behind his house that we climbed on a lot. One trick that I learned was how to quickly get on top of the shed by standing with my back to the shed and jumping up to the overhang. I would then pull up and throw my legs upon the roof. It would only take a second to get from the ground to the roof. This also worked good in climbing trees, as long as I could reach the first limb. We would go over the shed and jump to a tree on the other side to slide down again.

One day we thought it would be fun to pull a prank on the people walking the sidewalk under the large tree that overhung the sidewalk and road. It was a pecan tree. We would hide in the branches and drop pecans down on them as they walked by. We did not think that they could see us, but I often wondered if they really did see us.

We played a lot on the mountains that were on each side of the valley we lived in. One large pit we played around but never went down may have been South Pittsburg Pit, well known to cavers in the Southeast.

By the end of 1954 the mine on top of Aetna Mountain played out and we moved back to Providence for five months, where I finished out the school year.

In the summer of 1955, we moved to Spring City, Tennessee, where dad leased coal on the mountain just west of Spring City. To get to the new mine, you take Shut in Gap Road up the mountain then turn off onto Hard Rector Lane. Hard Rector Lane runs along the top of the mountain until you reach the mine.

Spring City

Spring City is one of three towns in Rhea county Tennessee located at the junction of the Cumberland Plateau and the Appalachian Valley with the Tennessee River and Watts Bar lake. Rhea County is named for Tennessee politician and Revolutionary War veteran John Rhea.

Rhea Springs was originally called Sulphur Springs before 1878, until the lower Piney Valley was flooded in 1942 by the Tennessee Valley Authority. Spring City was incorporated in 1890 after the railroad was completed. It now takes in the lake shore overlooking the flooded area of Rhea Springs.

A portion of the Trail of Tears ran through the county as part of the United States government's removal of the Cherokee in the 1830s. This is one of many places were I have lived that was near the Trail of Tears!

Store & post office in Rhea Springs, TVA Photo 1940

During the American Civil War, Rhea County was one of the few counties in East Tennessee that was sympathetic to the cause of the Confederate States of America. Rhea raised seven companies for the Confederate military, compared to just one company for the Union.

Rhea had the only female cavalry company on either side during the Civil War. It was made up of young women in their teens and twenties from Rhea County and was formed in 1862. The girls named their unit the Rhea County Spartans. Until 1863, the Spartans simply visited loved ones in the military and delivered the equivalent of modern day care packages. After Union troops entered Rhea in 1863, the Spartans may have engaged in some scouting for Confederate forces. The members of the Spartans were later arrested in April 1865 under orders of a Rhea County Unionist and were forced to march to the Tennessee River. From there they were transported to Chattanooga aboard the *USS Chattanooga*. Once in Chattanooga, Union officers realized the women were not a threat and ordered them released and returned to Rhea County. The Spartans were not an officially recognized unit of the Confederate Army.

In 1879, the Cincinnati Southern Railway was completed from Cincinnati to Chattanooga, running through Spring City and Dayton.

Rhea County was made famous in 1925 by the Scopes Trial, which resulted from the teaching of evolution being banned in Tennessee public schools. The Scopes Trial was one of the first to be referred to as the Trial of the Century. William Jennings Bryan played a role as prosecutor in the trial. In 1954 the laws were changed to allow teaching of evolution alongside Bible studies in school. On June 8, 2004, a federal appeals court upheld a ruling banning further Bible instructions as a violation of the First Amendment principle of "Separation of church and state."

On March 16, 2004, Rhea County commissioner J.C. Fugate prompted a vote on a ban on homosexuals in Tennessee, and allowed the county to charge them with "crimes against nature." The measure passed 8–0. Fugate's reasoning was, "We need to keep them out of here." Several of the commissioners who voted for the resolution chose not to run for reelection or were voted out of office. The resolution was withdrawn on March 18. In protest, a "Gay Day in Rhea" was held on May 8, 2004, with about 300 participants.[6]

One–of–a–kind Railroad

The City of Cincinnati is the only municipality in the country to own an interstate railroad. An Ohio law enabling the creation of the Cincinnati Southern Railway was enacted on May 4, 1869. Cincinnati voters adopted a resolution designating Chattanooga as the southern terminus one month later. Workmen spiked the last rail in place on December 10, 1879. The first freight train completed the route from Cincinnati to Chattanooga on February 21, 1880. The first passenger train followed on March 8.

The enterprise continues today under a long–term lease with Cincinnati, New Orleans and Texas Pacific Railway (CNO&TP), generating revenue annually for the city of Cincinnati.[7]

Discovering Spring City

In 1955 as a boy of fourteen, I was always looking for adventure, and unaware of all the social changes this small community was bringing upon the country. The mountains, streams and lake held all my interest. I rode my bike all around the area and explored the exciting place that we had just moved to. It was here that I found my first cave. Mother had taken me to several commercial caves, including Mammoth Cave in Kentucky, but I had never been in a wild unexplored cave. My first wild cave trip was one that I will always remember. I accepted Jesus as my Lord when I was nine, and from that time forward have had someone watching over me. Every time I had a close call or brush with death, I could thank God for sending an angel to protect me. I had three close calls in the six months we lived in Spring City, Tennessee.

My dad was a coal miner from west Kentucky, and during my teen years he opened several coal mines in Tennessee. One was on the mountain just above Spring City. Spring City in 1955 was a wonderful place for a teenager, with fishing at Watts Bar Lake, and parks and streams to play in. At the age of fourteen I was allowed to hunt alone with my .410 shotgun. I shot my first quail along Little Piney Creek, a small mountain stream just south of town that flows into the Piney River and Watts Bar Lake. It was this stream which I loved to explore, and I swam and jumped from the iron bridge. Just north of the bridge along the east bank is where I found the small cave.

There are only three caves listed for Rhea County in the book, Caves of Tennessee.[8] This cave is more than likely still unknown or ignored by the local caving groups. Before I describe my brush with death in this cave, I would like to share my other two close calls in Spring City.

First Close Call

During the school year I signed up for swimming. I was not much for sports, and swimming seemed to me like an easy sport. I even won a race in the breast stroke event. One Saturday we were swimming at the public lake, and toward the end of the day we had started to get a little wild. We had a boat and were using it for a diving platform. In order to get a little higher, we would stand on another swimmer's shoulder while they were sitting and dive into the water. The shore of the lake at the park was protected from the waves by large rocks which covered the shore line and extended down into the water. I was unaware that the boat had swung around to the edge of the bank, when I quickly jumped up on the shoulders of one of my friends and dove head first into the bank.

I am amazed that I was not knocked out. However, I walked up to the front of the concession stand and asked someone to call my dad. I rinsed my head under the water faucet that was in the front yard. I remember that there was a lot of blood and it seemed like forever before dad arrived. I was standing there alone, and I guess that everyone thought that I was OK. When dad got there, I slid into the backseat and passed out. Dad told me later that he was sure that he had lost me. I looked so pale from the loss of blood. At the hospital I had many stitches in the front of my forehead at the hairline, and unknown to me a large gash in the top of my head also. To this day I still have a lump on the head and two scars.

Second Close Call

Just before summer vacation started, on August 22, 1955, three days before my 14th birthday, dad was coming home from the coal mine upon the mountain. He told me later that he had the strange sense or feeling that something bad was wrong, and he was worried about his family. We lived in a small trailer park on the south edge of town and I walked to school.

At 3:00 P.M. on that partly cloudy day, a south bound Cincinnati, New Orleans and Texas Pacific Railway Co., freight train traveling at an estimated speed of 50 mph, struck a Rhea County School bus with forty nine students on board. The crossing was in the center of town, and I could hear the crash at our trailer. I had just gotten home from school. Everyone was walking toward the crash site to see what had happened. Sirens were going off everywhere, and there was a lot of confusion. I had walked those tracks many times after school, although I did not ride the bus. Just being that close to a major disaster can really make you pause and think.

The road from the mine crossed the tracks at that crossing, and dad crossed it twice a day. There were no crossing gates at that time, only lights. The school bus driver claimed the warning signals at the crossing were not in operation. However the train engineer reports—and one witness, along with several passengers on the bus—stated that the driver did not stop, and that the lights were working. Once the bus driver saw the approaching train, he attempted to accelerate through the crossing. Two school children on the bus said they saw the approaching train and warned the driver but he replied by saying he intended to cross ahead of the train.[9] Eleven students died. The bus driver and thirty three other students were injured.

Forty years later I was working in Kennesaw, Georgia for Ray Jackson, who was born in Spring City, Tennessee. Although he was not alive at the time, he remembered talk of the bus accident. I believe that God directs our paths and brings us into contact with others for a reason, even though we may never know why. And for some strange reason events and places play strong roles in these "chance" meetings.

Third Close Call

I had seen the cave on several occasions when I was hunting or just checking out the rocks in the stream. It was about five feet up the bank, and the opening was no more than four feet high and wide. I was alone, as I usually was when playing in this area near the trailer park. There were not many children my age living there. I brought a flashlight in order to investigate the cave. Of course I had not told anyone of my intentions or where I was going. At fourteen the world was mine and nothing was impossible.

I entered the cave and crawled a short distance, just out of the light from the entrance. I could still turn around but not stand up. The passage ended, except for an opening sloping off to the left that gradually became steeper as I inched into it head first. I soon realized that I could be in trouble if it got tight. I would be on my head and unable to back out. So I backed up to where I had more room, turned around and started in feet first, feeling around for a foothold as I got deeper into the hole.

I reached a point where I could not feel anything with my feet. It was as if I were dangling on the edge of some large void. Try as hard as I could with my feet, I could not touch the bottom or the sides. Had I come this far and still would not know what was there? I thought about my situation for what seemed like a long time, though it was no more than a few seconds, and then on some strange impulse which to this day I cannot explain, I let go!

Mystery Along the River Bank

Feet dangling over the edge, what's below?
Good hand hold, take it nice and slow.
Climb back up, or drop on down?
Come this far, I wonder what I have found.

Much older now as I look back,
I would have never been found, I left no track
at the bottom of a nameless cave by the lake.
I understand now the risks a teen will take.

Along the riverbank as a boy I played,
rocks and boulders, wherever I strayed.
A dark hole, a cave, a difficult climb,
each day, looking a little deeper each time.

Flashlight in hand to see what's there.
Was this a den, could there be a bear?
Alone, curious, not quite so brave,
like a mole I slowly entered the cave.

As I let go, it seemed like forever.
Now I thought, this was not so clever.
Everything still in place, no broken bones.
Could I climb out as I felt for large stones?

What had I found, a nice little room,
where maybe a bear slept or met his doom.
Struggle and push against both flanks,
free at last to explore the Piney River banks.

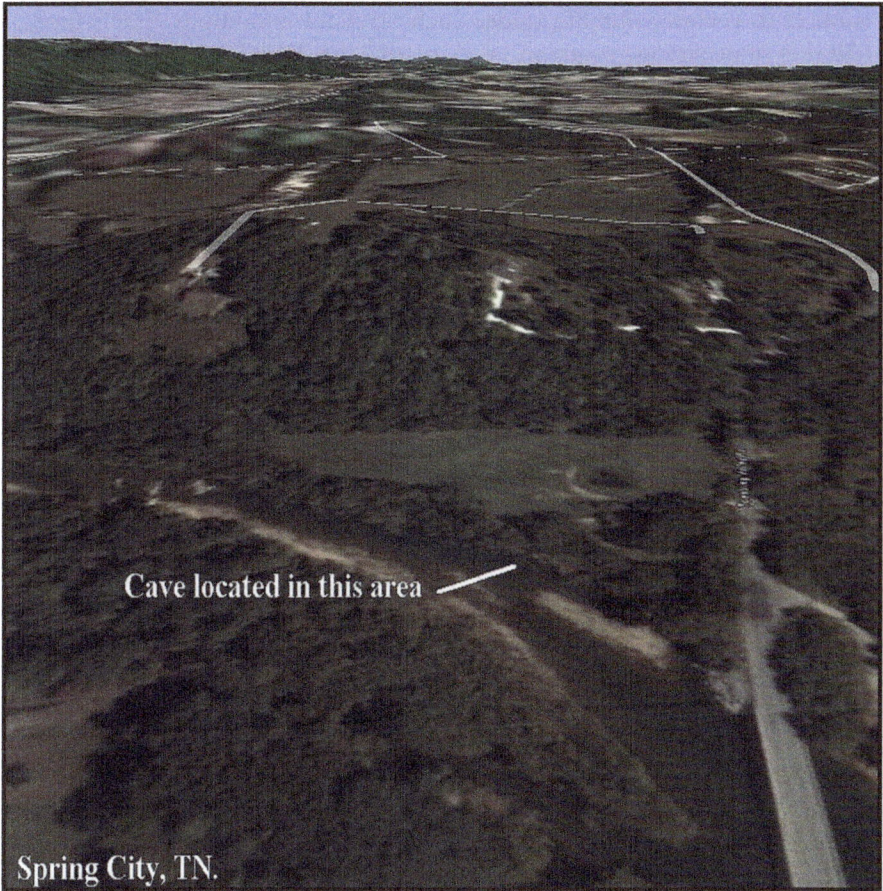

Little Piney Creek and new bridge. (Google Earth Image)

This was maybe one of two times in my life when my life flashed before me in a second. The drop seemed like eternity, and I found myself standing only a few inches from where I had let go. The floor was smooth and level. I got down on my knees and continued through the passage toward the river. After about Twenty feet I ended up in a small room that I could almost stand up in and about five feet around. It was a nice little hiding place, though I never returned. I managed to climb out by bracing against the opposite wall. I did not think much about it for the next twenty years. Looking back, my bones could still be in that small cave had someone not been watching over me.

It was a perfect place for a bear to hibernate, and I am sure that one did live there more than once in the past. I was just thankful that this time he was gone for the day. The other time my life flashed before me, I was involved in an encounter with a bear. While camping on the Appalachian Trail in upstate New York, I had a bear step over me. Twice in a lifetime is enough to review your life under such stressful conditions. Each time I had that same strange peace and reassurance that it was going to be okay.

Working in the Mine

That summer Dad would take me to the mine each day to keep me out of trouble. My chores consisted of odd jobs on the outside of the mine. I enjoyed filling dummy bags with dirt. A dummy bag is a long paper bag the size of a stick of dynamite that was packed in the hole to contain the explosion. I filled bags for several hours each day, then climbed on the tipple.

The tipple was a strange structure built on the side of the mountain. It served the mine in three ways: first, as a storage location for the coal, second, as a shaker operation that separated the coal by size. As the coal slid down a slight incline, it passed over a screen with small holes, and the smaller particles of coal would fall into a hopper as stoker coal. A stoker coal furnace or boiler would have an automatic feed system that used a screw to feed the smaller lumps of fine coal into it. We had one of these in our home in Kentucky until the natural gas line came through town. The coal then passed over another screen for slightly larger lumps of coal used in fireplaces, and then the remainder would go into the last hopper for commercial use at the power plant. Third, the tipple provided a convenient way to load the trucks when they came to pick up the coal. They would just drive under the hopper for the type of coal desired and pull a release rope or lever to allow the coal to fall into the bed of the truck, pulling ahead slowly to distribute the load.

Blasting during the daytime consisted of dynamite made up of sawdust and nitroglycerin to reduce the amount of smoke. At quitting time, black powder was used, as it was cheaper and the smoke would have time to clear out before work the next day.

In the place of a beltline, we used a three–wheel electric car to haul the coal out in trailers attached behind the car. Dad had twin brothers working for him, and they were experts at driving that car. They would come out of the mine at top speed, whip around and back a string of three trailers out onto the tipple. That always amazed me the way they could keep the trailers strait, backing up like that.

We had a big electric generator for powering the equipment in the mine, and it required a can of ether in the morning to get it started. The generator also charged the batteries on the electric car. The speed control for the car was a line of contacts on a lever, with each contact slightly offset from the next. As you pushed the lever forward, it engaged more of the contacts to bring more of the batteries into the circuit for the motor. There were no brakes, and you just reversed the power to the motor to stop. With one front wheel you could turn on a dime, which may be why they could control the backing of the trailers so easy.

The coal was loaded with an electric front end loader that had two arms to scoop the coal onto a belt that would feed the coal into the low trailers. The electric cable from the loader ran out of the mine to the generator. I also had the job of splicing breaks in the cable We always had to be on the lookout for copper thieves who would steal the cables for the copper.

Mountain Bobcat

On one of the summer trips to the mine with Dad, I got quite a surprise when on top of the mountain, Dad suddenly stopped the truck and jumped out. The motor still running and the door wide open, he ran off into the woods. I sat there in shock with the truck in the middle of the road. I did not know if should I get out, move the truck to the side of the road or just wait? After about five minutes, Dad returned. "Did you see that bobcat?" He asked. I had not seen a thing. "I sure wanted to get a better look at him," Dad exclaimed. Dad loved hunting, and lived in the woods about as much as he lived in the mine.

On the Dark Side

One other event that I remember about that summer in 1955, one I am not too proud of, was my first joy ride. Near the trailer park was an old pickup truck. I did not know who it belonged to and I played around it a lot. One day I tried to start it by crossing the wires behind the ignition. to my surprise I was able to start the truck and took it on a short joy ride around the countryside. After about fifteen minutes and afraid that something might happen or I might get stopped, I returned it to the same spot.

I learned to drive when I was about ten on my uncle's farm in Kentucky. He let me drive the tractor anytime he was working in the field. My older sister Pat also had a red Crosley convertible that I played around with. The older boys in town loved to pick it up and leave it on the sidewalk or other strange places. It was so small and light one person could turn it over.

I was also responsible for losing mother's yellow canary that summer. Mother loved that bird. You could open the cage and stick out your finger, rub his chest and he would hop right on. We walked around the trailer for hours with him on our shoulders. One day, forgetting that he was on my shoulder, I left the trailer–and that was the last we saw of the yellow canary!

Dad sold the mine that fall and we moved again, not too far, across the lake and south of Spring City to another small Tennessee town, Englewood. We moved the trailer and set it up next to the ESSO service station Dad bought.

I think that Dad tired of mining after opening those two Tennessee mountain mines, so he took a break and opened a gas station in Englewood, Tennessee.

Grassy Cove 1972

In 1972 I returned to the area near Spring City to explore a cave in Grassy Cove called Grassy Cove Saltpeter Cave. Take highway 68 over the mountain from Spring City toward Crossville, Tennessee, and you will pass through a very interesting place, a cove, a geological wonder. Grassy Cove is drained entirely by underground streams. The valley's main stream, Grassy Cove Creek, flows northward across the cove before dropping into Mill Cave on the slopes of Brady Mountain. It then winds its way southward through a series of caves before reemerging in the Sequatchie Valley to the south, where it forms the headwaters of the Sequatchie River. Grassy Cove Saltpeter Cave, located on the eastern slope of Brady Mountain, is the eleventh–longest cave in Tennessee and one of the 100 longest caves in the United States.[10]

Seventeen years after leaving Spring City, fate brought me back to this interesting area. My good friend and caving companion, John Wallace, suggested we fly up to Crossville and visit Grassy Cove Saltpeter Cave. On a cool March Friday in 1972, John Wallace checked out his four–seat airplane at the Charlie Brown Airport in Atlanta for a flight to Tennessee. My wife Kathy, our daughter Deanna and I flew up in John's small airplane, and John's wife Yolanda with two small children drove so we would have transportation to the cave. I would then drive back, and they would fly home to Atlanta.

The trip was quite a nice one along the interstate, and then we followed the state road into Crossville. It was after dark when we arrived, and the airport's lights were not on. The airport is on top of a mountain, and we were a little nervous about finding a place to land. John's wife was there but could not contact anyone at the airport. She turned the van lights down the runway. The excitement of flying was almost too much. We spent the weekend at Cumberland Mountain State Park and John, Art Smith, Jack Pace and I went caving on Saturday.

It was a large cabin at the park and we settled in for a good night of rest before the trip the next day. We planned to visit Devil Step Hollow Cave with the family, and then the four of us would explore Grassy Cove Saltpeter Cave on the other side of the mountain. Kathy and Deanna spent a lovely day hiking around the park while we went caving.

A few miles southeast of Crossville is Grassy Cove, a depression between two mountains that by all rights should be a big natural lake. The rainwater that falls in the cove runs north into a cave, then emerges at the Devil's Sink Hole, south of the cove and over the mountain. Grassy Cove

Saltpeter Cave is well known for being a dusty cave, and dust masks are handy to avoid histoplasmosis, a lung disease common in dusty caves and chicken houses. I did come down with a light case of this later, and it could very well have been from this cave. The doctor wanted to know if I had been around any chicken houses.

Discovery in Grassy Cove Saltpeter Cave

We entered the cave and debated about exploring the west dry passages or to venture down the waterfall at the east end of the cave. There were reported to be more caves below the waterfall, however more rope would be required and we were not prepared for that. The waterfall room sounded too good to pass up, so we opted for going down through the chasm and to the waterfall.

The chasm is a short drop that can be climbed if you chimney out to a narrow portion of the drop. We chose to use the rope for the drop. We continued down to the waterfall room and poked around looking for any easy lead to continue on. John was checking behind a large rock on the north side of the passage when he noticed air blowing from the rocks. We all got excited and started helping with the easy dig.

In less than an hour we had a small hole that looked to open up below. I was elected to give it a try. I am not sure why I was first but I was grateful. I went feet first into the hole, removing my hard hat in order to squeeze through. At the bottom there was a low craw that went to the northeast for about fifty feet, and then a ledge with a short drop of about five feet into a large room sloping downward. I studied the floor and could not make out any tracks. I sat there yelling encouragement to the others to come on down. We had found something big.

I felt like Neil Armstrong on the moon when I made that first step on the floor below and left that first footprint where no one had ever stepped before. The mud had a black coating on top, and when you raised your foot it left a very clear orange print about one inch deep. It felt strange to walk down into that huge room and then look back at the lonely set of footprints that would soon turn into a well–worn path.

We explored the new extension for the rest of the day, finding formations along the west wall and crystal gypsum flowers covering the floor as the ceiling became lower near the end. We crawled through some breakdown into a much smaller room at the end and could find no way to continue.

Tracks of Change
Air from a crack, a rock to move,
now a small hole, who would go?
What mysteries wait down in this groove?
Someone brave and small to check below.

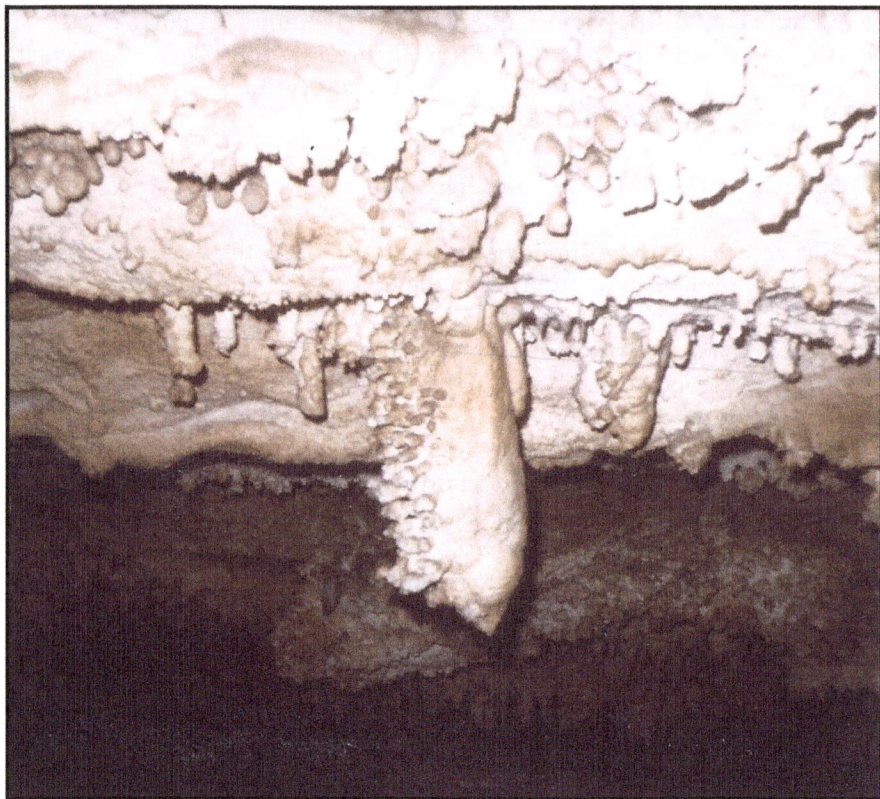

Popcorn in Grassy Cove Saltpeter Cave.

The dig was short, crawl not too tight,
as I sat on the ledge and gazed
at the dark void that had never seen light.
Several minutes passed as I froze amazed.

Enter a place never seen before,
sealed, never open, this special place,
where crystals grow and maybe more,
events that created it, left hardly a trace.

Layers of red clay, hid by a covering of black,
tranquil and quiet, but that would all change.
One small step, as I made the first track,
now it was done, this world we would rearrange.

Formation and flowstone in Grassy Cove Saltpeter Cave.

We were all very excited about our new find and planned to return to map this new section the following month. Unknown to us another caving group had just undertaken a major re–mapping of the cave and were in the process of publishing their map. When Jack Pace moved to Nashville and told the caving group there about the discovery, they quickly returned to the cave and called it the Nashville Extension.

We returned on Saturday, April 22, 1972 with the additional assistance of my wife's cousin, Bill Meier, and mapped the "March 18th Discovery." I was working for Eastman Kodak Company at the time and had access to the latest home movie cameras. I was trying out a new model with very low light capability for taking movies in the cave. We used a Coleman lantern for the light source and the shutter speed set slow to capture as much light as possible.

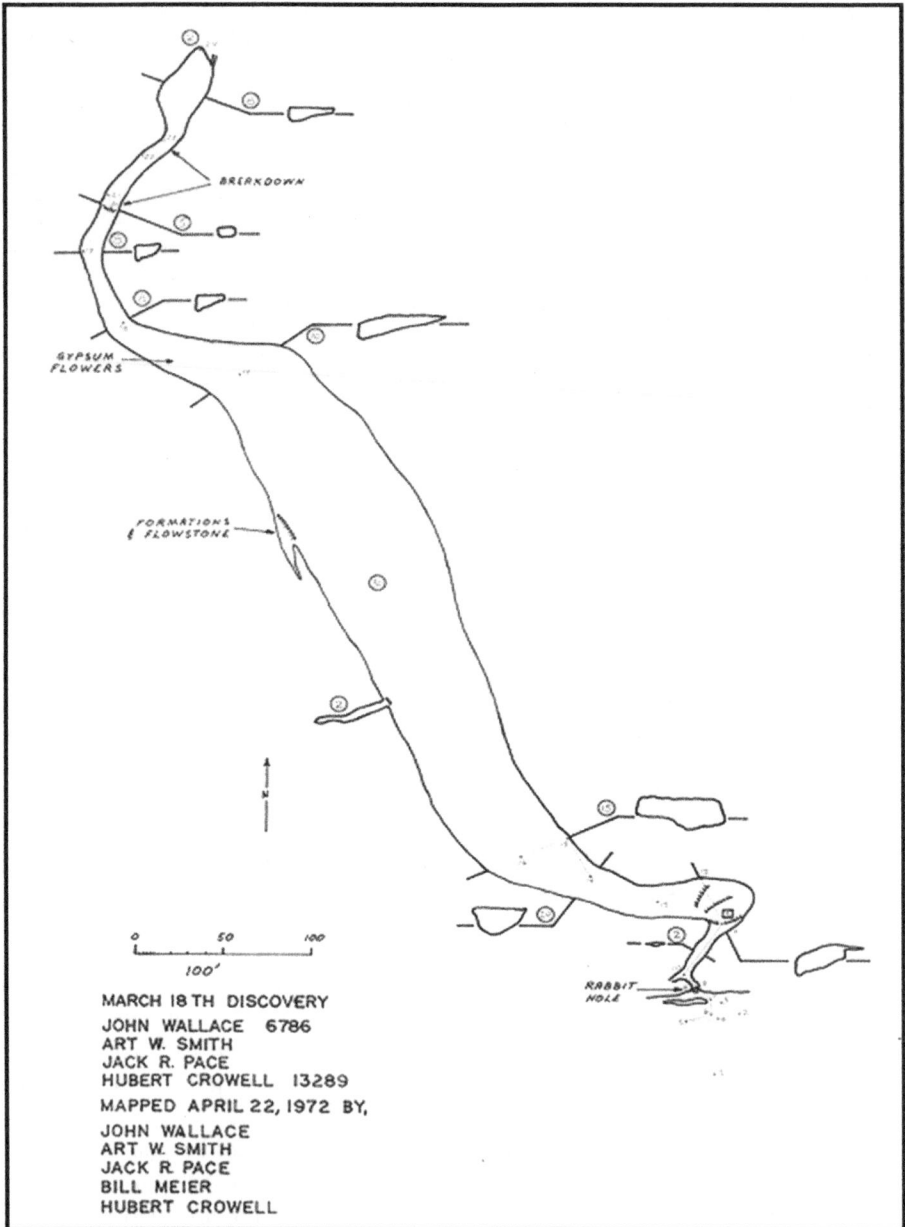

March 18th 1972 discovery in Grassy Cove Saltpeter Cave.

I placed this story online for other cavers to read and have gotten several informative comments back about the remapping and further exploration of Grassy Cove Saltpeter Cave.

Here is a great comment from a fellow caver on this story.

January 8, 2009

I just found your article, "Discovery in Grassy Cove Saltpeter Cave" while idly surfing different articles on the Cumberland Plateau and Grassy Cove.

I was an avid spelunker in the 1970's and early 1980's. I read about your discovery of "the Nashville Extension." I, along with Jeff Sims and Jay Cox, were the ones who mapped Grassy Cove and put the "Nashville Extension" label on your discovery. However, we were mapping the cave from 1975 to 1977. It was at a Tennessee Cave Survey meeting in April 1977 when Larry Matthews told us of the large room below the north wall of the Waterfall Room that you describe in your article. We returned the first weekend in May and found your room. The second weekend in May we returned to map it. On this trip a deep canyon chimney downward from "the Nashville Extension" led to a stream passage that ran for over 3000 feet under the full length of the dusty "Subway Passage" above. The passage was full of formations such as soda straws which was unlike any other part of the dusty saltpeter cave. On our map we named the new stream passage the "Knoxville Extension" as that is where we were from at the time.

However, this stream passage was very much like a stream passage I explored with Richard Schreiber and Marion Smith in nearby Gouffre (Blowhole in Tom Barr's book). We never dye traced the streams to see if the Mill Cave stream became the Knoxville Extension stream to become the Gouffre stream and finally the Run to the Mill Cave stream (that cave is on the Sequatchie Valley side of Brady Mountain), but that was the theory.

Anyway, it is great to read some missing history of Grassy Cove Saltpeter as I never heard the story of the "Nashville Extension's" discovery.

Thanks for the article.

Englewood

Englewood Tennessee was established in 1870 and originally known as Tellico Junction. Located in east middle Tennessee on a main highway running north and south, it had a fair amount of traffic and provided plenty of work for the service station business.

ESSO Gas Station

The service station had two service bays and a gift shop that mother used as a sewing room. There was just enough room on the south end of the lot for the house trailer. We moved there in January of 1956, from Spring City.

Pat was attending college in nearby Athens, Tennessee and was home on the weekends. She met and married Grandville Hooper from the Athens area while we were living in Englewood.

The service station kept me busy during the summer before school started. I learned how to grease cars and change flats, among other things.

There was no such thing as self service, and I pumped a lot of gas, cleaned windshields and checked the oil. You get to meet a lot of people working in a service station. One of the most interesting person I met was an elderly lady who walked south in the fall and then walked back north in the spring. I did not know how far she traveled, I believe it was from Florida to Maine. She never accepted a ride and pushed a cart with all her belongings, sleeping along the road. I talked to her at length about her travels. She followed the same route with the same overnight sleeping spots. I saw her again on her return trip back north.

Dad loved to go fishing, and he often took my friends fishing. Someone had to run the station, so I would get the job of taking care of customers while Dad and my friends took care of the fish!

Worst Moment

A close friend I met at church was a girl about my age, Becky Daugharty. She had a steady boyfriend that was keeping a close eye on who Becky was hanging around with, but I was careful, and we never had a run–in. He lived on a farm and had to work most of the time. I seldom saw him, but I would visit Becky during my breaks at the station. We talked for hours. On one visit her cat strayed out onto the highway and was struck by a car. The cat was in a lot of pain, could not walk and was sure to die. Becky could only scream and ask me to put the cat out of his misery. I will not go into the details of how or how long I tried to kill that cat, but it was the worst experience that I can remember. Even to this day I have a hard time killing even ants, it always brings back memories of that awful event. I later wrote to Becky during my years in the service and even visited her at college once when I returned from Germany. We lost contact after that, and I never knew how her life turned out, if she married that farmer or met someone else in college. I did enjoy the letters, it was great when mail call would come and I had some reading. I also corresponded with a girl a few years older that lived in Germany. She was a pen pal of my cousin, Anna Lelle Clark. More about that later.

Motor on a Bike

Working at the station I had access to a lot of tools and some idle time, so I was always looking for something I could do and still watch the pumps. Electric washing machines were replacing the last of the gas driven ones, and the motors were available for little or nothing. A gas washing machine motor had a horizontal drive shaft with a small pulley.

I got a motor that was in good shape and ran fine, so all I had to do was find a way to mount it on my bicycle. I found a large pulley that could be mounted to the spokes of the rear wheel. The luggage carrier over the back wheel was not very strong, so I reinforced it some and bolted the motor on top. I then mounted a lever with an idler pulley behind the seat. I was ready for a test run!

The road behind the station did not have much traffic, and it had a slight down hill for a good start. Leaving the belt loose, I took off down the hill peddling fast, then reached back and engaged the lever to tighten the pulley. The motor started right up and off we flew. I let the motor run at a constant speed and used the lever to control the speed. It worked out very well. I did have to be careful on turns as the front end was very light and would bounce up on the slightest bump.

If you got off the bike, the front wheel would come off the ground. After a while I got tired of struggling with it and wanted my old bike back. I am amazed that I didn't kill myself on that thing.

The Goat Below

My friends and I decided to go camping once and Mom said that it was fine, just don't go too far. We packed up our blankets and snacks and headed off to wherever the road led. We even walked the railroad tracks for quite a while. When night came, we had no idea where we were, only how to get back. We found an old barn that looked like it was about to fall down, and we climbed up into the second floor. Most of the floor was missing, so we had to be careful not to fall through. We spent the night there, and the next morning someone yelled, "look what is down below!" Right below us was a dead goat. He still had all of his hair, but he had been dead for a long time. I can't remember what we did the rest of the day, but that dead goat sure stuck with me.

Cave Trip and Wasp

My second wild cave trip was also in Englewood, I am not sure just where. We rode our bikes out of town to a farm, where one of the boys must have known about the cave. The entrance was a slide down about twenty feet into a good size room. We only had our flashlights, and I don't think that we stayed very long. I wish that I could remember where it was. I would like to go back and check it out again. I do remember that there was a spring down the hill just a short way form the entrance. On the way back we spent some time knocking down wasp nests in a barn and getting chased by them. That was always a challenge—to see how many nests you could knock down without getting stung.

We left Englewood in 1956 and moved to Lakeland Florida. Dad got a job as a welder in the phosphate mines there.

Lakeland

Kathleen, Florida, summer of 1956. This small community is just northwest of Lakeland, Florida were I rode the school bus to and attended middle school. My wife is also Kathleen, though there is no connection, at least I did not think so, until while writing this, I told her about Kathleen. She then told me something that I never knew, When she was in the eighth grade, there was a blonde boy named Clark. She said that she prayed that God would give her someone like him, but not him as he slept a lot in class. She always liked my middle name. I now know that God answered that prayer. I also slept a lot in class, and her prayer would have been around the time I was going to school in Kathleen!

Lakeland is one of the most beautiful cities I have seen, with a large lake in the center of town and a park along the lake with lights around the edge.

We moved to a trailer park on the north side of Lakeland and only lived there about six months, but once Mom got a taste of Florida there was no turning back. She would convince Dad to move back again later. He would do that after returning to the mines to get out of debt and save up a little.

Pilot Friend

The trailer park was on Lake Gibson, and the site of the Langford Seaplane Base. My friend from school lived on the south end of the lake. I would come over, and we would listen to his ham radio and talk to people all over the world. He was too young to have a drivers license, but he did have a pilot's license. I never got to go up with him, but just knowing him was a great learning experience.

Years later when I was working for Lockheed Air Craft, I took a course on single side band radios used in the C–141 cargo plane, and I thought back about those hours we spent on the ham radio. I was working at Lockheed when the President was shot in Texas. I guess everyone knows what they were doing at the time that happened.

The park had a club house, a dock and kids to play with. It was a great place for a fifteen–year–old. I could swim and water ski. You just had to watch out for the alligators.

Bowling Alley

This is where I found my first real paying job and got my Social Security card. I needed it to work setting pins at the local bowling alley. My Social Security records show that I earned $39.00 that year (1956).

Before the days of automatic pin setters in bowling alleys, they used a rack that one could throw the pins into, then push a lever down to set the pins in the correct position. This provided a good job for young men that liked a little excitement. The pin setter would sit on the edge of the pit with his feet clear of the bowling ball that would come crashing down the alley. Most of the time all the pins would remain in the pit, but sometimes they would fly out, and if you were not alert you might get hit.

When the bowler would throw the first ball, the pin setter would pick up the ball and place it on the return rail, then as fast as he could, pick up the pins and place them in the rack. If the pin setter was too slow and the ball reached the bowler before the pin setter was through in the pit, the person bowling may throw the ball and catch you in the pit. They usually cannot see you down in the pit, or maybe they can and like to see you jump! We would learn to pick up two pins in each hand and sometimes a fifth pin between the two hands. If it was a strike, you could then pick up all the pins by only bending over twice, five pins each time. The object was to always complete the action before the ball reached the return rack.

During the slack time and while waiting for the bowlers to arrive, we would gather around the pinball machine and see who could rack up the most games. We would set the front legs on the soles of our shoes to make the ball roll slower, until it would tilt, and end the game. Someone figured out where the solenoid for added games was located in the back and cut a hole there so we could save a nickel by pushing in just the right spot.

Now that I had gotten my first job, I felt that I could do anything and go anywhere and make a living. However, I had just turned fifteen! School was a problem for me, it may have been because we moved so much. I seemed to never be able to complete a full year at one school. And I believe that I also may have been bored. I spent two years in the seventh grade, two years in the eighth grade and was starting on my second year in the ninth, when I gave it up and left home at 16.

There was another family in the trailer park that had a problem son who ran away a lot, and there was a lot of talk about how hard it was to keep young boys at home. I was still fifteen when we moved again, back to my hometown of Providence, Kentucky.

CHAPTER 4 RETURN TO PROVIDENCE

I was working at a drive–in movie theater at night, cutting school in the day and always on the edge of getting into trouble. The owner of the theater rented our three story home in Providence, and we lived in the trailer, parked behind the house. My younger sister was getting older, and the trailer was getting crowded, so I was given the basement of the house for my bedroom.

Drive–in Theater

I would ride to work with the theater owner and run the projection equipment all night until the last show was over. The movies came in two boxes with two reels of film in each box. We would have to wind the film through our hands to inspect for bad splices before showing the movie. If you had a bad splice, the film would break or jam in the middle. The image would stop on the screen and a hole would start to burn in the middle. It would really look strange on the screen. Then the horns would start blowing all the time you cleared the mess out of the projector and re–spliced the film. One night during the second showing, I made an error and played reel number one followed by reel number three, then number two and ended with number four. No one complained, but if they were watching, I bet they were confused. Lots of time I would splice the cartoon or news on backwards and you would see the sound track running down the side.

The projectors we used produced light by creating an arc like a welding arc. You need a very bright light for a drive in theater. Two twelve–inch carbon rods were mounted on a slow–moving support that moved toward each other as the ends burned off. You had a smoked glass window where you could view the arc and make sure that the space between the rods was correct. If the space became too large then the arc would stop and the screen would go black, too close and the rods would weld together and the screen would go black. When the rods burned down to about two inches, you had to change them. Of course this could not be done in the middle of a movie. There were two projectors, and while one was showing one reel the other projector was being loaded with the next reel and a fresh rod installed. Then at the end of the reel a five second warning in the form of two circles would flash in the upper right of the screen. When the second set of circles would flash, one would switch projectors.

By the use of two knobs at the bottom of the lamp housing, the position of the rods could be adjusted. To start the arc, one just brought the two rods together to strike an arc and then backed them off to the correct space for the maximum light output. In order to save money, I had to splice the leftover ends onto longer rods with sheet metal squares wrapped around the two ends. I had to remember where these splices were and be ready when the splice burned off. In an instant I would move the rods back together, re–striking the arc.

Each reel had to be rewound by hand or placed into the rewinding box, film threaded for the next reel, new rods installed and splices made. This kept the projector operator busy all night and you could only see the same small sections of each movie over and over again.

During intermission time we sometimes had some kind of entertainment, and one night we had a group that bought junk cars and jumped them over each other and crashed them in the area in front of the big screen. They had trouble getting a 1948 Plymouth started that night and could not crash it. I offered them $60.00 for it and I had my first car, but no driver's license. You had to be 16 in the state of Kentucky to get a license. After the show that night a friend pushed me off and we got the car started so I could drive it home. Dad was slightly upset and said that it could just set there in the backyard until I was old enough to get a license.

I was back to walking home after closing the theater. The owners would usually not stay after the concession stand closed, and unless I knew someone that was at the movie I would be stuck with walking the five miles home in the dark. I don't know how many times I walked off the road and almost fell into the ditch on those nights when there was no moon.

In the storage space behind the large screen there were all kinds of junk, and I found some old 16 mm film reels of old B–movies. The owner had stored them there. Well I borrowed a few of them, and at home under our sunporch there was a crawl space of about five feet. I found an old 16 mm projector and set up my own theater. For the 50's some of the films were sexy, and by today's standards would be rated PG. The only problem with my theater was that I used a lot of cardboard for building material, and soon the termites were everywhere. Dad made me creosote everything that touched the dirt floor. Well the smell of creosote was just too much, so that ended that project. The owner reported to the police that someone had broken into the storage, and they questioned me about it. I was never sure if someone else had stolen something or if he was looking for those films.

I did drive the old Plymouth one more time. Some friends and I were going out to the coal mine strip cut to go swimming. There was a lot of strip mining in west Kentucky, and at that time they would just leave the big cuts open to fill with water. They made fine swimming holes. They were deep, usually over 100 feet, and had steep banks that we could dive from. We pulled the old Plymouth out onto the road and pushed it down the hill until it started. It had very little compression so you had to get up a little speed before it would start. After our swim we started back home on the long gravel road, and one by one the thin tires started to blow. I continued to drive it on the rims. If I stopped we would never be able to push it fast enough with two flats to get it started again. I think that Dad hauled it back to the junkyard after I left home at age 16 and joined the army.

Driver's License

After reading this account, I am sure that most parents will have second thoughts about allowing a sixteen–year–old to have a car. I am not proud of some of the things I have done or the close calls I have had, but I did learn a lot from those experiences. I only had a real car for less than a year before I left home, leaving the car behind. (I don't count that first junk car that I bought at the drive–in theater and only drove twice while I was 15.)

Shortly after my birthday, Dad took me up to the Plymouth dealer and helped me buy a good–running used 1950 Plymouth four door. He even let me charge the gas until I ran the bill up too high. I recall that I even had to drive myself to the county seat to get a license, and I was nervous that they might ask me how I got there. Having a car meant that I now became more of a leader than a follower, very few students in school had cars. You can do a lot of things with a car and get into a lot of trouble also. I would stay out late at night, drive up town and find anyone who wanted to play poker, drive out to the end of Leeper Lane, where no one lived and play on the back of the seats under the dome light for hours at a time.

Shotgun Prank

Some of my friends approached me about a prank they liked to play on some of the older students. Because I owned a shotgun and a car, I became one of the main players in the plot. We started spreading the rumor about a woman whose husband worked the late shift, and that she was entraining young men while he was at work. Out at the end of Leeper Lane in Providence, Kentucky where we lived, there was an old abandoned house. I drove out just after dark and parked around back, loaded up the shotgun and waited behind a tree. The others that were in on the prank gathered up some of the eager students in their car and brought them out. They made us some excuse for parking on the road before getting to the house and having them walk the rest of the way. I let them get almost to the front porch, and then I steped out and put a couple of shotgun blasts up into the trees.

We only used one car and would never let the victim drive their own car. It would usually take us several hours to find all the victims and calm them down. Of course they were then ready to pull the prank on the next group. After a couple of weeks we ran out of new blood and called it quits. Fortunately no one was hurt, except for their pride.

The Ditch

One Saturday I ran out of gas out on US 41 about five miles out of town. I walked home and borrowed the family Hudson, and picked up some gas. I now had a problem, I needed someone to drive my car back home so that I could return the family car. I drove up to the center of town, which consisted of one traffic light at the top of the hill in the center of Providence. There were a couple of pool halls down one street and the movie theater a half block up the street, a few stores and that was it. You could always find someone standing around in the center of town looking for something to do or someone to talk to.

I found a student that was more a friend of my cousin than I. He was older so I knew that he must have a license. For some strange reason he seemed reluctant to help me out, but I insisted, so he jumped in. We drove out to the car and I put the gas in the tank, got it started and told him to just follow me back to the house. Everything was going fine until we turned down this side street that had a ten–foot ditch on one side and sloped down to the water at about a thirty–degree angle. I was watching him in my rearview mirror and could not believe my eyes. He was slowly getting closer and closer to the ditch and then just drove over the bank and slid down to the bottom sideways. He started to get out on the bottom side when I yelled that the car might turn over on him.

I then found out that he did not have a drivers license. I also later found out that he had a mental problem that caused him to turn the car in the opposite direction that he wanted to go when he got excited. He had even rolled a pickup truck on a curve one time due to his problem. I am sure that there is a name for this, but I do not know what it is. I have never forgotten this, and I am very cautious about being on the side of the road. I think that this is why so many workers and police get hit when working alongside the road.

The police drove up to investigate what was going on, and I did not want to get my friend into trouble. I know that I talked my way out of it, but I cannot remember now how I explained the fact that I was driving two cars at the same time. One thing that helped me was that dad was well known in town, and almost everyone at one time or another had worked for him in the coal mine or played football with him in school. He was the football star and school hero. I guess that is the good thing about growing up in a small town. Everyone knows who you are, and a lot is overlooked.

Fort Campbell

Late one evening someone suggested that we drive down to Ft. Campbell, Kentucky and see what we could find. We drove down to one of the side gates which was closed. We parked on the side of the road and placed the jack under the car so it would look like we had a flat. Then we started out across a field toward the military post. There was a huge sign warning of prison and fines for trespassing, but that did not even slow us down. We found a parking lot full of tanks and climbed into one and played with the controls for a while. My friend had an open knife in his pocket, why I will never know. As he was climbing out of the tank, he put his hand in his pocket and cut it bad. We had blood all over everything. He finally got the bleeding stopped, and we left the tanks to check out the barracks. We tried several doors, and they all were locked. All of a sudden we heard sirens all over the base, and MP cars raced by as we hid. We decided it was time to get out of there, so we headed back to the car. The next day we heard that a plane had crashed at Ft Campbell. Someone must have been watching over us that night or we could have been in a lot of trouble.

Gun Trouble

A mile out of town, just before the intersection of US 41, was where another friend lived who stayed in about as much trouble as I did. We had a fort built across the field behind his house. There was a dirt road that leads to the field, and as it left the main road it had a dirt bank on each side close to the dirt road. I was spinning in the mud and had everyone jump out and push. Well the back doors on the Plymouth opened to the front of the car, and one of the boys left the door open while they were pushing. I got some traction and took off, catching the open door in the bank and tearing it off. Now I had to drive around with a missing back door, and two–odd colored finders that I had replaced earlier from the junkyard. My car was beginning to look pretty sad.

The skating rink was on the second floor of one of the buildings near the center of town, and it also doubled as the meeting place for the VFW.

They had some rifles used for parades, and for some strange reason, they stored the rifles in a hole in the wall of the men's rest room. I was told about the rifles and wasted no time, I drove my car around to the back exit, and we quickly moved the rifles to the car and out to our fort. The rifles were wrapped in grease and wax paper, and there were about five or six of them. I took one home and cleaned it up, and my friend was working on the rest at the fort.

A few days later as I pulled up in my friends yard, the County Sheriff was parked in the yard. He open the trunk of his car and asked me if I knew anything about the rifles he had in there. I explained that I did, and if he would follow me home I would give him the last one. Dad was home when we got there, and they started talking. After awhile I asked if it was all right if I went back up town and they said OK. Things were quiet for awhile and I was relieved. I found out later that my friend had ordered ammunition for the rifles.

I avoided him after that, and later in the year he placed some dynamite in a sewer man hole and blew it up. He was up at the theater bragging about it and got into a lot of trouble. After that the police would stop me after school and question me about drugs and other things, I guess they thought that I knew what was going on around town. I had never heard about drugs and didn't know there were so many problems in our small town. Dad warned me that I had better save up my money for cigarettes for when I went to prison. So I cut back on my wild activities after that.

Winter came and driving became more fun. We drove on the icy streets and cut the wheels to see how many times we could spin around. I am amazed that I survived that winter.

Leaving Home

I left home in stages. It started shortly after we moved from Lakeland, Florida back to our hometown of Providence, Kentucky. I had just turned 15 and felt very confident.

It was summer and school was out, so I decided to visit my older sister who lived in Athens, Tennessee. Mom gave me bus fare, but I decided to save the money and hitchhike to West Tennessee. I was really proud of myself, I made better time hitchhiking than the bus would have taken.

I had already figured out that there was an art to catching a ride. First I had to look neat and clean, and avoid being dropped off in cities or other places that it would be hard to catch a ride. I was also friendly and tried to get to know the people that I rode with.

One fellow that I caught a ride with would press the accelerator hard, then let up on it repeatedly until I thought I would go crazy. Most were just nice and willing to help with a ride. I had very little if any trouble. I stayed a few weeks and then hitchhiked back home.

The second time I left home had nothing to do with me. It was early fall, and my cousin Bobby and I were standing in the center of town talking when he starting talking about running away. I found out later that he had just broken up with his girlfriend and was upset. I did not try to talk him out of it, I just said sounds like fun to me, lets go. I think he had a few dollars in his pocket and I had some change. We started south down US 41 and decided to go through Alabama and onto Florida, I knew that if we made it to Lakeland that I could get my old job back in the bowling alley.

We got a ride through Nashville, Tennessee, but were not so lucky in Birmingham, Alabama. The ride let us out right in the middle of town. Bad mistake. We had to walk south to the edge of town before we could catch another ride. In Montgomery it was even worse. We were let out on the north side of town and had to walk all the way to the south side before catching another ride.

That night we crossed the Florida line and ended up just north of Tallahassee. An early cold front had pushed south, and we were feeling it. We found a lot full of school busses, and all the doors were left open. We picked one and tried to sleep, but it was too cold. Back out on the highway there was no traffic, and we tried again to hobo sleep. This is where you lay down head to head and use each other's shoulder for a pillow. After about thirty minutes we gave up again and started walking. We found an old abandoned house and it had a fireplace. We managed to build a fire and survived the night. The next day Bobby said that he had enough and wanted to go home.

We started hitchhiking back north and had better luck with the cities. One trucker picked us up and Bobby was setting in the middle, when the driver placed his hand on Bobby's leg. Well that did it. We were out of that truck in nothing flat, was that ever freaky. Back in Nashville our luck turned sour again and we were stuck in the middle of town again. We went into a diner and spent the last of our money, except for a dime that Bobby used to call home. Our dads drove down that night and picked us up.

After my close calls with owning a car and picking fights with my younger sister, I began to feel that I needed to get away. School was not going well, and it did not look like I would finish the ninth grade on my second attempt.

I have often been asked why I left home at the age of sixteen, and it has been a hard question to answer. I was bored in school and would usually start the school year making fair grades, but then I would slack off, play hooky or sleep in class. I tried sports and even joined the band, playing the cornet, but could not keep up an interest. I believe the teachers just gave up on me. My car was an escape, and I was taking more chances, driving greater distances looking for adventure. I think that more than anything I just wanted to see more of the world and get out on my own. The car would be more trouble traveling, and I could not afford the gas anyway, so I left it at home.

I was sixteen and a half and the weather was starting to warm, so I made some arrangements with Jim Zachary (nicknamed Sluggo) one of Bobby's classmates who was going on a senior field trip the next day to Paducah, Kentucky. The plan was that I would meet them about two miles out of town on highway 293 to Princeton. I had to be careful because that was close to where my aunt and uncle lived, and I knew that they would be up and out early. I was going to try to make it to St. Louis, Missouri on the first day.

That night I left a note on my pillow in the basement where I slept. Mom and Dad slept in the trailer parked just outside my window. Without a second thought I dressed, picked up my suitcase and started walking the back road out of Providence. About a mile out of town I climbed a fence and went down to the middle of a pasture near a small ditch and settled down for the night.

At daybreak the next morning, I shaved in the cold water of the ditch and washed off. I knew that I had to be back on the road and ready before eight that morning to meet Sluggo.

Here they came speeding like crazy, stopped and told me to jump in quick and get down in the back floorboard. I no sooner got down when the teacher pulled up alongside and demanded to know why they had passed him and sped off. I could see him, but fortunately he did not look down. After some lame brain explanation he pulled off again and they eased back to the back of the line of cars. Sluggo gave me a nickel and told me to keep it to remember the trip by. I did keep it until I got out of the service. Sluggo came to visit us in Georgia once after I was married. He was into insurance then and doing well. We had a good visit and talked a lot about that day I left home.

Pat's Letter to Mom

My older sister Pat, wrote Mom a letter shortly after I left home. Years later Mom gave it to me with a note on the back, "give this to Pat when her son gets to be fifteen years old (good advice if she needs it then), Hubert C. became a fine man!"

January 15, 1957

Dear Mom,

I received your letter yesterday and was very glad to hear from you. I have thought and prayed about your letter all night mom. And I know you are very concerned with Clarkie. I think it would be very unwise for me to say anything to Becky. She may want to tell me and yet she may think she could help Hubert Clark more by telling him we were praying.

Mom, I can't tell you what to do because I don't know all the facts. Even if I did know I still don't think I could tell you.

71

I will tell you what I think about Clarkie and you can do what you think.

When Clarkie was small you know I thought I should boss him just as much as you and Dad could. Well I was just like him, I didn't want him to boss me. It made me rebellious and I just wanted to choke him when he would tell me to do something. Well you know Cathy wants to tell Clarkie what to do too. And Mona you must admit Cathy has been petted and wants her way. Oh I know she is sweet and would do anything for Clarkie but she thinks Clarkie should do anything for her too. Just look back a little bit when I was home. I made good grades in school, I was active in church. Hubert Clark was always hearing you or somebody else bragging on me. Then Cathy makes good grades. Now that she is a Christian, everybody is saying she is the smartest, sweetest little girl I've ever seen. Maybe Clarkie should be proud of his two smart sisters. But Mom just think how he feels. He doesn't make as good of grades as his sisters or even his daddy. I think I realize now why he had to be best in basketball. He feels like he is the bad one in the family. Ok of course none of us feel like that but he does and you can't tell him different because he already thinks he has to prove himself. That is one point of why he is like he is. Another is that it's just like daddy says, "He's a Boy." Mama that's one thing that will never be changed. I was reading in Granville's Sociology book and it said boys between the age of fifteen and seventeen are the most difficult to understand and to discipline.

Mrs. Hooper said she thought she would never live through Granville and Avery at that age. They were always wanting to leave home, and Mom I think if you were to ask other mothers you would find the same thing true with their sons. The way I see it is not try to tell him what to do or act and just let him drift through these next two years and just let Daddy handle all the discipline problems. He was a boy once, he should be able to understand Clarkie better than anyone else. Boys are just different from girls at that age. I think probably what Becky was talking about being so shocked about was about Clarkie leaving home. I know I had to read your letter 2 or 3 times before I could believe it.

Mother, I honestly believe the best thing for you to do is just pray. Don't critize him about the things he doesn't do but let him know you appreciate the little things he does that's good. Clarkie has been brought up in a Christian home enough to know right from wrong. I don't think there is anything wrong with Clarkie but growing up. Mom all this I have written is just my ideas about Clarkie. What you do is up to you. I'll just keep praying for you and I'm sure in a couple of years you will know it was just a boy's way of growing up. I think Dad knows this and that's the reason why he hasn't said too much. Hope everything else is alright at home and I sure would love to see you.

Whatever you do don't let Clarkie know about any of this because he will think we are trying to run his business. Well Mom, I guess I had better close and get this in the mail. Try not to worry because if we have enough faith in God he will take care of everything.

Write soon and maybe we will get to see you before too long.

We love you,
Pat and Granville

I don't know if Pat really understood what was going on with me, but I am grateful for all her prayers!

CHAPTER 5 TRAVELING WEST

St. Louis

I caught a short ride from Paducah across the Mississippi River and into Missouri, then took US 61 north toward St. Louis. I was not sure where I was going, but for some crazy reason Salt Lake City sounded good to me.

I looked for a good spot to wait for a ride. I was well experienced at hitchhiking, and knew to keep a good view of the highway in both directions, look neat and keep a smile on my face.

Three young men that were a little rough looking said they were going to St. Louis, so I jumped in the back, a little nervous. I only had about sixty dollars on me, so it would not be a big loss if I were robbed on the first day of running away from home.

About halfway to St. Louis, we were pulled over by a state trooper and asked a few questions. I was never sure what all that was about. It may have just been God's way of making sure the boys did not try to take advantage of me.

They let me out in the center of St. Louis, with no possibility of getting a ride. It was getting late, and I would have to get out to the edge of town in order to catch a ride. The YMCA was nearby, so I decided that it would be best to check in for the night. I read my Bible and prayed that night. The room at the YMCA was nice, quiet and cheap. I settled in for a good rest after my first full day on the road.

I unpacked and looked over the few belongings I brought. My favorite treasure was a clay pipe with two deer stepping over a log. My grandfather Clark had given it to me a few years before he died, along with a .22 rifle used on the farm to kill hogs. I did not bring the rifle! The antlers were broken, but the rest of the pipe was in good shape and kept in a leather–hinged case molded to fit. Grandpa Clark told me that it was given to him by an Indian that was passing through. I often wondered what kind thing Grandpa must have done to warrant such a nice gift.

Early the next morning I packed up my suitcase and caught a city bus to the outskirts of town and a main highway to resume my hitchhiking west.

Kansas and Canada

The morning went well, and after a couple of short rides a man that was heading to Alaska picked me up. We talked about me riding along with him, but I understood that one needed at least a hundred dollars in order to cross the Canadian border, so we parted company around Kansas City.

The next ride turned out to be the last one, not only for the day but for a long time. The Youngs were traveling around the country working different jobs. They were working their way to Oregon where Mr. Young had a farm job waiting just west of Portland. Mr. Young was a full—blooded American Indian, and Mrs. Young was half Indian. They were both Christians and read their Bible every night. They were pleased to hear that I was also a Christian so we got along just fine.

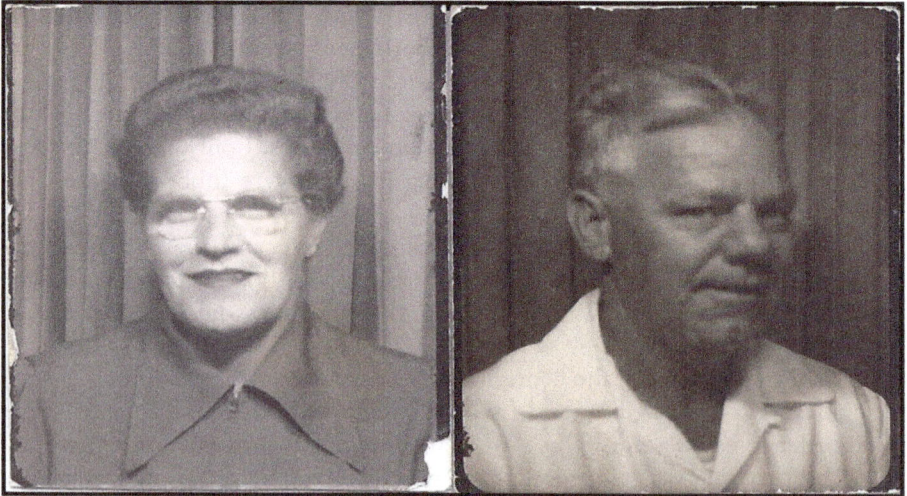

Mrs. Young and Mr. Young

I contributed what funds I had left for food and gas and changed my plans from Salt Lake City to Portland. Never knew what was so special about Salt Lake City anyway. We put our money together and fed the gas tank until we reached Wyoming. The first night we spent the night in a road side park and they read their Bible and prayed before turning in.

Each town of any size we came to, we would split up and look for work, then meet back at the car, then eat and sleep in the car.

74

The first town was in Wyoming, can't remember the name, but I do remember the elk dinner. As we split up to look for work, I knocked on doors in a well–to–do neighborhood, offering to wash window or any other odd jobs that needed done. After washing windows for this nice lady most of the afternoon, she paid me and then asked if I would like some elk. It sure was good, and it reminded me a lot of the wild game that Dad would bring in for Mom to cook.

The next day I found work digging ditches on a farm. I remember it being the easiest digging that I had ever done. The ground was soft, so it may have been just cleaning out old ditches.

Idaho

In Idaho we found all the work we wanted. The potatoes were rotting in a storehouse and had to be loaded on trucks to save as many as possible. We were offered work for as long each day as we could hold up. After a week of fourteen–hour days and tired nights, we went to collect our. The paymaster explained that we would have to wait a week for the money. It was their policy to hold back one week. We discussed the problem for quite some time, and then he said that he would have to guess at the withholding if we insisted on getting the pay that day. He kept about one third of our pay, and we had no other choice.

Portland

That was enough to get us to Portland and the farm. During the next few weeks I helped loading hay and applied for a job in Portland in a bowling alley.

The Tacoma River flooded that spring and covered the hayfield that had just been harvested. I could see the carp swimming in the shallow water, and I asked the Young's if they would like some fresh fish. I told them about grabbing for carp on the Ohio River after it flooded an island. A lot of people do not like carp because of all the bones. However I enjoyed the meat very well. It only took me a few minutes to wade in and grab a nice size one by the mouth and the tail. We ate very well that evening.

The old farmhouse had an old radio with all the tubes laying loose inside. I spent an afternoon playing with the tubes to see if I could figure out where they belonged. Before the evening was gone we had music and news.

I wrote Mom and Dad a letter, telling them that I was all right and letting them know where I was. The Youngs had been talking up the army and about enlisting, and I was thinking that I needed a little time to grow some with a little supervision. I was still sixteen, and even though I had only a few months to wait till my seventeenth birthday, I thought it would be an easier thing to keep up with one year instead of a month change. So I lied about my age by a whole year. I visited the enlistment office and obtained the papers for a seventeen–year–old to join.

I mailed the papers to Dad to be signed, explaining my desire to join the army. Dad had been in the army during WWII, and I knew that he would understand. Mom later regretted signing the papers and almost turned me in, but Dad talked her out of it. With the signed papers showing I was seventeen instead of sixteen, I threw away my driver's license and joined the army in Portland Oregon on May 26, 1958, three months before my seventeenth birthday.

US Army

The Youngs talked a lot about the army and how most of the boys they picked up had joined the army. They said that it was a good place for young men to grow up. A week later the army was ready for me. A bus was waiting for a ride to Ft. Ord California so that I could be processed into the service.

Dad realized that I had lied about my age, but he figured I would be better off in the army than drifting around the country. He did not tell Mom about the age problem when he signed the papers. Dad served in the army during World War II and trained in Ft. Fannin Texas. As a matter of fact one of my earliest memories was going to the latrine on the base when I was only three or four.

The Youngs had complained about the young men they helped out not staying in touch, so I wrote to them several times. They never answered, and I assumed that they had moved on to another job. This would explain the loss of contact with the other young men!

Basic Training

Three days of processing was quite an experience. I never knew where Fort Ord was, only that we were somewhere in central California.

After I enlisted in the army in Portland, Oregon, they wasted no time. I had to report for duty the following week and boarded a train for California. Fort Ord, located on scenic Hwy. 1 about five miles north of Monterey, was once home to 25,000 soldiers and civilian workers. Founded as a cavalry post in 1917, it became a major training post during World War II. Most recently, Fort Ord was home to the 7th Infantry Div., which deactivated in 1993.

The bus came to a stop and we all got out, lined up and answered a roll call. The first march to the barracks was a disaster. We were all out of step with bags and hardly in a straight line. It was late as we found a bunk and they turned the lights out.

Barracks at Fort Ord

I lost track of my personal belongs in the rush to leave Portland, and the thing that I missed the most was that Indian pipe my grandfather gave me. I should not have taken it with me when I ran away from home.

A New Start

Five–thirty came way too early with lights on and a whistle blowing way too loud. We were ordered to stand at the end of our bunks and given instructions for the day.

We were in lines all day, lines for new clothes, boots and shots between meals. Then we cleaned the barracks along–with other strange duties.

On the third day we were just beginning to find a routine of early morning roll call, exercise and instructions on how to march when we were told to pack up for our trip to boot camp and basic training.

A troop train was waiting, and we loaded up for the long ride to Texas. As we were about to leave California, the train came to a sudden stop. We leaned out the windows and doors to see what the problem was. A woman was under the tracks, assumed to be a suicide. After several hours and the mess was cleaned up, we resumed our trip.

After a couple of days on the train we arrived at Killeen, Texas for basic training at Fort Hood.

Fort Hood

As we departed the train, the heat hit us in the face. It was going to be a long six weeks. Fort Hood is in the middle of Texas, next to Killeen, Texas. The air was dry and hot for June, 1958. The cold war was in full swing. I felt safe entering the army at this time. The Korean war had just ended with troops still at high alert on each side and occasional shots beings fired at each other. Most of us thought that we would end up in Korea before it was over. We had not heard about Vietnam, and it was not until years later that I discovered that we had advisors there before I was

77

discharged. This qualified me as a war veteran and a free lifelong drivers' license from the state of Georgia.

We had no idea where we would be stationed and would not find out until we started what was called "Second Eight," or advance training. There was no leave during basic training, but we would get a two week leave at the end of boot camp.

All of us were very young, and I would guess that a lot of the boys were underage like myself. There were several that told their correct age so that they could get out and go home. There was a lot of joking about giving up. I never let on about how old I really was.

The PT Test

The second day, after we settled in to our new barracks, we were required to take a PT Test. This was to find out just how fit we were. The idea was to push each of us to our limits, counting pushups, situps and jumping jacks. Some of us got sick, and we were all exhausted, laying around on the ground. I could not remember a time when I was so tired, except for maybe the time I worked shoveling rotten potatoes. We all slept hard that night!

Picking Up Butts

"Smoke them if you got them!" This was the signal to take a break, and most of us did smoke. I started smoking at age thirteen, and small cigars were my favorite. Most of us did not have the money to buy cigarettes. When I could afford them I smoked about a pack a day. When the breaks came we looked for those who had cigarettes to see if we could bum one. If you did have a pack it usually did not last very long.

There were always a lot of cigarette butts laying around, and some of the guys would look for long ones to finish off. Before we would leave the area, the sergeant would line us up across the area at arms length and start picking up all the butts.

Sleepwalking

Long marches were made every day, we did not ride anywhere. Some were called forced marches. During each break we were required to take salt tablets to prevent dehydration. Soon some of the guys refused to take them. They then started adding the salt to the water. It was either take the tablets or drink salt water. After a few hours in the sun, our shirts would turn white from all the salt and sweat.

At the end of an especially long day, as we were marching back to the barracks, I went to sleep while walking. I don't know how long I marched that way. When I woke up I was laying in a ditch. I was told that I just drifted out of the column and walked right into the ditch! It was not uncommon, and we would sometimes take quick naps during the breaks if we had nothing to smoke.

Rifle Range

I looked forward to trips to the rifle range where we learned how to fire the M1 rifle standing, sitting and laying down. I already knew to squeeze the trigger and keep my eyes open, but taking a deep breath and holding it was new. Dad had showed me how to use a rifle and shotgun, and I even owned a shotgun at home. The M1 was an easy rifle to shoot, and I did fairly well with a marksman badge.

We were also taught how to field strip the M1 for cleaning–and even to do it with our eyes shut.

Tear Gas

The dreaded day finally came: gas mask training. We had to put on our gas masks, then enter a small building where tear gas was released. When the room was full of gas, we were told to remove the masks before being allowed to leave. There were a lot of red eyes for the rest of the day. I will never forget how my eyes watered so much that I could not see, but I did not get sick. We were all happy that the training was only one day and that we would not have to repeat the ordeal. And then there was the crawling under the live machine gun fire. I sure was glad to see those six weeks end.

Hand Grenades

The day of hand grenade training scared me the most. I knew that they would be heavy, I just did not realize how heavy.

We practiced with a few dummy grenades, then came time to get into the foxhole with the training sergeant and throw a live grenade. In the movies they pulled the pin, released the lever, counted to three and threw it. We did not release the lever or count to three. As soon as that pin was pulled I gave it all that I had to get rid of that explosive, pin and all. Then both the sergeant and I hit the bottom of the foxhole fast!

The biggest fear we all had was that we would get nervous and drop the grenade. I bet the sergeant was nervous about it too. He would be the one to find it and get it out of the foxhole before it exploded.

Compass Reading

The compass reading was fun also. we were taken out in small groups and told to find our way back to the barracks with only a map and compass. We would have to triangulate between objects we could find on the map to find our correct position, then plot a course to the barracks.

Green Hills of Kentucky

I still have not gotten over how green the hills of west Kentucky looked as the bus took me back home for the one week of leave. It seemed like I had been gone for a long time, although it had only been a few months.

A day on the road, five days with family, and then back on the bus to Ft. Hood.

Second Eight

After we returned to Ft. Hood, we went through a series of tests to see where we would fit in. There was the infantry, tank and artillery divisions, as well as a few other positions to be filled. And there were all the different jobs in each.

To this day I do not know how I ended up where I did. There was six of us chosen for the fire direction control in the artillery. We were sometimes called prima donnas, as well as a few other choice names because of easy jobs we had. We were always riding in a truck or personal carrier with charts and maps.

We spent a lot of time in a classroom studying maps and charts, plotting positions and learning about the artillery. We had lots of classroom training before going out on the firing range with the 105mm self–propelled howitzers. Fort Hood was the home of the 4th Armed Division, nicknamed Hell On Wheels.

Mischief

During this training period, passes to go off base were hard to get. One time I did slip out under the fence, but I got back before the wakeup call. Some others did not make it back in time and were charged AWOL.

I did get into trouble once, can't remember what it was over. The First Sergeant ordered me to dig a ten–by–ten hole ten feet deep under the headquarters building. There was about three feet of space to get started. It was sort of like shoveling coal in the mines. I never did finish that hole, and he let it slide.

One day we were scheduled to hold a full dress parade, and several of us decided to hide in the crawl space above the barracks. I remember seeing the sergeant stick his head up into the opening and look around, but it was dark so we all remained still. Later we came down and took naps while the rest were marching. Again they must have known who was missing, but nothing was ever said.

Elvis Presley entered the army on March 24, 1958, two months before I entered on May 26, 1958. he was finishing up basic training as I was starting, also at Fort Hood. Elvis was given a break to record new material for RCA in June before returning to Fort Hood to finish his tank training.

Elvis requested emergency leave to visit his mother who was dying and delayed his completion of training, he shipped out for Germany on September 19, 1958, within a few weeks of when I shipped out, and was assigned to the 3rd Armored Division in Friedberg, Germany. He was seen by many of my friends, however I only thought that I saw him once, we all looked alike in our uniforms, so I could not be sure. Elvis returned to the States on March 2, 1960. I had enlisted for three years and had another year to serve.

CHAPTER 6 GERMANY

After a long speech in the post theater by the commanding officer, we lined up at the bulletin board to find out where our assignments would be. Everybody was dreading Greenland, and a few were sent there. Some went to Korea, but most, including myself, were assigned to Germany.

I turned 17 in my second eight weeks of basic training at Fort Hood, Texas and was too young to appreciate a tour of duty in Germany. I did visit some of the sites, but most of my free time was wasted. I should have taken more leave while there and toured more.

Me with a 3.5 rocket launcher, Wildflicken, Germany.

Hanau, Germany

We boarded a train for New York with no stopover, and the train rolled right through New York City and stopped at the docks. It was in the middle of the night so I saw nothing of the city. Early the next morning I was assigned KP duty and had to remain below, even missing the view as we sailed. I pulled KP duty every other day for the 20 some days at sea before landing at Bremerhaven, Germany.

After the troop ship landed in Bremerhaven, Germany, we loaded into a train and headed south to a small town near Frankfort, Germany. Hanau would be my home for the next two years. The Cold War was building up, and we were warned about riding the trains too close to the border. You could get on the wrong train headed for East Germany, and it would not stop until the first station inside East Germany, and then it would be too late, and it might take months for the military to get you back.

Army Post, Hanau, Germany

After small arms target practice one day about an hour drive from Hanau, two of us decided to skip the target duty and hitchhike back to the barracks. Large targets would be raised for the solder on the firing line to shoot at, then you would lower the target and mark the bullet holes. If they missed the target altogether, they would get a "Maggie Drawers," a red flag would be waved from the pit for everyone to see. Sometimes if you didn't care for the person on the line, we would give him "Maggie Drawers." We walked out to the main road with our rifles over our shoulders and put out our thumbs. In no time we were back at the barracks and no one said anything. I guess that we were not missed.

The barracks at Hanau were built by the Germans before WWII, and the base was well laid out in a half circle with the motor pool and equipment on one side and the barracks on the other side. It was a short walk to the motor pool, but it seemed longer when you were carrying all your gear and a 30–Caliber machine gun or the barrel of a 50–Caliber. We had red alerts about once a month, and we would jump out of bed, rush down to the arms room in the basement, grab the equipment and run to the motor pool to await further orders. Our barracks was on the corner with a good view of the athletic fields and lower buildings. The room was also on the top corner floor. It was great except for a low support beam that ran at an angle from the floor to the ceiling. We soon learned to duck under or avoid it.

The Fourth barracks from the left was home for two years

We were trained for an atomic war if hostilities broke out. One or more of the atomic warheads for the Honest John Missile were stored in the basement of our barracks. We always knew when they were moving them, because they would warn us about taking pictures out of the windows. I did take a few pictures of the crane that lifted the warheads, but not of the warheads. Shells for the Atomic Cannon were moved around all over our area and could have very well been stored in the basement as well. One end of the basement was restricted, and we had our classroom and arms room in the other end. There were rumors that we also had atomic rounds for the 8 inch and 155 mm guns, but I never knew for sure.

Atomic Cannon, only fired once in US

Artillery

B Battery, 3rd Armored Division, 2nd Howitzer Battalion, 73rd Artillery, consisted of six 155mm M109 self–propelled howitzers and an armored personnel carrier for fire direction control. Except for direct fire practice, the artillery would be shooting blind under the control of the Fire Direction Control Center. The Fire Direction Control Center would receive information by radio from the forward observer who would be watching the rounds hit the impact area. The pack of charges for firing the 155mm shells came in a pack of seven. They would then be told what charge to use, for example a charge five would mean that two charges would be removed and thrown into the fire pit. As a safety measure, one of the gun crew would count the discarded charges and repeat out loud to avoid mistakes.

Modified APC, raised top for standing at map board

85

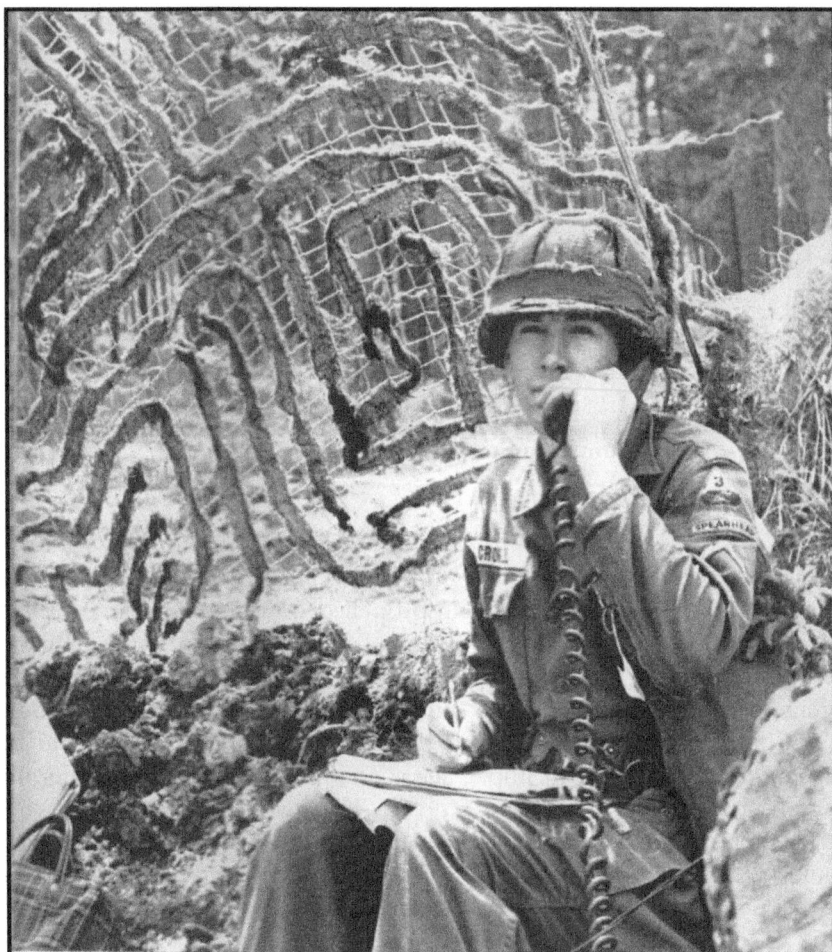

PFC Hubert Crowell

A recorder on the phone between the fire direction group and the guns would record all the information sent to the guns in case there was a mistake or someone misunderstood, then verification could be made. This was my job, Battery Recorder. I would ride out ahead of the battery with the First Sergeant and we would align the aiming circle, a device which had a compass and a scope for sighting in different angles. We would use this to obtain the correct direction for the guns and place stakes for them to line up on when they pulled into position.

Great care had to be taken to insure that all six guns were pointed in the same direction parallel to each other. You aligned the device to magnet north by looking through a hole at the end of the compass needle. The danger here was that you had to be sure that you knew which end of the needle you were looking at. If you had the wrong end, then the guns would be laid out 180 degrees and you would be shooting backwards.

One of the Honest John rockets was laid out backward in Grafenwohr during practice. The rocket, with just enough explosive to blow the head apart, hit a building in a nearby town. No one was hurt.

155 MM note round in the air!

The Fire Direction Control Center consisted of two drafting tables set up in the armored personnel carrier with field telephone contact with the guns. Each table was identical except that one used a plain paper chart and the other used a topographic map. The first order of business when we set up in a new position was to zero in on a known target. We would fire one round toward the target, and the observer would then give us corrections over the radio. We would bracket the target with usually only three rounds. From this information we could then aim at any other target within our field of fire. The drafting equipment consisted of a metal scale for the elevation and protractor for the azimuth. There were other calculations that determined the proper charge and weather reports that gave us the air density. This information was sent to the guns in a string of information as charge, elevation and azimuth. The recorder wrote down this information as it was being given to the guns.

2nd Lt. Phelps, in charge of FDC   **PFC Green on FDC radio**

After setting up the alignment stakes for the guns and while waiting for them to arrive, I would dig a foxhole and set up the command station for our lieutenant who oversaw the operation. In practice I could get away with digging a shallow hole and erecting a tent or camouflage over it, depending on the weather.

Lt. Weske and I in command center Fox Hole

My cousin, started writing to a pen pal in Germany when she was in high school and asked if I would look her up while I was in Germany. We wrote several letters back and forth, and I was invited up to Hanover when I got some leave. Hanover was in the British sector, and they were not used to seeing American solders. Annamarie's father was a soldier in WWII, and I am not sure how he felt about his daughter seeing me. A friend of theirs owned a hotel, and they provided me with a nice room. We went to the movies, took long walks and toured Hanover. Nothing more became of the relationship, and we lost touch. I am not sure if Anna Lell is still writing to her.

I also corresponded with Becky, my friend from Englewood, Tennessee, while I was in Germany. It was nice to get letters while away from home. Once shortly after I arrived in Germany, I took a week of leave and went camping. I did not have much money, so it seemed like a good idea. I fit right in with the campers and my pup tent. The locals at the camp ground were friendly, and they had a nice swimming hole.

I was not much for drinking. I might go out on the town with some of the other solders and just sit on one drink all night. However one evening I thought that I would see what it was like to get drunk. I persuaded Zink, who did not drink, to go with me. Funny how we used only last names in the service and seldom first names. I guess it was because our last name was always there on the front for everyone to see. Zink took good care of me that night. I sure don't remember much and was very sick the next morning. I hated not knowing what was going on around me, and I don't recall ever trying that again.

From left, Pfc. Rudolph, Pfc. Crowell, Sp4. Zink, Sp4. Morgan

Operation Winter Shield

Operation Winter Shield took place in February 1960 with over 60,000 members of the Seventh Army at the Grafenwohr training grounds. The weather was cold and dry. This was the cause of a major motor pool fire at the start of the training. A returning jeep driver was refueling one night from a tanker parked in the motor pool, when a static spark started a gasoline fire. We were called out in the middle of the night to evacuate the motor pool. It was quite a sight with all the vehicles moving past the burning jeep and fuel tanker with the tires blowing and flames reaching hundreds of feet into the night sky.

One of the batteries experienced a shell going off just after leaving the barrel of the gun. There was a road some 100 yards in front of the position and a lieutenant in a jeep had a close call. We got the cease fire on the radio and listened to the excited chatter over the radio. The shell is set for an air burst by placing a tool on top of the shell and setting a dial for the correct time. There are safety limits on the dial, so it had to be a defective shell in order for it to go off that soon.

We would go to Grafenwohr about every six months for training, and that summer we returned.

General Colin Powell writes in his 1995 autobiography, "My American Journey," about his time with the division in 1958–60 and about the Cold War and the army's mission in Germany.

Colin Powell was assigned to the 3rd Armored Division on December 1958, the twentyone–year–old 2nd lieutenant joined the 2nd Battalion, 48th Infantry Regiment, at Coleman Kaserne. After a promotion to 1st lieutenant and training in Grafenwohr, he related the following story.

(The following is from General Powell's book)

While working as Louiseil's exec, I got a foretaste of what hot war could be like if the Cold War ever ignited. It was a morning after payday in the summer of 1960. Our brigade had gone to Grafenwohr for field training. The troops were to be billeted in over six hundred general–purpose tents. Our company had not yet arrived in force, but a sister unit, the 12th Cavalry, had come in the night before. Its tents were full of troops, still asleep at this early hour.

I was returning from a bartering mission with another company's exec., bringing rations I had traded for back to our mess hall. My ears pricked up at an odd, whistling sound overhead. In about a nanosecond, I realized it was an artillery shell that had strayed wildly out of the impact area. I stopped, frozen, and actually saw the 8–inch round come in. It struck a tent pole in the 12th Cavalry's sector, detonating in an air–burst. The roar was deafening, followed by a terrifying silence. I dropped the food and rushed toward the blast as dismembered legs, hands, and arms thumped to the ground around me. Money from payday came fluttering to earth. Some other soldiers joined me, wading through the acrid smoke and fumes. Inside the tent, I zipped open a sleeping bag, and what was left looked like an illustration of viscera in a medical textbook. In an instant, a dozen lives had been snuffed out and more men wounded. The tragedy was later found to have been caused by human error in aligning the gun, and the battalion commander and other officers were relieved of their duties. I had seen a hundred war movies, but nothing had prepared me for the sights I saw that day.

(End of account from General Powell's book)

I was also in the field at Grafenwohr that fateful day. We were in the middle of a firing mission with our 155's when the radio broke open with a command to cease firing, hold all positions and maintain radio silence.

(Account of the accident from the History Web Site of the 3rd Armored Division)

Accidents in an actual shooting war, as well as a Cold War, are inevitable. This one, however, stands out as apparently the worst U.S. ground training accident of the entire Cold War. Just after roll–call, on a rainy Friday morning on September 2, 1960, sixteen solders were killed and 27 were wounded when a 200–pound artillery shell landed amongst them at Camp Kasserine, Grafenwoehr. All of the men were from the 3rd Reconnaissance Squadron, 12th Calvary, 3rd Armored Division. The shell, which had an incorrect charge due to human error, was fired by a V Corps Artillery unit — Battery A, 3rd Battalion, 18th Field Artillery.

(End of account from History Web Site)

8 Inch similar to the one that overshot the impact area from the 18th Artillery

I knew exactly what happened that morning, someone misunderstood the correct charge and the round overshot the impact area. The big fear in that tent area that morning was that they all knew that usually a fire for effect would follow, and that would mean six more rounds could be following the deadly misplaced round. But that did not happen.

Vacation

I tried to take a typing course during my time in Germany. I started the course three times and each time when I was about halfway through the course, we would pull out for field training. I never did complete the course. However the typing lessons have helped me over the years.

I took a couple of weeks leave and visited Copenhagen, Denmark. I saw a lot of museums and towers. One tower was built for a queen to ride up in a carriage that had a circular ramp all the way to the top. I saw Tivoli Gardens and the Littlest Mermaid. I loved the food. They had a lot of dairy products and everyone was friendly. The bars rotated hours, at midnight half would close and another group would open. Copenhagen had a lot of night life, and although I did not dance much, I enjoyed watching. I was a loner, maybe because I was younger than the others. I took this trip and others by myself.

Put to the Test

Near the end of 1960, the majority of our unit rotated back to the states for discharge. These were the drafted men who only had to serve two years. The enlisted who had to serve three years had to take over the operations for another six months. At the same time the Nike Missile sites in Germany were being turned over to the German Army. The men who still had the remainder of their tour to serve were transferred to units like ours who were now short of men.

I was promoted to Sp4 and placed in charge of the fire direction control center under a new 2nd Lt. Phelps. Even though I had received advanced training at Butzbach, Germany, in January 1959 in fire direction, I had been acting only as the battery recorder up until this time. Now I had a new crew with no experience or training in the artillery. I conducted classes, but it was hard to hold the interest of displaced men with only months left to serve. I was very cautious, remembering the accidents that had occurred. I did not want any blood on my hands.

During the winter of 1960–61, we were involved in more tests at Grafenwoehr, and I am proud that we completed the exercises without incident. However, we were slow in performing the tests. I was given an article fifteen and reduced back to private and 2nd Lt. Phelps did not get his 1st Lt. bars. I fought the article fifteen with the help of barracks lawyers, until it was almost time for me to ship back to the states. One of the guys at headquarters told me at the end that if I had not fought so hard, he could have torn up the papers and no one would have been the wiser. But it was too late at that point, so I stripped off all my rank from my uniforms, except one set that I saved for the trip home. This would keep me off any picky details that were dished out along the way.

We were fortunate to fly back to the states, and I had a month off to visit family, now living in Florida, before reporting for duty at Fort Lewis, Washington. I was hoping to be stationed closer to my home, however you are returned to the nearest post that you enlisted. As I enlisted in Portland, Oregon, then Fort Lewis would be where I would be discharged.

On the way to Florida, I stopped in Tennessee to visit Becky. She was attending college at the time. We had a nice visit, talking about old times we had in Englewood. I took her to a drive–in movie and the next day continued on to Florida. There did not seem to be any strong attraction between the two of us, and we did not write to each other again. Many years later, when I was working in Atlanta, I was on a service call at Rich's department store. They have a bridge over the street connecting two of their buildings, as I crossed over I noticed a young lady sitting at one of the tables on the bridge. As I continued toward my service call in the accounting department, I kept trying to figure out why she looked so familiar. Then it hit me–it was Becky, I am sure of it. I was so positive that I went back down to the bridge to see her, however she was gone!

Fort Lewis

My two–year tour in Germany was over, and I was grateful for the commercial flight back to the United States. With thirty days leave to spend with my family, now living in Florida, I was ready to relax. Dad was commercial fishing now and hunting alligators. Mom was happy with her beach house on the lake and her painting, and my little sister was in high school. Dad took me out running the trout lines in the daytime, and at night we would load up the boat and go alligator hunting.

Alligator Hunting

In 1961 it was still legal to hunt alligators. We would use a boat or wade through the swamp shining a light around, looking for red eyes. If the eyes were high off the ground then it would be a cow, and you had better not shoot any cows. Dad shot a five–foot alligator one night, and I was dragging it back to the boat when it came back to life. The tail is the strongest part, and I could not hold on. Dad finished him off with the .22 magnum pistol he carried, and we had alligator tail for dinner the next day. The trotlines were for catfish, and he would usually bring in a tub full each day and skin them on a nail board next to the canal that ran alongside the house.

The trailer that we had lived in for two years before I left home was parked behind the house. Dad kept bait in the freezer for maggots he collected and froze for bait. Visitors who stayed in the trailer were warned to not open the freezer! Dad also used Camay soap, the catfish liked the smell I guess. Only a year before, fish traps were used on the lakes by the commercial fishermen and had just been outlawed due to fears of over fishing. Trotlines were all that were allowed, and it was a lot more work. My sister had the job of baiting the lines that were set in box frames with the hooks hanging from groves around the outside. Dad would set the stack of frames on a turntable mounted on the edge of the boat. The boat would then be driven fast across the lake with Dad picking off the empty frames as they turned feeding the line out into the lake. He would attach a milk jug for a float every once in a while to hold the line off the bottom. That afternoon we would bring the lines and catfish back in with a few turtles to create a little excitement. We usually ate the turtles and alligators, and Dad sold the fish.

Driving West

After about a week of this, I was ready to get on the road. The old family car was a 1956 Chevy station wagon. Dad had moved up to a Volkswagen, and he gave me the Chevy wagon. It ran good, but the tires needed balancing, so I could only drive about fifty-five miles an hour. I drove up to west Kentucky to see my aunt Pauline and uncle Paul before heading across the country for the second time. But this time I was traveling in style. My aunt packed a sack of sandwiches for me and I would drive, eat sandwiches and sleep in the back of the wagon when I got tired. I had an old army gas can for back up, and it came in handy on the long stretches between towns.

Three days later as I was crossing Idaho, it started snowing hard, and it was dark. I pulled off the expressway and down the ramp to what looked like a safe place and crawled into the back. When I awoke the next morning, I was parked in the middle of an intersection. The snow had no tracks and the intersection had not been used all night. I eased back upon the expressway through the fresh snow and continued on to Washington state.

Ice Skating

I arrived at Fort Lewis a week early and with little money. Not wanting to check in until my leave was up, I drove through the post and would pick up soldiers looking for a ride into Tacoma. A few bucks extra helped with the gas, now all I needed was a place to stay. I found out about the officer's hotel nearby and talked my way in. They had empty rooms and said that if I did not tell anyone I could stay for the week.

During the week I continued my taxi runs and found an ice skating rink to spend the afternoons. I had never ice skated before, and it was quite an experience. After building up a little strength in my ankles, I decided to never roller skate again. Ice skating is so smooth and quiet compared to roller skating. By the end of the week I could skate backwards and stay on my feet for several hours at a time.

My assignment at Fort Lewis was easy. I was assigned to drive a jeep for officers on duty at headquarters.

Party Time

I enjoyed the heavy wet snows that are typical along the coast of Washington. On the weekends we would drive down to Portland. A friend I met lived there and knew where all the parties were. We would party all night Saturday and then go to Mass early on Sunday morning. Being Baptist I did not quite understand the logic of Mass. I would not drink as I was driving and did not like drinking that much anyway. We would again party Sunday night and drive back to Fort Lewis early Monday morning to arrive before roll call. When the fog rolled in on those early morning drives from Portland along the coast, we would sometimes have to hang our heads out the window to see the center line of the highway.

Snow Skiing

During one weekend I drove over to Mount Rainier to try out snow skiing. The snow was so deep that the road looked like a tunnel with the snow piled so high along the side of the road. The parking lot had a tunnel entrance to the ski lodge, and only the roofs of some of the buildings were visible above the snow. I had never been in snow that deep. I started out on the beginners slope and never made it any higher. On the second day I ended up with one ski pointed up and the other ski pointing down, both stuck in the snow. This was before they had the quick release shoes, so my feet were still attached to the skis. My knee was sore for two years after that experience.

Our unit was on standby for trouble spots around the world, and each time trouble broke out we had a new round of shots. I have never been stuck with so many needles. We would load up our equipment and board the train, then wait for orders. Although we never had to leave, when trouble broke out in Lebanon that year, we were all sure that we would be sent. Vietnam was heating up at this time and we had advisors there, but at the time we were not aware of the problems, and it was not until after I was discharged that I learned about Vietnam.

Discharged

Due to cutbacks in the budget I was discharged a few months early on April 12, 1961. On the day I was processing out, one of the soldier's working in the discharge area swore that I had a twin bother there. I never met the fellow, and it remained a mystery never to be solved. They say that we all have a look–alike somewhere, and I guess that I came close to seeing mine.

The drive back to Florida was a little faster after I had the tires balanced on the Chevy. I had to keep all my uniforms for three more years to complete my six–year obligation to the Army, but I was never called back. I did have to register for the draft because of my age, but would not be called as I was in the reserve.

Getting my military experience over at an early age was a great advantage as I started looking for work. With Vietnam and the draft, the first question asked when I applied for a job was if I had already been in the service. Once they found out that I would not be drafted, there was not problem getting a job. After a short visit with family in Sebring, I moved to Bradenton, Florida to work and attend the junior college there. The college was new, and they would take students with no high school diploma. The GED test results were all that I needed.

CHAPTER 7 SEBRING

I never lived in Sebring, but I listed it as my home when getting out of the service and registered for the draft there. My family moved there while I was in the service, and when I got out I headed straight back there for a few weeks while I decided were I was going to live.

Sebring is the home of the Sebring International Raceway located on an old air base runway and is well known for an annually held American Le Mans Series race.

After a several years of saving up for Florida, Mom, Dad and Cathy moved to a house on Lake Istokpoga. Big Mac drive ran along a canal from the lake, and the house was at the end of the drive on the lake. There was a boat dock and a small shed next to the canal. The trailer was parked behind the house. Mom loved the lake and beach, and Dad was in his element, fishing during the day and hunting alligators at night!

Preacher's Daughter

From the moment I arrived Mom was trying to match me up with the preacher's daughter. We did go on a few dates. The one I remember most clearly was at the teen club house in Sebring. I parked the Chevy wagon in front, and we were inside for about an hour. When we came out, I saw my car moving slowly down the slight grade toward the lake. I ran and caught up to it, jumped in and pulled the brake! I just could not believe that it took that long to start rolling. I had left it in neutral and the wheels straight, instead of pointing toward the curb.

I did not care much for her, and it was difficult to see anyone else. I knew that I should find a trade and work on my education. There was nothing in Sebring.

Bird Island

Out in the middle of the lake, due east of the canal, was a small island that had nothing but birds, goats and trees. There were birds everywhere of all kinds. You could not walk without stepping on nests or small birds that had fallen out of the nest. The sound was deafening, and there was movement everywhere. Dad loved to take visitors out to the island. Many years later, Kathy's uncle Bud was in the middle of a divorce, and we were all trying to convince him not to leave aunt Evelyn. In a last ditch effort I convinced him to go to Florida with me for a break from it all to sort things out. I was young and thought I could influence him to stay with Kathy's Aunt Evelyn. I took him down to Sebring and out to the place on the lake. It was a rush trip, and I found out that Mom and Dad were visiting family in Kentucky. I loaded Uncle Bud into the fishing boat, and we headed out across the lake to check on Bird Island.

You could not see the island from the shore, and when you got to within sight of the island you could not see land in any direction. Lake Istokpoga is the second largest lake in Florida! It is also very shallow, about eight feet deep over most of the lake–great for the trout lines Dad would put out. We checked out the island, and it was just the way I remembered it, goats, birds and all.

When we started back, a fast moving storm came up. The shallow lake got very rough in a hurry. All I could do was head west and hope for the best. We were soaked, and the boat was half full of water. I remembered how Dad got the water out of the boat, so I removed the plug and kept the engine running wide open. By the time we reached the canal, the boat was empty, but we were cold and wet. Dad had let me know where the key was, so we were able to clean up and get a good rest.

All the way down and back I tried my best to talk some sense into him, but it was no use. I had seen the way a nurse at the hospital he was in charge of had looked at him and knew from the start that something was up. He had a good job as administrator of the Hospital in Villa Rica, Georgia and was about to throw it all away over an affair. Katie was nice enough, I just think that she was alone and desperate for help with three children and no husband. Uncle Bud always did have a weakness when it came to women, and as he was good looking, he made a good catch. They went ahead with the divorce, and he and Katie were married for several years, until his health began to fail.

I learned a lesson on that trip, you cannot change someone once they have their mind made up. I never poured that much effort into trying to change someone again.

Fish Traps to Trotlines

When Dad started fishing for a living, all the fishermen on the lake were using traps to catch the catfish. The trap was a small wire cage with one end open. The open end had a taper down to a small opening into the cage. The back end could be opened up to dump the fish into the boat. They would use anything dead for bait to draw the catfish into the cage.

The cages were placed all over the lake with floats to mark the location. Each fishermen has his own area and respected the location that the others used. If you looked closely you could see milk jugs bobbing all around the shore. The cages remained in the water, and the fishermen would make the rounds each day pulling up each cage, dumping the fish, throwing in a piece of meat and tossing it back into the lake.

The state of Florida eventually thought that the lakes were being over fished and outlawed the use of traps. Like most things in life, as soon as someone starts making money, the government has to step in and control it.

Dad was very skilled at running trotlines from his days of fishing in Kentucky. When checking the trotline the line for catfish, he would locate a float, lift the trotline and feel for movement. Bringing the fish up and over the side and shake him off or using pliers remove the hook. When all the bait was gone he would pull in the line and hooks placing them into a five gallon bucket.

Strange Fish Bait

Dad was always looking for the best bait to use on the trotlines. Camay soap worked very well, and the fish liked it, but I think that Cathy liked it best. It was my sister's job to bait the hooks for Dad. When we visited there we would never open the freezer in the house trailer, that is where Dad kept the other bait. Dad took me out on the lake to show me how he produced his other special bait. We pulled up along the shore and into a swampy area between the trees. There Dad had set up a five–gallon bucket tilted at a forty–five degree angle. Just below the lip he had another bucket attached. He would throw some fish heads into the upper bucket where flies would blow it. As the maggots matured, they would crawl up the side of the upper bucket and drop into the lower one! Dad would then bag them up in ziplock bags and place them in the freezer in the trailer until Cathy was ready to bait the lines.

Bobcat and Roadkill

Dad's neighbor across the canal had a large garden. They had a clothesline running over the canal so Dad could send over fish, and in return the neighbor would send over items from the garden. There was a power pole at the edge of the canal that one end of the line was attached to. One day they discovered a bobcat hanging on the power line. He had climbed up and electrocuted himself.

Dad had a thing about seeing what different wild life tasted like and wanted to skin out the cat, however it was cold and stiff, so Dad decided to pass on bobcat stew.

Now road kill was another story. Highway 98 was busy, and if a stray calf was hit, it would not stay on the road long, so you could usually count on it being fresh. Dad would tie it on the bumper of the Volkswagen and make steaks. We always asked where dinner came from when visiting. Dad did most of the cooking of the wild things. The large catfish we would eat and the smaller ones were sold to restaurants. Turtles also brought good money and were often caught on the trotlines. The shed was used for skinning catfish and cleaning turtles. Dad had a board with one large nail driven through from the backside. He would stick the head on the nail, make two quick cuts below the gills and with a pair of pliers pull the skin off. One more swipe with the knife and all the insides were removed. Cut the head off and he was done.

Dad fished and Mom painted lake pictures for several years. Cathy got married and had two boys. She married a son of one of Dad's best friends that I used to play with on those hunting and fishing trips Carlton and Dad would take.

I registered for the draft and was told that because I had already served almost three years, I would only have to keep my uniforms for another three years and then my six year obligation to the Army would be complete.

After four months, I decided it was time to be moving on and making a life for myself. Bradenton was only about an hours drive away, and I could come home on weekends if I wanted. There was a junior college there, and I needed to finish my education.

We made many more trips to Sebring over the following years, back and forth from Bradenton on a long stretch of country road. after we settled down in Georgia, there were many long trips down Interstate 75 and Highway 27. It was interesting to see the changes in the landscape over the years. There used to be miles and miles of orange groves in north Florida, then there was a big freeze. For a few years afterward it was nothing but fields of dead trees before they were all cleared.

We loved to stop at the rest stop north of Gainesville and check out Paynes Prairie, a dry lake bed that Interstate75 crossed. At first there was clear water on each side of the expressway, then there were times when water lily's bloomed all along the way, and at last the trees and brush took over as the dry lake bed began to grow. Maybe someday the sinkhole will plug up again and Paynes Prairie will be a lake once more!

CHAPTER 8 BRADENTON

I had been warned about Bradenton, "watch out for the women!" They told me that when you go to Bradenton, you will end up married! Bradenton, Florida looked like the perfect place to start civilian life. The Gulf beaches were only a few miles away on Anna Maria Island and Longboat Key. The Manatee River was even closer, emptying into the Gulf at the entrance of Tampa Bay. Now all I had to do was find a job and a place to live.

Almost immediately I met Dave Owens, who was working as a salesman in a local shoe store. We were both looking for an inexpensive place to live. I don't remember exactly how we met. It may have been that he had the apartment already and as I followed up on an ad the landlady introduced us. Dave was a good cook, and I tried to keep things picked up so it worked out well. I believe that I took the couch, and Dave had the bed. Later on I got a job at night, so I would sleep during the day and Dave had the apartment at night.

Tropicana and Gulf Station

My first job in Bradenton was at Tropicana Products, Inc. I got a job in the popsicle department on the night shift. The machine that froze and molded the popsicles was a huge rotating freezer with seven holes across for the syrup. As it would rotate and stop, the seven holes would be filled, and when the syrup started to thicken, sticks would be inserted. It would then continue to rotate to the exit station where I worked. Claws would come down and grab the ends of the popsicle sticks and remove them seven at a time. They would slide into paper, get sealed and fall onto a conveyor belt. When I started there were two workers required to pack the popsicles into boxes. Each box contained six popsicles, however there would be seven at a time coming down the belt! One person would pick up six at a time, and the second person would pick up the extra one until they had enough to fill a box. I soon found out that I could work quickly by using my thumbs to flip the two in the center, and scoop up six faster than the belt was moving. I would fill six boxes, letting the odd popsicle stay on the belt, then pick up the odd ones three in one hand, then another three in the other hand, leaving three rows of six still moving. I would then go back to scooping up the six at a time. They found something else for the other person to do!

Every once in a while the machine that removed the popsicles would jam. You could not stop the rotating freezer without losing hundreds of popsicles, so we would quickly remove all the broken sticks between the stop and start cycles. I know that God was looking over my shoulder that day along with my supervisor. The claws would come down and close, leaving a very narrow space. After dropping the popsicles, the jaws would be open, and you had about three seconds to reach in and remove the jam. As I reached in with my right hand, I was late, and realized that I did not have enough time to remove my hand before the jaws came down. On reflex I started to pull my hand back, when my supervisor grabbed my arm and held it tight. The jaws came down and closed on my wrist with just enough space to keep from breaking the skin. After it raised up it opened again, and I was able to remove my hand. If he had not held my arm, it would have torn up my hand very badly. That was a long couple of seconds waiting for the jaws to come back up! About a month on that job was enough.

At the end of the street was Bud Diemer's Gulf Service Station on Manatee Ave. in West Bradenton. I was able to get a job there pumping gas and fixing flats. It was August 1961, I just turned twenty, put in my time in the Service and not likely to be drafted. This all looked perfect on a résumé. The first question I was always asked, will you be drafted? I was never in a better position to enter the work force.

John Deimer was a good employer, and gave me a good letter of recommendation to look for a higher paying job. I also found a non–paying job with Bus Strong, a small radio and TV repair shop. It was great experience, and I knew that it would pay off later. I was looking for anything that would improve my odds at finding better and higher paying work.

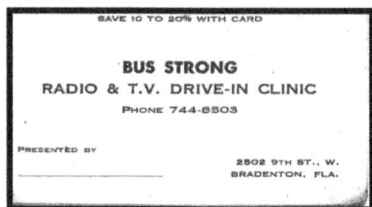

I also signed up for the Fall semester at Manatee Junior College. They accepted my Army GED for a high school diploma, and my GI bill would cover the cost. The high school in Providence would not issue a diploma for a GED unless you had finished the eleventh grade, and I had only completed the eighth grade! Now if I could only keep a passing grade in the subjects I was taking.

During those few months I dated a few times. One friend I met lived on Anna Maria Island. Their home was on one of the canals with a sailboat. She would take me out into the bay, sailing through the narrow canal as if it were a motor boat. We did not get too serious, and I cannot even remember her name. There was another girl I took to the movies, but that did not amount to much either.

A&W Root Beer Stand

One of our hangouts was the A & W Root Beer stand on the Tamiami Trail just south of town. Dave and I would park, talk and exchange phone numbers with girls that were doing the same. One evening we met two girls in a convertible, and the four of us exchanged phone numbers. They were just out of high school and attending the local beauty school. We debated which number each would take, and we later found out that they did the same. Dave called Jean, and I called Kathy. Lots of times girls will not give you the right phone numbers, but this time it worked out.

I met Kathy, and we dated almost a year. Kathy's mother worked at the time for the Eli Witt Cigar Co., in town and felt that someone dating her daughter needed a better job. She got me on as a driver making the rounds through Sarasota, Bradenton and the Islands. After our dates I would go in and watch TV with her mom long after Kathy retired for the night.

Dave dated Jean, and there was a lot of discussion about who would marry first. Kathy and Jean were comparing notes, but I don't believe Dave and I talked much about our dating. I proposed first, but Jean and Dave were married first. Kathy and I were married on December 16, 1961 after less than a year.

Fishing Under the Bridge

Dave and I sat there for hours, talking and watching our corks. The night was quiet, with an occasional car passing over the bridge above. Crappie fishing is best at night with a Coleman light out over the water to attract bugs. As the bugs hit, the water minnows start to swim around the light, and then deeper the large crappie come after the minnows. On a good night, fifteen or twenty would be considered a good catch and great eating with a sweet unique taste that only crappie have.

However many nights we sat and talked until daylight catching only a few crappie, and then if we were not careful a snake or turtle would eat our catch right off the string.

The reason for these all night visits were not for the fish, although it made it worthwhile. The real reason we spent the night under the bridge was to catch up on each other lives. We both got caught up in our jobs and raising a family and did not see much of each other, so about once or twice a year we would plan a fishing trip under the bridge.

Dave and I remained best of friends and I later learned that he was from Marietta, Georgia. It was after we both moved back to Georgia, that we spent those nights under the bridge. They say we only have about seven close friends in a lifetime, and I am proud to count Dave Owens as one of my close friends. I want to thank Jean and Dave for sharing their home with us when we were young and for being there when I needed to talk.

Eli Witt Cigar Company

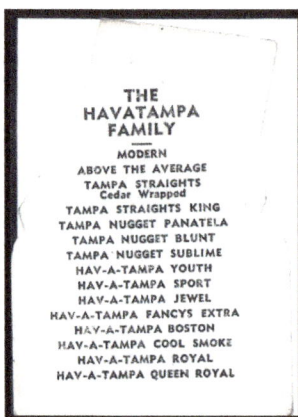

I started work at Eli Witt on 10/9/1961 with help from Andree, Kathy's mother. She worked in the office, and I worked in the warehouse, and later was given a route and truck for deliveries.

I would stop along the back roads for lunch and go through the coins I had taken in, and swap the rare ones out for my coin collection. The bars on the route would have tax jars on the counter, and they would pay me with the change from the jars. The hottest item for the bars was large jars of Pickled Pigs Feet. I would circle through the farm country west of town, then cross over to Longboat Key and work my way up to Anna Maria Island, then back to East Bradenton.

The 56 Chevy station wagon held up well, and Kathy and I spent lots of time on the beach, and running out of gas late at night would keep me in trouble with her mother.

We went on camping trips together with the Tinl family. Johnnies Tinl was Kathy's age, and we all had great times together. Kathy's maiden name was Coriell, and there was a lot of confusion about Coriell and Crowell. The first time I introduced Kathy to Mom, she thought I was marrying a girl with the same name as my sister Cathy!

I was only twenty when we were married, and the State of Florida required that the men had to be at least twenty one, and the girls seventeen. Kathy was nineteen, and we were thinking about going to Georgia to get married where the age limit was lower. However we wanted a church wedding, so I used my discharge papers to show that I was twenty–one. It was several years before I straightened out my age on my drivers license and other documents.

After we were married, Andree found a larger apartment, and we moved in with her and Kathy's sister, Rae.

I thought college was going well until my English instructor called me in and told me that I would be wise to drop out instead of getting a failing grade. What a shock that was, I was sure I was making good progress. English was the only subject I was having trouble with, and I ended up with twelve credit hours. We left Bradenton in the station wagon for New Jersey in August of 1962.

CHAPTER 9 RED BANK

Kathy's aunt Marie owned half interest in a beauty shop in East Keansburg on Highway 36, north of Red Bank. They had an apartment over the beauty shop and Kathy had a job waiting. I wanted to get into electronics and had heard that New Jersey had plenty of electronic jobs.

Elastic Stop Nut Corporation

I signed up for unemployment and was able to draw a few checks from Florida while I looked for work. I got a job through the employment agency at Elastic Stop Nut Corp. in Union, New Jersey. It was a good paying job but nasty work. I had to clean the bins that they used to move the nuts around the factory in. When the bins would get rusty, they would come to me, and I would use an overhead electric hoist to lower them one at a time into a barrel of acid. The acid would eat away the rust–and the lining of my nose! I had to keep a good coating of A&D ointment in my nostrils and visit the company doctor each week for a checkup. After less than two months I was laid off due to a reduction in personnel. However I figured it was more a matter of having to join the union which would have made it harder to let me go. I believe that due to the health risk of that position, they rotated new employees out to avoid trouble. I was not sorry to be leaving. The drive was long and the traffic heavy.

H. J. Bailey Company

Within a week I landed another job at H. J. Bailey, this was the same type of company as Eli Witt. I worked in the warehouse and help run the cigarette tax stamping machine. It was not bad work, but not the electronic experience I was looking for. The guys would have a poker night once a month, and it seemed like a good group to work with. I had a three month trial period before being required to join the union. You had no choice in New Jersey. Once the Union was voted in everyone had to join. It was a closed shop. During the three months the boss would ask me to work on Saturdays for a flat $15.00, which was straight time, not time and half! But I did not mind and needed the money, which brought my weekly pay to about $90.00 a week. After three months the boss came to me and informed me that I would have to join the union. I had never belonged to a union and was not interested in joining, one boss was enough for any job. I informed him that if he wanted me to join, that I would have to have a raise to cover the dues. He obliged, and the next week he asked if I would work again on Saturday, I said sure, for time and half!

The shop stewart would get depressed or upset at times and leave work, going to a local bar across the street. This happened one day while I was working there, and the boss asked me to go across the street and bring him back to work. Now I was a little nervous about pulling someone out of a bar! As I approached him I thought about it and decided it was best to just pull up a stool and join him. We talked for a good hour, and then I returned to work. He showed up the next day as if nothing happened and nothing was said about my not bringing him back to work!

Charles E. Coriell

On the weekends we would visit Kathy's dad and his wife in Pluckemin, NJ. They lived on Washington Valley road. Before modern roads this was the main route east to New York City and was near were George Washington had a winter camp during the Revolution. Charlie had turned the farm into a nursery. there was a large barn up the hill and a large yard. The front steps were large blocks of sandstone, very similar to the ones at my grandfather Clark's house in Kentucky. Kathy's step sister, Jean, lived just up the gravel road that crossed over the mountain and by the barn. The ditch along that road had once been used as a landfill, and during a huge rain storm it washed out, and all that junk ended up in front of the house that Charlie grew up in.

Charlie loved to tell stories, and we have many of them that we will publish for the family called " O Charlie", by Charles E. Coriell.

Charlie and Andree were divorced when Kathy was young. Kathy prayed over and over that they would get back together. Several years after Charlie's second wife passed away, Kathy was able to reintroduce them to each other and her prayers were at last answered.

When young and starting out in life, things are simpler and you have fewer things! We packed all our belongings in a station wagon when we moved to New Jersey, and when we left we had to rent a U–haul! One item we collected from the barn and has been with us to the present was an old RCA Victrola made by the RCA Victor Talking Machine Co. It stood on tall legs, had two set, of doors in the front, one for sound and the other for storage of the records. I later cut the legs off to make it into an end table, and it now sits at the foot of our bed, still working! I would sure hate to move again from our home in Marietta. We would not be able to pack all the stuff!

Charlie and Andree settled in Georgia and during his later years lived with us. Charlie lived to 95 and Andree is now 96, as of September, 2012.

Electronic Assistance Corp.

At last in March of 1963, I was able to find work in electronics. The Electronic Assistance Corp. built radios for the air force. This was a non–union shop, and I was grateful for that. I started out on the assembly line but was soon put in charge of checking the line for problems and trying to keep production running smoothly. There were always little problems that would slow down production, like the time the front knobs would not align correctly. I started inspecting all the knobs and rejecting all that were a problem. The holes for the set screws must have been drilled free hand from the vendor. Very few were at the same angle. After returning a large number we finely got it straightened out. Most of the time it was just a matter of pulling a problem radio off the line and making repairs.

After three months it came time for the union vote, and the company shut down for two weeks to avoid the union. If you have vacation time coming then you got paid, but if you had not earned any vacation then you did not get paid.

The beauty shop business was also slow, so we rented a U–haul trailer and in June of 1963 we headed for Georgia.

CHAPTER 10 SMYRNA

Kathy's uncle lived in Smyrna, Georgia, a small town just southeast of Marietta. I started looking for a place to live that would be nearby. On July 25, 1963 I signed a contract with the FHA for a FHA repossession that was empty and needing many repairs. The FHA would replace the roof and broken windows, as well as the flooring, so for $8,000.00 and only $125.00 down as a deposit we got the house. With payments of $60.00 a month, we were on our way to becoming homeowners. It was very close to Uncle Bud and Aunt Evelyn in Smyrna. We called it our crackerbox. It was small, only two bedrooms and one bath, a small kitchen and living room. Several years later Kathy was trying to plant something in the front and found a sidewalk leading up to the front porch! It did have a nice backyard and I later fenced it in for Panda, our dog. We were not able to move in until after the repairs were made, seven months later.

We moved in with Uncle Bud and Aunt Evelyn until they moved to Villa Rica, Georgia. We stayed with them in Villa Rica for a while. During that time I found work in a service station east of Marietta. I had to be to work early and drive from Villa Rica which took over an hour in the dark early hours. I would do OK until I reached Marietta, then more than once I fell asleep at the wheel. I would wake up when the tires hit the curb. If I had fallen asleep before getting into town, there would have been no curb to wake me up. Someone was looking over me, I am sure.

I enjoyed the time spent them, and we had fun building a metal storage barn he bought in kit form. He often talked about the whole family moving to Australia. I never knew how serious he was.

Dave and Jean Owens were living in Georgia with two children. They invited us to stay with them until our house was ready. It was a little cramped in the three room, one bath cottage near Lake Allatoona north of Marietta. Dave worked at Lockheed, a large aircraft plant in Marietta. I applied for work there and waited.

The job opened up at Lockheed, and I started work there September 1, 1963. The money was good, and it qualified for the loan we needed for the house.

At last we were able to move into our crackerbox on March 6, 1964. Aunt Evelyn's sister Ethel and Dub Westbrook gave us a refrigerator they had used for years, and forty–eight years later it is still working as good as new with never the first service call. We use it now in the basement to keep water cool and as an extra freezer when needed. You see, it is a gas refrigerator with no moving parts and only the light bulb inside is electric. We have never lost gas service so it has never stopped!

I do get a lot of comments about when the utility men come by for other repairs. I found out later that they were all recalled and sent to Mexico due to not being vented. There are a lot of them still working south of the border!

Threat of Nuclear War

We lived under the threat of a nuclear war, and a lot of people were building fallout shelters. Uncle Bud was no exception. He had one installed off the basement and below the basement level. There was a small door and steps that lead down to a 12 X 12 room with a vent to the surface. It was not well stocked, so I don't know how long we could have lasted. Most fallout shelters were expected to hold you only for a few weeks until the radiation levels dropped. Lockheed was a prime target, and it was only a few miles away.

I had training on nuclear war survival and books on the subject, but I knew that we could never be fully prepared.

Lockheed Aircraft Co.

Working at Lockheed was a good experience, I even took a course there on single side band radios that were used on the aircraft. I worked on the wiring harnesses that were placed in the C141 cargo plane. My job was running the machine that stamped the number on the wires. I would key in the length for the wire and the number, then watch it stamp the numbers, first close together, then space them out, and again close together at the end. There was a rhythm that almost would put you to sleep. The wires were assembled on a large peg board to build up a harness and then pulled through the aircraft on the assemble line.

I was sitting at my work station on that Friday, November 22, 1963, when the announcement was made over the PA that the President had been shot! All work in the plant came to a halt, and I think the whole nation was in shock.

In the evenings at the close of work we would walk out the long tunnels to the parking lot. There was one black fellow that I would usually talk with on the way out. The subject of prejudices would usually come up. I tried my best to convince him that I was not prejudiced, but it was a lost cause. That is when I began to understand that most blacks were convinced that all white skinned people looked down on the darker skinned ones. However I knew differently. I had played and grew up knowing several as good and equal friends.

I do recall once in Providence of being caught up in a mob, and when I realized that all the whites were on one side of the street and a group of blacks were on the other side, I quickly got out of there and went home. I did not want any part of what was developing, and I never knew what was going on or what stirred it up. I have had a slip of the tongue now and then that got me into trouble. I have trouble telling people apart, most women look the same to me, and most blacks look similar, I think it is only because the most distinguishing feature sticks in my mind. Well I commented to someone at work one day that all blacks looked the same, I was having trouble placing someone. The word got out and I had to write a letter of apology or lose my job! I thought it was only natural, and if I had heard it from someone about whites I would not have had a second thought about it. It did teach me that this was a very sensitive subject.

Noble Concrete, Inc.

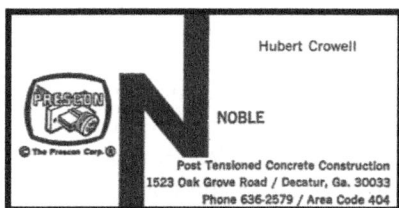

A career side step, construction work for three years! In September, 1964 I went to work for Bill Noble, sometimes referred to as "Will Bill" by his friends. He married a Westbrook, one of Aunt Evelyn's sisters. We would talk at family gatherings, and one day he approached me about working for him. I had been working at Lockheed for about a year and was beginning to make a fair salary. He offered me a couple of thousand more a year if I could come to work for him right away. I turned in my notice at Lockheed the next day. They were upset because I did not give them any notice and told me not to bother applying back for a job.

It was a long drive from Smyrna to Decatur, as the interstate around Atlanta had not been completed. Each morning I would have to cross a one–lane bridge over the Chattahoochee River, then drive the backroads to Clairmont Drive in Decatur. At first we worked out of his small office behind the garage, and later he bought a house on Clairmont Drive for an office. On the first day, he showed me a drafting table and a file for an upcoming job and said if I had any questions just let him know!

We bid on construction jobs all over the Southeast that required Post Tension steel cables. The cables were supplied by the Prescon Corp. out of Corpus Christi, Texas. During the first year, Bill was running for the state senate. I had to help him campaign by riding around in the back of a pickup and shouting through a bullhorn!

Villa Rica

Uncle Bud, being the administrator of the hospital in Villa Rica, thought it would be great if Kathy had our baby in his hospital so he could sign the birth certificate. We moved in with them again when the baby got close. Deanna was born on November 15, 1964, and grew up in our crackerbox. We had some good times there. Family would visit, and we would have people sleeping all over the floors. Christmas time was special, and we would always fill the house up. We visited Uncle Bud and family often in Villa Rica and always had fun.

Where is the 13th Floor?

If you visit Plymouth Harbor Retirement Community in Sarasota, Florida and enter the elevator of the spectacular 25 story tower, you will not find a 13th floor. The building is really only 24 stories high. The 13th floor was shipped back to the factory!

In the mid–sixties, while I was working for Noble Concrete, Inc., in Chamblee, Georgia. We sold and installed Post tensioning cables for heavy construction projects throughout the southeast. The cables are made up of 1/4 inch cold drawn steel wire from Japan and cut to the correct length, bundled two or more together for the designed size, and wrapped in a lubricated paper at The Prescon Corporation in Corpus Christi, Texas. These cables are placed in the concrete forms at the proper height along the length of each beam, and then after the concrete has cured to the proper strength, stretched about 6 inches for every 100 feet of cable.

There are two common methods for stretching cables. Stranded cables use gripping fingers to hold the cables at the correct tension. With the 1/4 inch wire, a steel plate and collar is drilled with the required number of holes, one for each wire, and a button is formed on the end of the wire to hold against the collars and plates at each end. The sizes of the plates are determined by the number of wires and the area required to prevent crushing the concrete. When the concrete has set for about three days, A hydraulic jack with a hole in the center is placed over a steel–threaded rod with a device on the end that fastens to the collar. A steel chair is inserted between the jack and the steel plate. The cables are then stretched to the proper elongation and monitored by gauges on the hydraulic pump. When the correct tension and elongation have been obtained, two steel shims are slid into place between the collar and the steel plate. The jack, chair and rod are then removed.

When I started working for Bill Noble, I had some drafting experience but not much else in the construction field. Bill said that he would teach me all that I needed to know. The first day he showed me the drafting board and laid out a job to start on and went into the other room saying just call when I had a question. Well I did have plenty of questions over the next few years. I learned a lot from Bill Noble and some things that at the time seemed trivial, such as not to wad up trash when you throw it into the trash can as it takes up too much room. I still practice that today.

As I grew more familiar with the construction business, I started doing estimates on jobs that we would bid on in the southeast, and one of those jobs was the Plymouth Harbor Retirement Community in Sarasota, I was excited about the job because I met my wife in nearby Bradenton, Florida and was looking forward to visiting the job site. However we now had a full crew to make the installations, and my onsite services were not required. I did not see the building until 2005. And after 40 some years it still looked as good as new.

With a large job like the tower, we would study the drawings, calculate the material required for the first floor and multiply by the number of floors. We had the contract for placing the forms, installing and providing the steel and overseeing the pouring and stressing of the beams. I was in constant contact by phone with Jim, our supervisor on location, and he would let me know of any problems that he encountered and when to order the next shipment of cables. All was going well until he reached the 23rd floor. I received a call and Jim seemed confused, he said that it looked like we may have too many cables on the site for the job.

I discussed the problem with Bill and reviewed the drawings to see what had happened. Bill was a wonderful person to work for. He always said that we learn best from our mistakes, just try not and make the same ones twice. I had made more than my share of them while learning about the construction business, but this was going to turn out to be my most costly mistake to date.

A lot of buildings use the 13th floor for heating and air–conditioning equipment due to the fact that most people tend to avoid the 13th floor and space is hard to lease there. I had encountered a few projects where the 13th floor was ignored and you have to check very closely to find the notes on the drawings. I had overlooked the note on this tower!

Bill took the mistake I had made very well and we proceeded to contact Prescon Corp. to see if we could salvage any of the extra material. They said to ship it back and they could re–cut the cables for other jobs. This was another good lesson that I learned from Bill, to come forward with mistakes as soon as they come to light. Throughout my career I have always brought any mistakes made by me to my superiors as fast as possible and they always understand. It is only when someone tries to cover up or hide the mistake that the problem grows.

In 2005 we attended my wife's 45th class reunion in Sarasota, and while driving out to the beach, I recognized the tower. We went in and talked with the management, took pictures and read the articles in the hall way about the construction. I told them of my involvement in the construction and promised to share some of it. They were excited and said that they get a lot of questions about the building and its construction, but did not have many of the answers. I am pleased to be able to share this article with them and I hope that they will include it in their archives.

Plymouth Harbor Retirement Community, Sarasota, FL.

Over Design

Many of our large projects would be stressing ring beams for dome concrete buildings. Domes exert a large lateral load on the walls of the buildings upon which they set. The ring beam is what holds the walls from falling outward from the weight of the dome.

In concrete construction there is usually a large safety factor built into the construction in the way of extra steel bars. Post Tension concrete is a little different, as too much of a good thing can cause trouble.

The design engineer will note on the plans how much tension is required, and suppliers like Noble Concrete would bid on the jobs and then make the shop drawings showing the placement and size of the cables required.

We got the contract of a church dome in Jacksonville, Florida, and all was going well. When the concrete had been poured and reached the proper strength, I loaded up the stressing equipment and headed south. Our time on the construction site for a job like this was usually no more than a couple of days, and this one could be completed in less than a day. Of course there is always the problem with the unions. They insist on having one of their people do the work. However, they never have anyone trained in this type of work. We give them a call, and they send us a couple of workers, we tell them just to stand there and watch, and we complete the job as fast as possible.

We were making our second trip around the ring beam, bringing the stress up in stages to prevent damage to the columns. I had planned on connecting to each cable four times during the stressing procedure. Suddenly there was a large pop, and all that I could see were workers scrambling down off the building!

We stopped the stressing and inspected the columns for cracks. I also climbed to the top of the support for the dome and checked the top of the form. We had raised the dome about one inch off the top of the form. The columns were pulled to the point that one of them had cracked!

I got on the phone to the engineer and asked him what we should do next. His reply was, "Is it holding up the dome? Then your job is through." He had over designed the ring beam just as he over designs when using steel bars and if he was aware of what would happen, which I doubt, he did not warn us. We relayed the information to the contractor and packed up for home.

Construction Nightmare

Varsity gymnasium, Boone, NC

For more than 40 years, the 8,000 seat venue at Appalachian State University in Boone, North Carolina has stood up to heavy snows and tough winters. When it opened in 1968, the facility was North Carolina's largest indoor athletic facility west of Charlotte and Winston–Salem.

Crowds have visited Varsity Gym to witness various circuses, the Harlem Globetrotters and Herrmann's Royal Lipizzan Stallions of Austria. The list of entertainers and concerts to step on the stage in Varsity Gym is a diverse group, covering several musical genres. Bruce Springstein, Chicago, Bob Dylan, Rod Stewart, James Taylor, Linda Ronstadt, The Jimi Hendrix Experience, Steppenwolf, The Allman Brothers Band, The Fifth Dimension, Andrew Gold, Dionne Warwick, Bread, Phish, The Atlanta Rhythm Section, Pablo Cruise, Kenny Rogers, The Carpenters, The Nitty Gritty Dirt Band, The Cornelius Brothers and Sister Rose, Ronnie Milsap, Edgar Winter, Gary Puckett, The Lettermen, The Chairmen of the Board, The Four Tops, Frankie Valli and the Four Seasons, The Temptations, The Beach Boys, Jimmy Buffett and Ray Charles all made appearances in Varsity. Several public speakers, ranging from educational to political to comedic, have addressed large crowds in Varsity Gym. John Houseman, Jane Fonda, US consumer advocate Ralph Nader, entertainer Bill Murray, Harry Reasoner of 60 Minutes, US Army General Thomas Kelly, as well as Grammy Award–winning poet, writer, composer and actress Maya Angelou, all stood behind the Varsity Gym podium.

But in 1967 when I was working for Noble Concrete installing the Post Tensioning cables in the thin deep beams that support the roof, I was having nightmares over the safety of the building. This was one of the main factors that helped me decide to find another line of work and get out of the construction business. And it was one of the last jobs that I was involved with.

Varsity Gym under construction 1967

116

The beams were so thin that we could hardly find room to place the steel—much less the cables—which were encased in a flexible metal tube. The beams were almost 8 feet deep, and the cables ran from the tops of the columns to the bottom of the beam at the middle. Any misalignment would result in the beam twisting when the stress was applied. After a nervous few days we had the cables stressed to the correct tension and locked into place.

The problem we now faced was filling the long metal tubes with grout. There was a hole in each end of the cable plates where we connected the grout line and proceeded to pump the grout under high pressure until it sprayed out the other end. However it never came out, the span was too long or there were crimped places in the tube that prevented the grout from filling the cable housings. We were told to pump all the grout that was possible from one end, plug the hole and then go to the other end and do the same thing.

The grout bonds to the cables, but I had no way of knowing how much of the cables were covered in grout and how much were just laying in water! I could picture the cables rusting and breaking at some point under a heavy snow. But I was not an engineer, and I was assured that it was safe. I never liked the grouted cables, the cables that were greased and wrapped in heavy paper always worked as planned. For years after completion of the job I half expected to hear of a collapse. I am thankful to God that it has stood up this long. The good thing is that the longer concrete sets, the stronger it becomes, and I assume that the cables, if in water, would need air in order to rust.

Trips with Bill

It was always exciting when traveling with Bill. Once while I was driving and Bill was with me, we came to a railroad crossing that had a slight uphill grade before you reached the tracks. The car in front of us would not move, and there was no train coming. Bill said, "Blow you horn!" I said that I did not think that would be a good idea and told him about the time when I was a kid in Providence and a farmer was stopped in front of me at a stop sign. I tooted the horn and he got nervous and put the pickup into reverse, then backed into me.

I have always been very careful not to blow my horn at someone, just take my time and wait until they get it together.

Well Bill insisted, so I blew the horn and sure enough, the car rolled back and bumped us!

Another time we were traveling to a job site in Augusta, Georgia, the expressway was under construction, so Bill insisted that we take it anyway. There was no traffic and it was a great—drive until we reached a bridge.

The concrete dropped about eight inches, and we were airborne! You would think that I had learned my lesson about driving on closed roads, but no. We returned from Villa Rica once while they were constructing Interstate 20, and I took the uncompleted expressway again and the same thing happened. In both cases we were fortunate, no one was hurt and there was no damage!

Bill was great to work for. Once when Kathy and I were visiting with our baby, we left her blanket at Bill and Earline's. This was before cell phones. Bill jumped in the car and caught up with us on the way home. He said he understood how critical a blanket was to a baby!

Appalachian Trail 6/30/1967

I was a Boy Scout leader at the Smyrna Presbyterian Church, Troop 733. Kathy was attending the Episcopal Church in Bradenton when we met. and I was Baptist. We agreed that the Presbyterian Church was one we could both agree on as it was sort of in between the two. I was involved in scouting for several years. One of the more challenging things we did was hike the Appalachian Trail in Georgia. Five of us, after long warm up hikes around Kennesaw Mountain, were dropped off at Amicalola Falls State Park to start our week–long trip on the Appalachian Trail. Lowell Reed, my assistant, and his son Tim, two older scouts, Guy and Pat, all joined us in our long climb to the start of the trail at Springer Mountain.

Marker on Springer Mountain

We had planned to hike at least ten miles a day for six days, with one extra day if we needed it. We would come off at Unicoi Gap and try to catch a ride down to Helen and call home for a pickup. We were lucky just to make it to the start of the trail hiking six miles uphill all the way.

Guy and Tim

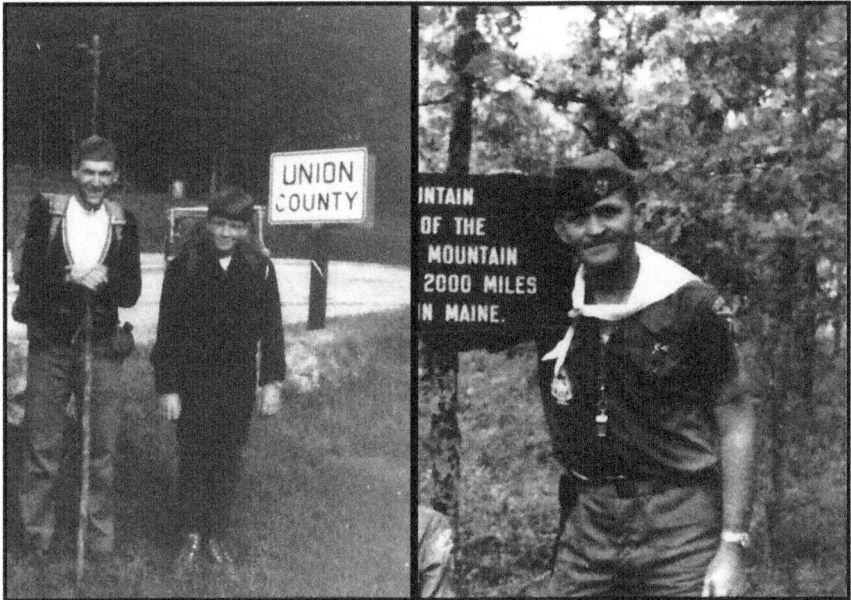

Pat and I   **Lowell Reed**

By the third day our muscles loosened up, and we climbed up Blood Mountain without stopping. The view from the top was great. We all spread out on a rock and almost got a sunburn! Neels Gap was a nice break. The trail went through the porch of a restaurant there, and they had real restrooms!

Jim's knee gave out on him, and he had to leave us, so I took the boys on to Unicoi Gap where we caught a ride down to Helen on the last day.

I returned in 1968 to complete another section of the trail in Georgia, Unicoi Gap to Dicks Creek Gap.

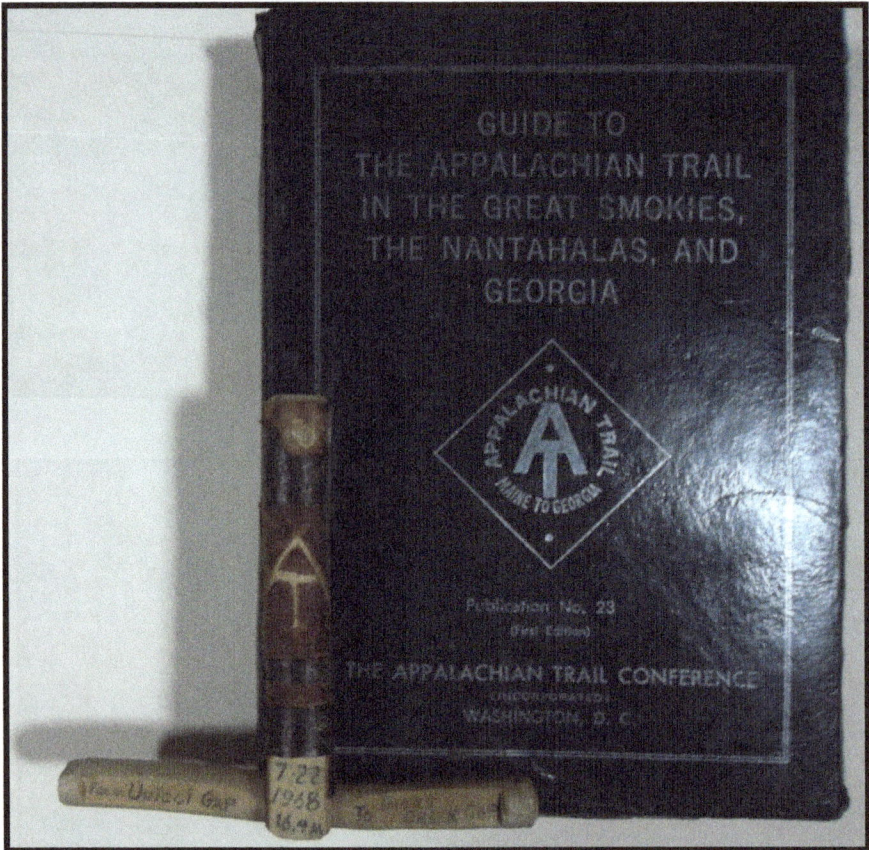

Wood Carving to mark the event!

I dream of hiking more of this great trail in the near future.

Run–in with the IRS

As the money sometimes would get tight in the construction business, our company was no exception. A lot of times Bill would tell me to cash my check right away or I may have to hold it a few days until a deposit was made. We were behind on the payments for tax withholding, but our lawyer had worked out a payment schedule with the IRS–or so we thought!

I arrived early one Monday morning to pick up the company truck and head out to a job site, when as I was looking down at the key and starting the truck, something hit the windshield. Two men in suits opened the door of the truck and grabbed my arm, pulling me out. The sign on the front of the truck read, "Government Property!"

They wanted my key to the office and placed another sign on the door. That is when I started talking fast. I explained that I needed to call the owner and that I was only a worker there. They finally let me call Bill, and when he arrived he was, able to talk them into letting him remove some personal files. He retrieved the job files needed to conduct our business, and I drove my car to the job site while he returned home to conduct the business from there.

In a few days the lawyers were able to straighten the mess out, and the IRS backed off.

In December of 1967 Bill cut back on the work force, and I decided to return to my love of electronics. Although we never missed a paycheck, the waiting sometimes made it hard to pay our bills on time. I was offered a position with The Prescon Corporation in Corpus Christi that looked very promising, with profit sharing and other benefits. However I decided not to make the move away from family and friends.

I applied for and got a lower paying job with the RCA Service Company in Atlanta.

Years later as I was arriving at the Atlanta Airport from a business trip, I was saddened by the sight of the old Delta terminal building being torn down. I had stressed the cables that ran under the round terminal, and as I thought about those days I began to feel just a little bit older.

RCA Service Company

RCA sent me to Coral Gables for what was called color crossover training. Color television sets were quickly replacing the black and white sets we were so used to. We watched Neil Armstrong step onto the moon on our black and white television set in July of 1969. Shortly after that I picked up a discarded color TV alongside the road, repaired and built a cabinet for it.

The training was only one week long, but very intensive. I also signed up that same year for night courses at Marietta Cobb Area Vocational Technical School, just up the road from where we lived, For four hours each night from 6PM to 10PM. I started out with radio and TV, and then moved on to advanced electronics courses. When there were no more courses to take, I convinced them to let me take on a Honeywell computer that was donated to the school. It was my own special class. I worked on it each night and got the punch card reader working again as well as most of the other functions. After that I applied for a position teaching electronics at night. They were looking for instructors that were working in the areas that they were teaching, and the night instructors did not require a degree. I had graduated with 1335 hours in Electronic Technology in September 1971. I continued to teach there for several years.

One of my classmates was employed by Eastman Kodak Company, and we talked about the possibility that I might be able to get a job there in the future.

RCA Service Company was a union work place just like Lockheed was, however Georgia was and still is a Right to Work State, so I could not be forced to join a union. Lockheed was no problem, we were not even asked about joining the Union. RCA, on the other hand, was a different story. Management was ex–union people, and all were pro–union. I was told right from the start that I would not get any of the better service calls as long as I did not join. I was asked to attend a meeting with one of the members and thought that I would go and see what it was all about. When I walked into the room, it got silent. Then someone spoke up and asked if I was ready to join. I told them that I would like to sit through a meeting first to see if I was interested. They then asked me to leave. I told my friend that I would wait for him in the car. I never did join.

I later learned that they were planning a strike for higher wages. When I did hear the details, I was amused. They were asking for wages that were less than the non–union repair centers were already getting. I think that the union and management were a little too close. The next thing I knew was my windshield was getting marked up. Then the phone company came out to disconnect the phone. I had to call all the utilities and stop all the cut offs. We also got many strange calls. I had to ask myself, who in their right mind would want to join an organization like that! I knew that soon I would be moving on to a much better job, and told my manager that I was only working there to gain some experience.

Making Service Calls

I started the morning by picking up my calls for the day, typically about 12 to 15. I would spread them out and with my map and lay out the route for the day. If I had picture tube replacements to do, I would try and place them close to the end, or at least in the afternoon. I would start the day knocking out the easy stuff, trying not to spend more than twenty minutes on a call. A lot of the problems were easy, like cleaning the tuner or replacement of a small tube. Adjustments were made with one eye on the customer and the other on the screen. As soon as I got an indication that the customer was happy, I would close out the call. If I tried to get it to looking the best for me, I would be there for hours! A picture tube would require an hour or more, so it was good to be caught up before starting to replace one. Sometimes we would have to pull the chassis into the shop for repairs, but not very often, and when we did you had to call in first to make sure you had not missed anything. When we ran out of calls, we would call in and take one of the calls that had come in during the day.

It was fast–paced work, and I liked that because it made the time pass faster.

Eastman Kodak Company

During my classes at night I was always looking for a large company where I could build up some retirement and benefits. Hewlett Packard was my first choice, however they were looking for someone already skilled in computer technology. They also wanted someone to do sales as well as service work. I was not too keen on sales work.

At the same time I had applied at Eastman Kodak where my previous classmate, Bob Futrelle was working. They called me in for an interview, first with Joe Thomas who was over the reconditioning center at their Chamblee, Georgia location, and then a second interview with Jack Ingram, who was over all the technical operations in the southeast. He had at the time three people working for him who supported all the service engineers in the southeast and conducted training as well. They were called Regional Specialists. Joe Thomas and Jack Ingram had worked closely together for many years.

In November, 1968 I started what was to become a long and satisfying career with Kodak. I started out in the recondition center with my friend Bob and soon became good friends with the other workers there. We were rebuilding from the ground up older microfilm equipment, replacing all worn parts and repainting the cabinets.

Kodak was a very unique company. They were all non–union, except for one lens division. They had a very good profit sharing plan, except for the union group at the lens division. We would get our bonuses each year just before Christmas. All benefits were fully paid for, health insurance and life insurance, including dental insurance.

George Eastman, the founder of Eastman Kodak, even designed a special calendar for the company, made up of thirteen periods instead of twelve months. It had four weeks in each period. All schedules were based on this calendar of an even fifty-two weeks.

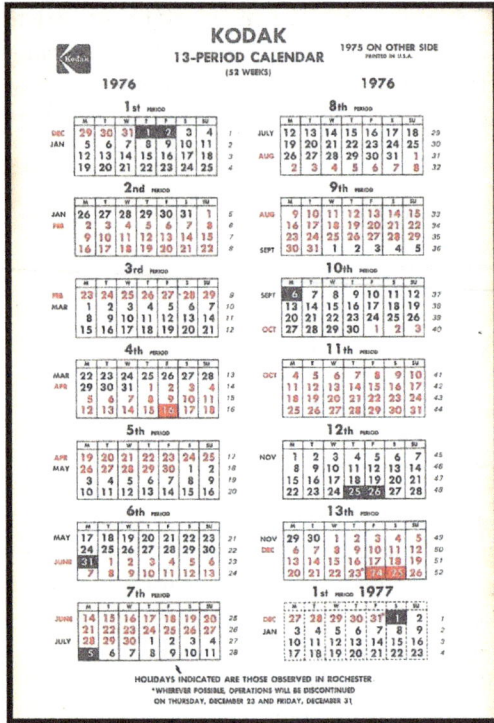

It took me awhile to get used to living by two calendars, but I do have to admit that it was much simpler keeping up with things.

Panda

Panda was a good dog for Deanna. He loved to grab the knot under her swing seat and stop her in mid air. We had the yard fenced and a nice doghouse for him. He seemed to be happy as an outdoor dog. When he was older and I returned from a long business trip with a beard, he would go into his house every time I would come out to feed him, and he would have nothing to do with me until I finally shaved!

Panda would bury his bones in the backyard, and if you stood on top of one, he would get upset and bark or pull at your pant leg until you moved.

By 1970 the neighborhood started to decline. A repair shop and truck dealership went in on South Cobb Drive and backed up to our lot on the side. The workers would throw their beer bottles over the fence, and we had to keep the blinds closed on that side all the time. The owner wanted our place real bad, and at last made me an offer of twice what we paid for it. We signed the deal on a hand written agreement with $100.00 deposit, $4,900 at closing and the balance to be paid within six months.

We found a new location, and I took out a builders loan for the contractor. It worked out that they did not wait the six months, but paid for the old house in full at closing. It was a good thing because I needed all the funds to close on the new house early. Later we learned that he turned around and sold all of the property to a bank that needed a parking lot where our house once sat! When they graded that lot for the parking lot, they must have been surprised. I had buried two fifty–five gallon drums vertically in the front yard with holes in them to spread out the wash water from our clothes washer. Kathy would place the drain hose in a line I installed by the back door and the waste water would run around to the sunken drums to water the front lawn. It never worked too well since the Georgia clay was just too hard!

Lice in the House

To cool the house I had picked a used fan that was about three foot square and installed it in the attic in front of the end vents. We would then open the pull–down stairs to the attic and let the fan pull the air through the house. One year birds found their way into the fan and built a nest. Kathy started having trouble with her hair itching and went to see the doctor. The problem was a case of Lice. But we could not find out where they were coming from. I finally checked the fan and had to remove the large nest. My arms were black with lice. We sure were glad to get rid of the birds!

On the day we were moving out of the house, I was unloading the attic when I slipped and my foot went through the ceiling!

I moved into the new house alone about two months before it was completed and slept on the floor. I had to be up and out before the workers arrived. The reason for staying there was to try and get a lawn started in the front so we would not have all the red clay. I found out the fastest way to get a new lawn in was to spread chicken litter over the fresh seed and water it twice a day. The chicken litter stunk and feathers blew everywhere. I tried to avoid the neighbors and prayed for the grass to come up quickly. We did get a good start on a lawn before moving in and the smell died down!

We closed and converted the builders loan to a thirty year mortgage on September 5, 1970. Because I helped out the builder who was over extended and wanted to keep his crew busy, we got the three bedroom, two bath ranch for $23,500. Other homes in the subdivision were going through realtors for $30,000 and up.

CHAPTER 11 MARIETTA

Our new home was in East Marietta, a quiet farm that had been turned into a subdivision. A friend told me later that he used to hunt where our subdivision was located. A strand of barb wire is still embedded in one of our largest trees in the backyard along the creek. I leave it there as a reminder of what was once there. The lot I chose was one that no one else wanted. It had a ditch along one side and Lost Creek across the back. I loved it and looked forward to building bridges and dams!

We had the basement roughed in for an apartment and had them replace the metal post in the basement with studded walls. One end of the basement under the kitchen above was narrow, nine feet wide and in the other houses with the same floor plan this space was left as a dirt crawl space. We did not want the dirt smell getting into the basement, so I talked them into continuing the concrete slab into that area. It made a great play room for Deanna.

The apartment was a daylight basement with windows in each room. Where they normally put a garage door, we had a double door instaled and a concrete pad outside with an outdoor light. The plumbing for the apartment kitchen and bath were roughed in so that I could install everything later.

We found a new church, Covenant Presbyterian Church, only a few miles away and new friends there as well. The closest grocery store was on Sandy Plains with what we thought was a dirt floor. Another one was on the corner with a wood floor, both are now gone. The school was near by, Mountain View at Shallowford and Sandy Plains. Deanna had to ride the bus and was very happy to do so. She finished the first grade there. Her first grade started while we were living in Smyrna. The school backed up to our Smyrna lot with an alley along side the house were the school kids could walk to school. For the first half of the first grade she had only to walk the length of our lot to school, but she did not like the teacher and was glad to be moving.

Bill Meier, Kathy's cousin from New Jersey, left his home one morning to get a paper and showed up on our doorstep. Bill was eight years younger than I and we got along fine. He stayed with us for a while until he found a job and a place of his own.

Wetumpka, Alabama 1971

Uncle Bud had divorced Aunt Evelyn and married Katie, the nurse from Villa Rica. He got a job as an administrator of the hospital in Wetumpka. They bought a farm just west of town. Katie had three children, and we visited with them about once a year. This year Bill was with us, and it was a very exciting trip. First there was the fire in the pasture next to the house. Bill took the trash out to a barrel they used to burn the trash and was not watching it. The field was ablaze before we knew what happened. We fought it with everything we had, but at last the fire department came out and settled it down.

There was an old barn out back, and it had a shallow well inside covered with boards. Bill stepped out onto the boards and they broke. He caught himself with his elbows and his feet were in the water! All he could think of was that it was a septic tank and it was full. Of course it was not, but we could not convince him otherwise. He would just yell, "Get me out of here!"

One of Uncle Bud's neighbors had talked about a cave that they had on their property and that stirred up the interest of Bill and I. We searched all over that property and never found a cave.

When we returned to Georgia, we were still excited about finding a cave and going caving. I called around and found out that there was a caving group in Atlanta and that they were having a meeting the following week. Bill and I attended the meeting and started learning about caves in the southeast. They had a weekend trip planned that coming weekend, so I pulled out my construction hard hat and we joined the group. The Dogwood City Grotto loaned us a light, and I picked up a few items from the army surplus store for the trip.

Howard's Waterfall Cave, Dade County, Georgia

Our first trip was on Saturday to Howard's Waterfall. On the way we learned that a few years before a caver had died there rescuing a group of scouts who were trapped in the lower section by gas fumes. The underground gas tanks of a local gas station were leaking down into the cave. The scouts were using electric lights, but the person trying to rescue them had a carbide light. The explosion burnt up all the oxygen in the surrounding area and he suffocated. All the boys were able to get out, and no one else was hurt.

With this bit of information fresh on our minds, we suited up in front of the waterfall entrance and crawled into the dark, low, wet cave. Not only was there water running over the top of the entrance, but a fair size stream was running out of the cave.

Entrance to Howard's Waterfall Cave

Three cavers that we got to know on the trip were John Wallace, Bill Hardman and Norm Briehime.

Bill and I were quite impressed with the cave. We saw most of the upper part of the cave and looked down into the lower section from the second entrance room. We even stuck our heads out of the third entrance, but was told that the property owner was not too friendly and had been known to shoot at trespassers.

The popup was one of the more interesting spots in the cave. It required that you lay on your back and inch your way down under the rock and back up into another passage on the other side.

Bill and Norm invited us to camp out with them up on Lookout Mountain and check out another cave the following day. We camped under the stars with no tent and the next morning watched as Bill and Norm dropped a pit on top of the mountain. We did not go down.

Kudzu Cave was the next stop, and we were about to experience some real hard core caving. They told us they would show us how to climb the rope and let us use their equipment. We tried on the equipment at the entrance and climbed a short distance to get the feel of it. Then with help from the experts, we repelled down the rope for about sixty feet into the cave. After what seemed like a long passage through a fissure, we climbed up into a large well–decorated room with formations all around us. I am afraid that we were hooked on wild caving from that moment on. We did not go down the next drop, and after about an hour returned to the entrance for the climb out. That weekend was the start of more than forty years of caving.

Our next trip was the following month, May 15 at the invitation of John Wallace to see a cave discovered only ten years earlier in northern Alabama.

Fern Cave System, Alabama

On May 15, 1971, John Van Swearingen, IV introduced us to New Fern Cave. John Wallace, Bill Meier and I were excited to see what all the cavers in the nation were talking about at the time. A huge cave system had been discovered in north Alabama. Vertical cavers from all over North America were coming to drop the deepest pit at that time in the eastern United States, Fern Cave.

Nat Mountain

The Fern Cave System is located in the west side of Nat Mountain in North Alabama. Fern Cave was discovered June 4, 1961 by Jim Johnston,

Bill Torode, Louis Fox, Chris Kroger, and Butch Dill. It consists mostly of Surprise Pit, 437–foot deep and more than 200 feet long.

Morgue Cave was discovered June 9, 1968 by Bob Clark, John Cole, Jim Johnston, Don Myrick, Arch Swank and Lynne Swank. It consists of several pits 100 to 200–foot deep. The Morgue is a hibernating and nursery cave for roughly 50% of the entire Gray Bat species and perhaps 75% of the Gray Bat population in the southern United States.

On January 11, 1969, New Fern Cave was discovered by Jim Johnston and is commonly referred to as the Johnston Entrance to the Fern Cave System. New Fern Cave consists of more than 15 miles of horizontal cave with three main levels connected by pits and canyons.

John Van Swearingen, IV and John Wallace at the Elephant Ears, 5/15/1971.

New Fern Cave was connected to the Morgue in January of 1969, and in April of that same year the lower level of New Fern Cave was reached.

There was found evidence of past visits to the cave by torch barriers and large animals, some that are now extinct. Searches were made for a lower entrance, but none has been found. Caving in the Fern Cave System involves a long hike up Nat Mountain, or if you know the roads, a drive to the top and a hike down to the entrances. It seemed strange to climb the outside of the mountain, then go inside and climb back down the inside of the mountain.

Me studying the helectites

Finally on October 10, 1971, the lower stream passages of Fern Cave and New Fern Cave were connected by digging out a stream in the cold water. This completed the Fern Cave System by connecting the three main caves and a few minor ones on the mountain. The map and most of the exploration of the Fern Cave System were completed by Bill Torode and members of the Huntsville Grotto.

Our group consisted of horizontal cavers, only getting involved in vertical work when there was no other possibility. We made several trips in

1971, 1972 and 1973, at a time when the last discoveries were being made and the mapping was completed. I experimented with some movie taking in the cave, but was not pleased with the results. One scene shows the Elephant Ears shortly after being broken, and on the first trip I have a picture of the Elephant Ears before being broken with John Van Swearingen, IV and John Wallace.

On November 20, 1971, we made our second trip into New Fern Cave. We parked by the river at the foot of the mountain and hiked up to the Johnston entrance. Just inside the entrance there is a drop of about eight feet where a wooden ladder was installed.

John Wallace in a Fern Cave canyon

We continued to the southeast to the upper formation rooms filled with helectites growing in all directions. We also visited the Red Lily Pad Room. The room had round formations that looked like Lily Pads in a pool of water, and some of them had stalagmites growing up from the center.

The helectites are formed when the wind blows through the cave, forcing the water droplets to blow off the sides of the formations, leaving mineral deposits. At different times the wind blows in different directions, causing the odd shapes.

After exploring many of the formations areas, we continued south to the Elephant Ears and the Green Passage. The Green Passage is a smaller crawl and walking passage that leads to the Blowing Hole. The Blowing Hole is a shortcut to the middle level of the cave. Bill Torode cleared the dirt from around the hole, placed a bolt in the wall and installed a cable ladder. The hole is about four feet around and an easy place to belay climbers as they go down the ladder. The last person down has to be belayed from below with the rope going up and through the carabineer at the bolt.

Formations along the Green Passage

At the bottom of the middle level we continued down the canyon of the Gold Passage to the Crystal Room, where large, five–inch gypsum crystals jut out from the wall. The wall is more than ten feet high and almost as wide with these crystals side by side all over the wall. The crystals are pointed with smooth sides, making the most striking formation room that I have ever seen. From the Crystal Room we continued to the Balcony Room. You literally can sit on the edge of a balcony and look into a huge round room about eighty feet high that contains a massive flowstone called Myrick's Monument that reaches from the bottom to the top of the room.

On July 21, 1973, I returned with Jack Pace, and we spent eight hours exploring upstream from the Johnston entrance. We passed the second dome and climbed over a ledge and into a virgin room. The room had many soda straws and helectites, and no tracks or signs that anyone had been there. We left the formation room and reentered the stream passage at survey mark #18, just to the left of a dry stream bed.

John Wallace 1971, at the Reflecting Pool in the Red Lily Pad Room

On October 20, 1973, John Wallace, Jack Pace and I returned and went directly down to the Green Passage and the Blowing Hole. We continued to the Lunch Room, then climbed down the waterfall drop, rigging a rope for the return climb. We noted the white glacier flowstone and the small cave pearls. We climbed down into the first Big Room, and after exploring it, exited the cave after another eight–hour trip.

Tumbling Rock Cave, Alabama

Of all the caves that I have explored, Tumbling Rock Cave in Alabama ranks number three on my list of favorite caves. My first trip there was July 24, 1971. I have made many return visits to this famous—and Alabama's most visited–cave. Tumbling Rock Cave is over 6 miles long and is mostly walking passage. At one time it was referred to as Blowing Cave. There is a stream that flows almost the entire length of the cave and that forms a spring just below the entrance. This is the only cave that I know of that contains oil. The Asphalt Ooze occurs in Allens Alley near the back of the cave and covers the floor with a layer of dust hiding it. It drips from the ceiling and flows down a long slope to the floor of the cave. I keep a sample of it in a bottle labeled "Alabama Crude!"

Alabama Crude

After a visit with the owners and paying our parking fee, we climbed a short distance up the side of the mountain, opened the gate and crawled through the three–foot–high entrance. Note: The cave is now managed by the SCCi (Southeastern Cave Conservancy inc.). The first room, Ante Room, is a large walking passage that crosses over the stream. Care must be taken from the start. If your eyes have not adjusted to the Dark, you may step into the crevasse that crosses the path. This is a three foot–wide drop that you step over. You then follow the stream to the Saltpeter Works. These are large Civil War vats which have long rotted away, leaving the square mounds of dirt remaining.

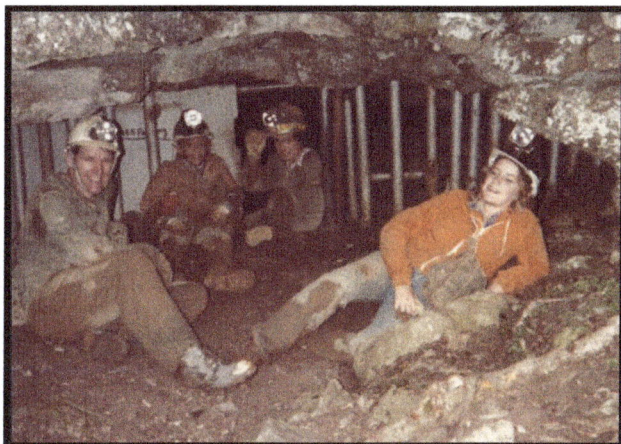

Left to right, me, Stanley Schmidt, Jerry Hill and Debbie Schmidt.

Dogwood City Grotto at the Saltpeter Works

My first visit was in July of 1971 with the Dogwood City Grotto, and it was on this trip that I became more acquainted with John Wallace. We became friends and caving partners for years to come. John shared that when he was dating his wife, Yolanda, he spread out a tablecloth near the Saltpeter Works and set up a candlelight dinner that he had carried into the cave.

John and Yolanda always wore white overhauls when caving, it was sort of a status thing I guess. John would call me about once a month and start the conversation with something like, "Have you had too much sunlight? Ready to go caving?" I always said yes. John played a big part in shaping my life. He always encouraged us to do more. I credit my cave mapping software to his encouragement. Now anytime I take on a new project, I think of John and how he looked at life. I know that he had the same effect on his students at Georgia Tech. He loved to play the viola, rode a motorcycle to work and of course flew his plane whenever he got the chance, often to a cave somewhere!

We caved together almost every month until his death in 1994. I had the honor of writing his obituary for the NSS News, October, 1994. [11]

Dave Hughes, a fellow caver, shared with me how he met John.

"On returning to the vehicles after a wet caving trip. John was approached by a young college student who had participated in the adventure. The student had never been in a cave before and was cold, wet and hungry. In the hustle of loading the vehicles and leaving the area, this individual had become separated from his ride home, from his

change of clothes and from his wallet. John took the novice under his wing, loaned him some dry clothes and began to drive him home. Along the way, John bought the student a good dinner and delivered him right to the doorstep of his dormitory. When the student asked John what could be done to pay him back for his kindness, John replied, "You've already paid me back. It's good to visit with a new and enthusiastic caver!"

I miss John and those monthly calls to go caving. I began to slow down after that, only caving a few times a year, and most of the time to my other two favorite caves.

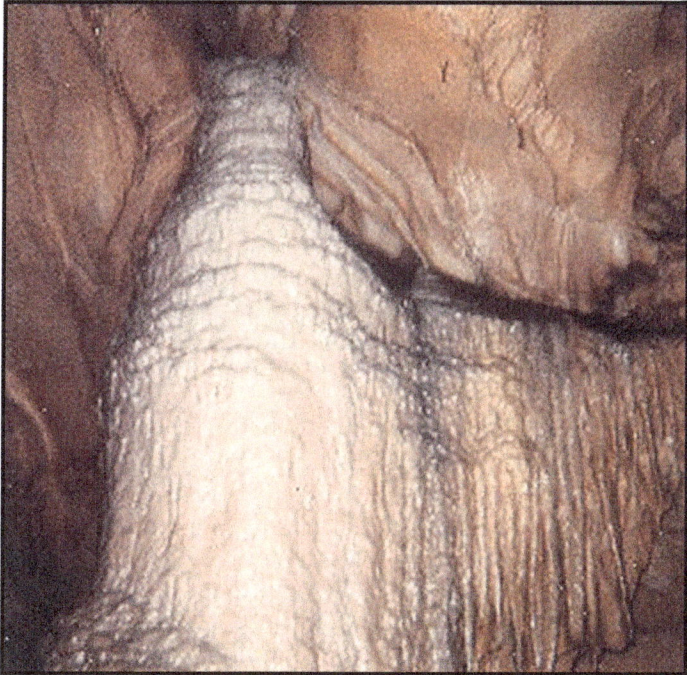

One of the two Elephant Feet

A short distance from the Saltpeter Works we climbed up out of the stream passage and into a large room with two large formations called the Elephant's Feet. If you climb up to the top of one of the feet, near the ceiling one can enter a small crawl space that goes up above the ceiling and over the stream passage into what is now called Vujade' Extension.

Continuing upstream, we climbed over the Wildcat Rock pile and past the Little Hall of Mysteries. Formation Grotto is off to the left, and we explored The Sewers to a 15–foot drop. We then returned to the stream and went through the Wind Tunnel to the Totem Grotto, Craters of the Moon. Chucks Music Box is in a side passage to the left and well worth the visit to view the tall thin columns. At this point you need to be with someone who is familiar with the cave in order to locate the Hidden Door.

If you miss the Hidden Door on the way back out of the cave, one ends up in a dead-end stream passage.

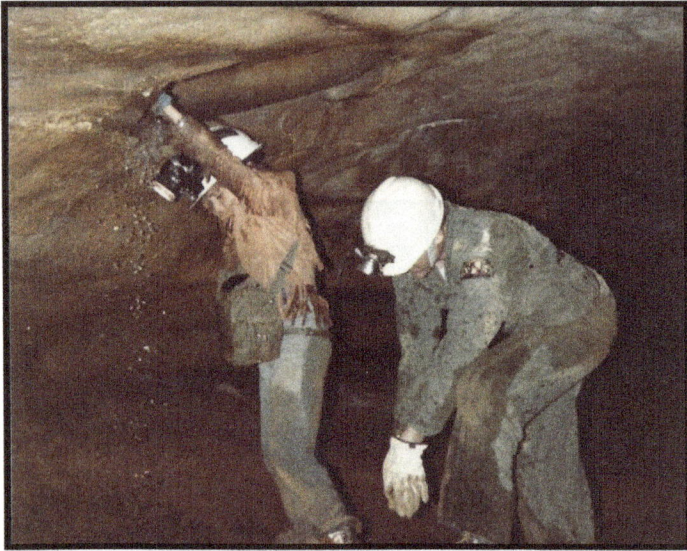

Stanley getting some assistance up through the Kings Shower

Just beyond the Hidden Door and just before entering the Great Hall of Mysteries is the Kings Shower. When the upper passage to the Topless Dome and the lower passages were mapped, it was found that there were only inches between the two. So a sledge hammer was used to make a shortcut up to the Topless Dome. The stream from the Dome now runs down and drops through the hole creating the Kings Shower. Pulling up through this hole and going a short distance to the right brings you to the bottom of the Topless Dome.

The Dome is 396 feet high and was climbed by Don Davison and Cheryl Jones around 1979 over a two–year period. The climb is 555 feet long, which makes it the longest underground technical route in the United States. Read about Topless Dome Revisited in the October 1982 NSS News.

For a long time the Great Hall of Mysteries was the end of the cave. Now there are two passages to continue to the back of the cave. Both are challenging. I will describe the Blue Crawl first as it was the first to be discovered. Straight across the room, to the left of the Christmas Tree formation and up the mud slope, is Johnston's Junction, a short squeeze into the Emperors Room. Cross the Emperor's Room and climb up in a crevice and into a 75–foot long round crawl. One must decide which arm goes first at the start, because you cannot change positions again until you emerge out the far side of the Blue Crawl. When exiting the Blue Crawl, it is a narrow ledge, and in order to get your body out of the hole one has to extend out over the ledge. I have made the crawl one time, but never again. However I think that everyone should try it once.

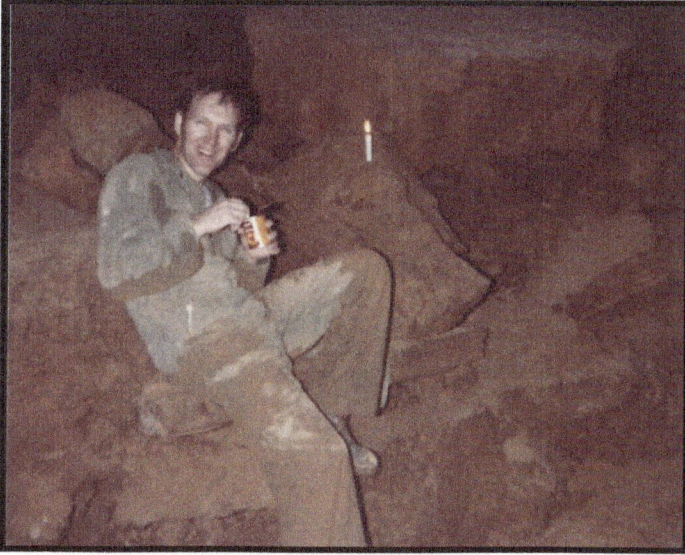

Me taking a lunch break

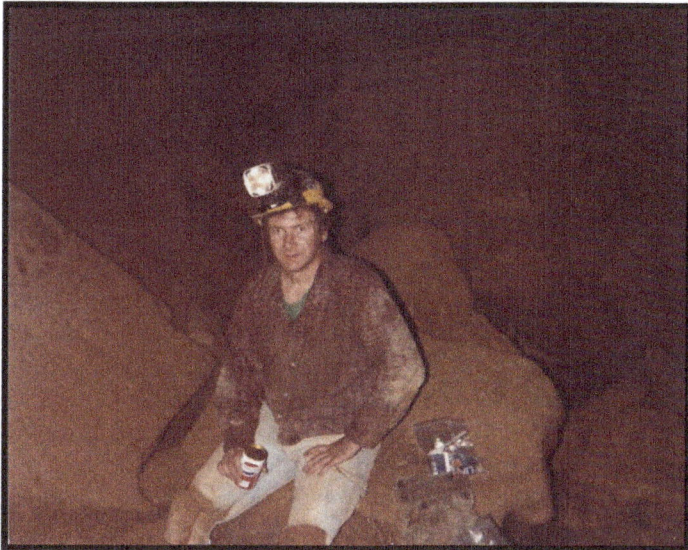

Ed Schmidt taking a break

Ed Schmidt was my coworker at Kodak, and this was his first, and maybe, only caving trip. We also hiked some in the North Georgia mountains until we came upon a rattlesnake and that was pretty much it for hiking. Ed was from Germany. His family came to America shortly after the war. I will never forget how excited he was when they tore down the Berlin Wall! He told me that he did not think that he would see that in his life time!

We exited the Blue Crawl and went into the Inter Sanctum breakdown room, and on the far side we climbed down and under the Surprise Waterfall into Allens Alley.

John Wallace just taking in the cave

The second route that was discovered, or I should say was dug open, is the Suicide Passage. Back in the Emperors Room, climb down and along the right side of the Christmas Tree formation to the stream level. Follow the sandy crawl along the left side of the stream until you can climb up into the rock pile. After several tight bends and climbs, one enters Allens Alley. This is a shorter route and is usually preferred over the Blue Crawl.

Allens Alley is a nice long canyon passage with the stream flowing down below. About halfway through one has to climb up near the ceiling and crawl through a two–foot restriction. It then opens back up again into a huge long room. Watch out for the Asphalt Ooze along the right side, which crosses the path.

There is a small lead off to the left side of Allens Alley about halfway to where it lowers to two feet. It appeared to have some traffic, and I wanted to check it out at a later date, but never did. I took a nice picture of John Wallace setting there.

The reward at the end is the Pillar of Fire, and it is well worth the climb up Mt. Olympus. This large, bright red formation sits at the top of a mud mountain called Mt. Olympus. This is where most cavers stop after a four-hour trip in and another four hours to get out. If one wants to see the bitter end, Terry's Tiger Teeth, then just before climbing Mt. Olympus, go over to the right side of Allens Alley and look for the D–T passage. This is a tight break down crawl for about 300 feet. After emerging back into a walking passage again in Grant's Tomb, the stream is down and to the right, called Grant's Pool. Terry's Tiger Teeth is on ahead to the left.

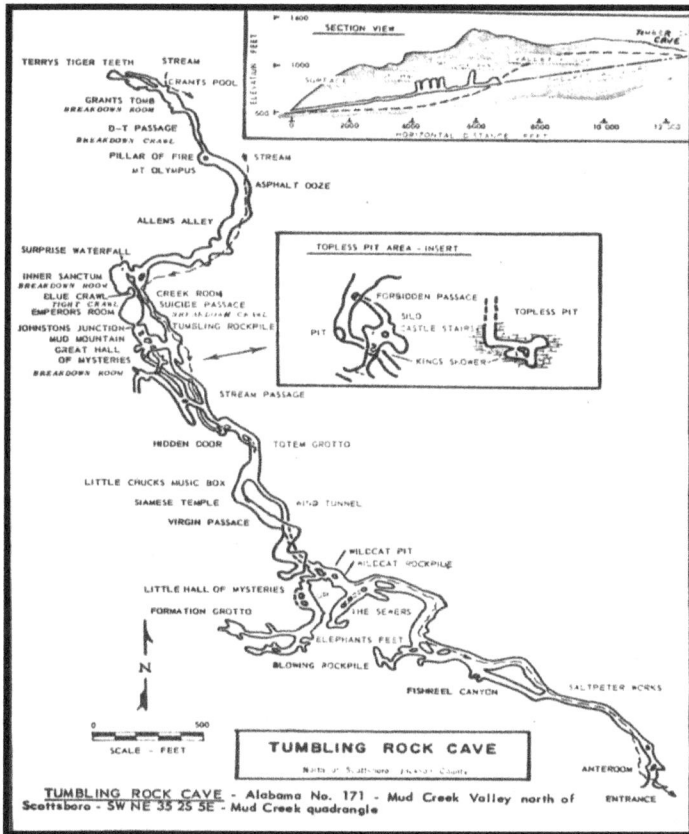

Early map of Tumbling Rock Cave

The cave continues, though the passage may not be discovered, more than the length of the known cave to a small cave called Timber Cave on the far side of the mountain. Dye tracing of the water entering Timber Cave was traced to Tumbling Rock Cave. If you are looking for a good eight hour wild cave trip, then I would recommend Tumbling Rock Cave.[12]

Kodak Job Change

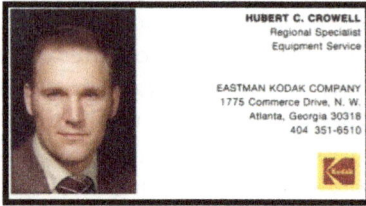

When I first started work at Kodak, I attended training at their Southeastern headquarters in north Atlanta. Fred, our instructor, was also the Regional Specialist for the micrographics line of equipment for the southeast. I was intrigued by his job from the start. I had met his boss Jack Ingram on my interview.

In 1974, just a little less than three years after starting, Fred took a supervisor job in Birmingham, Alabama, and his job became open. I had just recently moved from the shop in Chamblee to the Atlanta district, making service calls. I discussed the opening with Jim Turner, my supervisor, and he said that I did not have enough time with the company to get the job. I was currently teaching nights at the vocational school and felt well qualified for the job, so I put in for it anyway. Now if this had been a union job they would have also blocked me. The company was going through some budget problems and there was a wage freeze for the year, however if you changed jobs, they would make sure that you were at least at the bottom of your new pay scale.

I believe that God intervened. The job was offered to at least two other employees that I know of, and maybe more. One I knew well, Jim Strange, told me that he turned down the job because he was sure that a supervisors job would be coming soon and he was going to wait for that. Before the year was over I got the job, along with the biggest increase in pay I had ever gotten with Kodak–and during the wage freeze!

Teaching Kodak service reps was a breeze, as I was already teaching at night. I knew the equipment very well from working in the recondition center and tearing them completely down to rebuild them each and every day.

I worked in the shop very closely with Bob Crouch. he was older and had been with Kodak a long time. He showed me many tricks and repair procedures. Bob's wife, Wilma Crouch, was the company nurse in the same building. She was great, and would help me out when my ears needed cleaning or any other minor medical need. Years later when I was teaching blood analyzers, I would send the students down to her to draw blood so they could get a real feel for how the analyzer worked. We built a homemade centrifuge to spin down the blood sample and test the serum.

Bob got cancer the second year I was there and was out of work for a whole year with pay. Kodak's sick leave policy was that after your first year you could take up to one year sick leave, then only work one day and be out another year if need be. Bob came back to work for about a week and then was gone again. He passed away about a month later, and I was one of the pallbearers at his funeral. That is when I started to feel like I was getting old. The more friends I lost down through the years, the older I felt.

Jack Ingram often referred to our small office behind the training room as the pit! When you came in the main entrance of the training facility, you would open a side door and go down a set of steps that was inside of our office. My desk was just at the bottom, and a doorway to the right went into the training room. Ed Schmidt sat across from me. Jack was to my right, alongside the stairs, and on the other end was Bob Morthrop and Larry Remy. Each of us had our own line of equipment that we covered, with Jack overseeing the whole group. We were very close, not only in the cramped space but also as friends as well. When we would all be on the phone at the same time, it became very interesting. You always knew all about the problems everyone was working on. That was good because toward the end of my career with Kodak, I had to step in and take Bob Mothrop's place after he died of a heart attack.

Several years later Kodak expanded into the copier marker and added two more specialists for that market. We did not have room for them, so we all got to move upstairs with the brass. Things changed somewhat after that. There were no walls, only dividers, so we had to keep the noise level down, as well as the jokes.

We traveled a lot, and most were rush calls. We had a four, four, four system that required a problem to be declared a Red Alert when eight hours were spent on a problem. The service rep had four hours to resolve a problem. If at the end of four hours, he did not have the solution, he had to call one of us. We would talk them through it, and if we could not solve the problem over the phone in the second four hours, we had to declare a Red Alert. At that stage we made airplane reservations, notified our Rochester counterparts of the Red Alert and head to the customer site. We then had about four more hours with discussions with the main office in Rochester on the problem. If needed, engineers from Rochester may also have to be called upon to help out on site.

Ed Schmidt and I backed each other up, and the same was true with Larry and Bob. I could tell a hundred stories of calls we were involved with, but for now I will only share this one!

Laying On of Hands

The main product that Ed supported was a large computer output microfilm machine called the COM–80. I was familiar with most of the common problems, and when Ed was doing training or out of the office, I would take his calls. We also overlapped with other regions as well. This particular call came in from Washington, DC. The equipment was shutting down or would just act up at random, the worst kind of problem to have. After several hours I declared a Red Alert and jumped an airplane for DC. The service rep picked me up at the airport, and we headed straight for the job site. I walked into the air–conditioned computer room and as I listened to the operator explain what was going on, I leaned over and placed my hand, for some unknown reason. on the panel that contain the fuses for the COM–80. I knew something was wrong right away, the panel was just too warm. I interrupted the operator and told the service rep that I thought I knew what the problem was. We shut the equipment down and removed one of the fuses. The end was black from lack of proper contact with the back of the fuse holder. A weak spring in the fuse holder was the problem.

The service rep almost blew his top. "You can't just walk in here and lay hands on this thing and fix the problem in five minutes!" I knew that I had nothing to do with it. God had intervened again just as he did many times before, for just what reason I don't know, other than to show me just how powerful He is!

I caught a flight back home that afternoon and never heard any more about it. Problem solved!

Ed could tell many stories also. Ed had a bad experience with a preacher when he was young. He overheard the preacher telling his dad he should be giving more to the church, and Ed knew that they did not have it to give. I am sure that Ed misunderstood, or at least I hope that was the case. Anyway Ed was against the church and Christianity. He did not want to have anything to do with it.

Kathy and I were invited over to meet Ed and his wife, Debbie, one evening, and during the evening the subject of God was brought up. Debbie pulled Kathy into the kitchen with some excuse and told her how shocked she was. Debbie was a Christian in spite of how Ed felt. Ed at one point had thrown Debbie's Bible into the fire and told her that he did not want to have anything to do with it and not to bring the subject up again when he was around. Debbie had been praying that God would place someone in the workplace with Ed that was a Christian! I knew as soon as Kathy told me about the conversation why God had made a way for me to get the job that I had. It was an answer to her prayer!

He would always remain quiet and not respond. Well not only did I get to witness to Ed, but God continued to place Christians in his path. Out of the blue one day Ed told me, "Guess what Bill asked me the other day while we were working on his problem? Do you know Jesus?" Now Ed knew about Jesus very well. He was raised in a Christian family and had read the bible as a child.

Years later, while we were still working together, Ed developed cancer. Although he smoked, he believed that it was due to the Sweet and Low he used. He showed me the warning on the label about it being known to cause cancer in lab rats! They opened him up to remove the cancer, but it was too late, it had already spread through his body, so they just closed him back up without removing anything. He went through a series of radiation treatments, and the doctors told him that they could give him one good year.

Ed loved to play golf, I did not know it at the time, but his partner and golfing friend was a preacher. Ed golfed a lot that year, and called me one day and asked me if I could pick him up a Bible. I wasted no time, bought him one and took it to him. He had divorced Debbie by then and remarried, living in the country north of Canton, Ga. We went for a long walk, and he shared with me his life story, which I had never heard before. He apologized for not coming to me first, but explained that he had told the preacher that he golfed with that if he ever accepted Christ, that he would come to him. The preacher never brought up the subject again.

Ed, with less that a year to live, turned to the preacher friend and was lead to the Lord. Now at the end as he was dying, Ed explained that the hardest thing he had to accept was the fact that Jesus would forgive him. It was as if he were one of the thieves on the cross.

We had many more good visits during that year, and both Kathy and I were at his bedside when he told us that angels were standing beside the bed, waiting for him. He died with a smile on his face and with many of his friends standing by his side!

Glory Hole, South Georgia

On September 25, 1971, a member of the Dogwood City grotto was going down to take some pictures in Glory Hole and was looking for someone to go with him. The two of us drove down and back the same day.

Glory Hole has records dating back to 1855. It was then called Blowing Cave, it is now referred to as Willder Cave, or Glory Hole.

An article from the *Atlanta Journal Magazine* published on March 22, 1931, discussed "breathing caves" in Georgia. It stated, "One of the caves is 10 miles north of Whigham in Grady County. The cavern continuously inhales and exhales great puffs of air. Accompanying its breathing is a shrill whistling sound, and at certain periods of the day and night the whistling changes to a long, rumbling groan, as though a giant is struggling to break through the stone walls that pen him in. This phenomenon is due to slight changes in atmospheric pressure, and the whistling sound can be heard more than 30 feet away from the cave." [13]

We entered the cave through the bottom of a sinkhole. The cave was low and muddy, however the walls were covered with crystal white formation, all the way down to the mud. I explored while he (I cna not remember his name), took pictures. At one point I crawled down into a small room, turned around and could not find my way out. It is just as easy to get turned around in a confined space as it is in a large maze. This was my first year of real caving, and I was learning to respect caves. After what seemed like a long time, I made my way back up through a small opening and into the main part of the cave again.

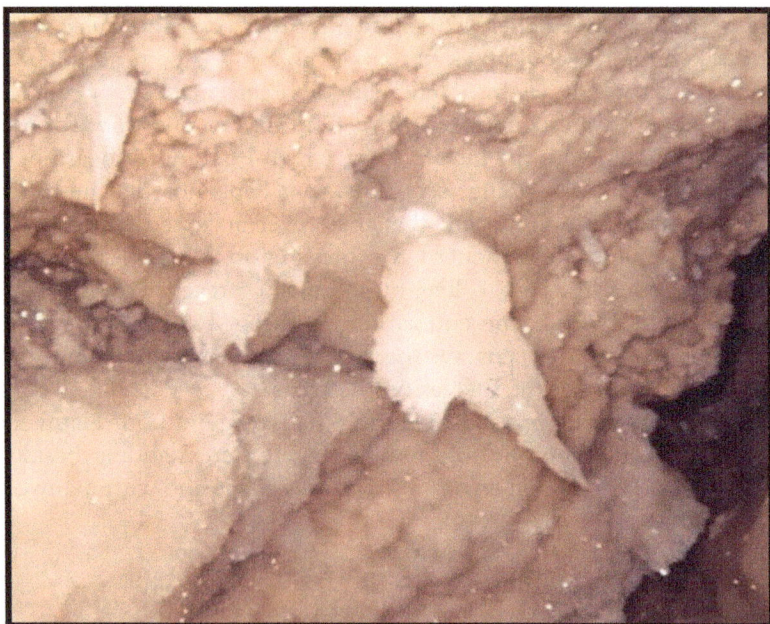

Six–inch angel wings in Glory Hole

During the ride home I was exhausted and fell asleep several times. It was a long day.

My First Caving Convention, June 1973

Bloomington, Indiana NSS Convention was a great trip. It was convention time in Indiana, and this would be my first NSS (National Speleological Society) convention. John Wallace, Jack Pace and I flew to Indiana in John's small plane. Landing a small plane at a commercial airport was quite exciting. They directed us to the runway from the side as large jets were landing, and at the last moment had us make a sharp 90–degree turn and land as quickly as possible, then taxi at top speed to the nearest taxi way to get off the runway before another jet landed.

The 1973 convention was being held at Indiana University in Bloomington and was a huge success. It was capped off by our banquet speaker, Roger Brucker, relating the exciting story of the discovery of the Flint–Mammoth cave connection, making it the world's largest cave system. I was also excited over winning third place in the prusik contest. I climbed 100 feet of nylon rope in one–minute–and–forty–two seconds in the 30–39 age group. I believe that there may have been only three contestants in this age group!

One of the caves open to the convention attendees was Sullivan Cave. The three of us decided to have a look at the cave. We entered the cave and went through the small narrow passage for a short distance before connecting with the Back Breaker passage. This was a long passage with a ceiling height of about 3 to 4 foot. This finally intersected the main trunk passage at the "T." Following the map from the convention guide book we found the Mountain Room passage, then after a short distance the Mountain Room. We spent some time exploring the Mountain Room, and as we were about to leave, some very wet cavers appeared. They shared that they had entered the cave through the Speed Hollow entrance.

This was a very tempting choice, to leave by another entrance and avoid that long trip back through the Back Breaker passage. They left a good, easy–to–follow trail as it was wet from their passing through. We traveled about half the distance that we had come thus far and reached a room called the Spiral Room. Crossing over a flowstone floor through a short crawl, we found the Manhole.

Looking down the Manhole, all we could see was water. We turned off our lights and let our eyes adjust to the darkness, and then leaned down into the Manhole as far as possible. There was a very slight glow of light shining from the far side of the underground lake. John dropped in first and could not touch the bottom. After struggling for a while he finally found a spot where he could touch the bottom. We all followed behind, dropping into the cold water, and headed for the light as fast as possible.

As we sloshed through the water the waves reached the ceiling, getting us completely soaked, ears, eyes and all. There was no turning back now. We just gulped air between waves and continued. Near the exit the passage became lower until we were crawling in the water with only a few inches of air space. When we climbed out of the water and into the daylight, it sure felt good.

Now we had another problem. We did not know where we were. There was no road in sight, only an open field and the wooded hills. We did not even know which direction we had gone in the cave. After exploring the field we found the main road and took a guess at the direction to walk. It was quite an adventure, but I believe we will try a little better planning next time.

Manhole in Sullivan Cave

The water lapped against the ceiling as I tilted my head,
bad decision, should have gone the other way instead,
admiring the Spiral Room and resting after the long trip,
cavers appeared looking like they had just taken a dip.

A choice, Black Breaker passage or swim out Speed Hollow,
finding the way should be easy with a wet trail to follow.
As the trail began to dry, strange sounds ahead could be heard,
the three of us continued on hands and knees, not to be deterred.

The hole in the middle of the passage, dark and black below,
which way and how far to the exit are things I wanted to know.
The size of a manhole without the cover and full of water so cold,
who would be first, as we studied our plight, would I be so bold?

With lights out and hat removed, leaning in till I almost fell,
I strained to see if there was any daylight between each swell.
At last after looking all around, a dim slight glimmer of light,
now I knew the direction and just thankful it was not night.

John went first and made a big splash, his orange hat out of sight,
over his head until he paddled to the side, giving us all a fright.
I followed into the cold water, gasping for air between the waves,
then I began to wonder just what makes us venture into caves.

Close to the stream exit I had to crawl with only inches to spare,
at last I was out, cold, wet, confused, but glad to be in the fresh air.
Nothing familiar, getting late, no road in sight. Are we lost?
Could that be a fence, did they mention a field to be crossed?

Tired and wet, finding the road, luckily taking the right direction.
I wonder how the ones we met climbed with no rock projection
from the water through the manhole with the water so deep.
A stop for dinner, discussing our adventure, and ready for sleep.

Mustang Momma

In 1969 Andree and Rae moved to Georgia to be closer to family and found a job in Atlanta. They lived in an apartment not far from us in Smyrna. Mom bought a new Mustang, a dealer demo, a 1968 red Mustang coup. We joked about it a lot and called her Mustang Momma! When Andree and Uncle Bud moved out to California to be with their sister Marie, she gave the car to me.

Caving in New York State

During July 1975, I drove the red '68 Mustang from Atlanta to Rochester, NY for a month of training with Eastman Kodak and was looking for something to do on the weekends. I found John Freeman, who also worked for Kodak, and he invited me on a caving trip for the weekend.

I followed him to the top of a hill where the cavers had a small shack with a fair sized cave nearby. The group had a band, and they played most of the night. The rock group was good, but I was not into that kind of music, a little too loud for my taste. I started out sleeping in a small tent, then it started to rain and turned colder. The rain got so hard that I moved into the Mustang. I pushed the passenger seat forward as far as possible and tried to make a bed between the back seat and the front seat. I was not too successful and stayed up most of the night. The rain and lightening were strange. It was running sideways through the clouds, like nothing I have ever seen.

The next day Jack took a few of us that were from out of town to show us a new cave. One of the couples was visiting in the States from Australia. Jack thought that we would be leaving and so the cave location could remain a secret for a while. I believe that the name was Raccoon Cave. There were many raccoon tracks in the cave and even high on the walls.

The entrance was small and tight, just a crack along the side of a small rock wall. The cave was small but had some nice formations. There was even a possibly that it could be pushed through a large crack to deeper levels.

Jack was a member of the Cave Research Foundation (CRF), and he gave me a copy of the CRF Personal Manual. The CRF was the major force behind the exploration of the Flint Ridge System in central Kentucky and the connection of this system with Mammoth Cave. Jack was also a member of a group that explored the 7.5 miles of Lee Cave, in Kentucky, beneath the northeastern edge of Joppa Ridge, in Mammoth Cave National Park a few years earlier.

New York caves are colder than the ones in the south, and much wetter also. I purchased a 3/4 wet suit and used it each time I went caving in New

York State. The cave behind the shack followed a stream passage to a small room at the back with few formations. You could see the complete cave in about fifteen minutes.

Herkimer, New York is the home of the Herkimer Diamonds. These are large crystals, and not real diamonds. We walked across a farmer,s field, kicking up a few diamonds along the way, until we reached what looked like a mine shaft. The pit had a ladder, and we climbed down about twenty feet to the floor of the cave. The passage was cold and damp as we crawled along around several turns. It also kept getting smaller and lower. My friend who brought me to this cave was up ahead and pushing hard. Being young and with a lot to learn, I told him to keep on going. He rolled over and said that I was welcome to past him and go ahead. I inched passed him and headed for the next turn in the passage to see what surprise might be waiting there.

Hard hat off and slowly pushing it ahead, exhaling to move forward, I finally gave up. It was just too tight. I announced that I was coming back. With no room to turn around there was only one thing to do, back out the same way I went in. When I cave, I carry an army gas mask bag with all my gear. And an army belt with the battery for my head light, All this fits nicely at my sides. When I started to back out, everything started going wrong. All my gear started moving toward my chest where it was already so tight that I could hardly breathe, and I had to release all the air in my lungs just to move.

My arms were in front of my head, and I could not move them to release my belt. I could not turn around. I was stuck! Panic set in as I lay there against the cold rock, and I wondered if this would be my grave. Over the next twenty minutes or longer, I would exhale as much air as possible and dig my toes into the rock, pulling backward a fraction of an inch at a time. Each movement only resulted in the Chinese finger getting tighter. At last, the passage relented and gave me a little more room and I eased on back with my toes. That was the last time that I egged on a fellow caver. I had learned my lesson.

Stuck in Herkimer Cave

Cold and damp, unable to move,
why was I here, did I have something to prove?
Like Floyd Collins in Sand Cave,
would this also become my grave?
Caught in a Chinese Finger Trap,
so tight I had to remove my caving cap,
would there be a media circus with me below?
I can only move with the use of my toe.

150

Curiosity drove us on around each turn,
of the danger we had little concern.
My friend in the lead pushing hard
with me urging him on with little regard.
"You're welcome to pass and go ahead."
I would live to regret what I had said.
Pride drove me beyond my limitation,
with curiosity adding to my fixation.

Arms and hard hat pushed out in front,
I slowly inched forward with a grunt.
Unable to turn or even look ahead,
how would they get me out after I'm dead?
Exhaling to move forward, like a snake,
I thought this cave would be a piece of cake.
Unable to breath against the unforgiving rock,
time to rest, reflect and take stock.

I finally gave up, it was just too tight,
started to push back with all my might.
Panic as my belt, battery and pack
would not budge or move back.
As I moved backward they wedged tight,
now I was stuck in this awful plight,
like a Chinese Finger Trap, tighter than ever,
only now I am the finger as I struggle to endeavor.

Giving up, struggling to breath in a cold sweat,
it was over, no point in being upset.
I was nothing, nothing mattered anymore,
this was it, no one could help as I lay on the floor.
Now I knew the true meaning of helplessness,
what had I done, how did I go amiss?
Using my toes and pulling back with all my might,
it all seemed useless. Should I give up and not fight?

Thoughts rushed through my mind of loved ones never to see,
quick prayers as I took inventory with such degree.
searching for anything that would move,
anything to push against, any rock or groove,
like a tight glove that would not expand.
Force out a little more air and move my toes and hands,
relax, rest awhile, remain calm, think small.
I could still move my feet as I searched for the wall.

Pull with my toes, something has to surrender,
maybe my clothes, belt or pack, wish I was slender.
At last an inch in the right direction, though tighter,
the situation is beginning to look a little brighter,
twenty minutes later and a little more room
around my chest. Deeper breath, as I leave my tomb.
Maybe an hour or more later and breathing normal,
giving up on Herkemer Cave, after all I am only mortal.

My friend, I cannot recall his name, took me to several small caves around Albany that weekend and even showed me his old swimming hole, which turned out to be the city water reservoir. No swimming was allowed, but that did not stop us—or the local kids we ran into along the way. We took the well–worn path along the low brush to the edge of the lake. There was a high bank with a tree that reached out over the deep water. Attached to a limb was a rope. One of the young boys climbed the tree, and by swinging the rope over to the bank, we were able to grab it. It was a long swing out over the water and very high. I also did not know how cold the deep water would be. I hit the water hard and went deep, gasping for air. The cold water took my breath away. I tried it a few more times but was not having as much fun as the younger boys.

I had two or three good and exciting weekends on that trip, and I learned a lot—mostly that I was not as young as I thought I was.

Wildcat Oil Well

My first experience with oil exploration was in 1970 with a Canada company called Brilund Mines Limited. I invested $365.50 in ten shares of stock. They owned Etosha Petroleum Limited of South Africa and were searching for oil in the Etosha Basin, Namibia, Africa. I ended up with ten shares of worthless stock and did not learn my lesson.

Having been bitten with the "Oil Bug," I was ready when my boss told us about an oil well investment in Louisiana. Our whole work group at Kodak went down to listen to the offer, and five of us bought in. I invested $2,700.00 in what promised to be a return of $1,200.00 or more a month.

The proposal was to reenter a 1939 oil and gas well called the H. M. Branton #4 in Webster parish, Louisiana. The 1939 well was drilled to a depth of 9,203 feet to find free flowing oil. Reports indicated that several reservoirs of oil and gas were drilled through in this attempt to find deeper oil deposits. Cities Services' well, Hearn #A–1, which was nearby, was a success, and the recommendation was to deepen the Branton #4 another 400 feet.

We were given an offer to be flown down to Louisiana by Mr. Wayne Fleming, who chartered for us a small plane. It was a cool November Saturday in 1983 when we left the Peachtree Dekalb airport, flew down to Springhill, Louisiana and met Mr. Fleming. We were given a tour of the existing oil fields and a steak dinner at the Branton #4.

Dave Reissig, Larry Remy and I on the Branton #4

We were introduced to Perry Branton, the land owner, and Carl Sinclair, who was in charge of the drilling, and showed us around the operation, which was very impressive. We spent the day watching the drilling and casings being lowered into the now enlarged well.

The drilling started on 10/7/1983, and we received daily reports up to and following our 10/15 trip. On the 19th, at a depth of 8,500 feet, they started getting gas and oil as the well tried to unload the mud. They temporarily capped the well for safety and ordered a larger rig capable of containing any possible blow out and of drilling down to a total depth of 11,500 feet.

In late October, I invested another $4,650.00 and bought 500 shares of stock in the company at $1.00/share.

On December 22 drilling resumed, but sleet and snow stopped the operation on the 24th, and the crew was sent home. The mud was frozen on the 27th, and they could not work for the next week. On January 2nd they started back to work and more problems followed. First a blown engine from a frozen block. On January 6th 1984 they reported making oil and gas from the Sexton zone. Then more problems with the equipment, a tool called a packer, had to out to be redressed. On January 12th the well unloaded with 2,815 feet of mud oil and gas and 85 feet of clean oil and no saltwater. On the 18th they twisted off the drill bit. Four days later they recovered the bit and reached 9,487 feet.

More problems continued as they pushed the well deeper. The last report we received from the drilling operation was on February 3, 1984.

Ed Schmidt and I were on a Kodak service call in southern Arkansas and decided to drive down and check out the well site on our own. We arrived after dark on February 21, 1984 and found the site gated and the well capped.

Magnola Branton #4 on February 21, 1984

We received a letter from Bob McCarthy on February 28, 1984, complaining about return mail and asking us to return an address card with our correct mailing address to expedite our production checks on the Brandon #4 well, and we should start to receive checks within ten days! We knew that as of seven days earlier, there was nothing on the site. There could not have been any production of oil. It was starting to sound like a scam.

On May 7, 1984, we were advised that Antilles Petroleum Corp. had moved to a new location in Brownsville, Texas. Still no checks in the mail.

We later received an undated letter from Mr. Wayne Fleming, explaining that the state of Texas was challenging the joint ventures and enclosed a stock certificate to cover our investment in the joint venture, with the promise to exchange it for any future share of another drilling operation.

On November 18, 1984 I called Mr. Perry Branton, the land owner, and he stated that the well was still shut down with a broken pipe still in the hole. The mud pump motor blew up and was in for repairs. He said that Mr. Fleming was now living nearby in Shongaloo, Louisiana.

On December 2, 1985, I was able to get in touch with the State of Texas Charter division and found out that Antilles Petroleum Corp. had lost their charter with the state of Texas due to not paying taxes. A law suit for fraud in gas and oil leases was filed on 4/23/1984 against John Fleming and Perry Branton, and bank accounts were attached totaling $400,000. John Wayne Fleming, President of Antilles Petroleum Corp. was arrested on drug and fraud charges in Haynesville, La., according to the Tuscaloosa News, March 30, 1985.

John Fleming started out working for a large oil company checking on wells that had broken down. He found that sometimes the well would not be producing for the time limit spelled out in the lease, and the well would revert back to the property owner. Mr. Fleming started working deals with these property owners and looking for investors to pour money into his new found problem wells. In trying to go too deep with small equipment, he got into trouble. I believe he started out with good intentions. As problems mounted, the temptation of easy money in flying drugs into the country with his plane led to his downfall. Was he a scam artist? I don't think so. He spent too much effort in trying to reach the black gold!

Yellow Gold in Our Backyard

Down through the years I have searched for gold in north Georgia. Kathy would tell me, "Why don't you try the stream out back of the house?"

I have estimated that when I am working the streams in north Georgia for gold, I can earn about $0.50 an hour at the current price of gold. I understand completely how hard it was for prospectors to make a living looking for gold. However, there is something exciting about finding that shiny speck of metal in the ground. The gold of north Georgia has a deep golden color and is the purest found anywhere. The thrill of that gold appearing in the bottom of a pan of black sand can be addictive. Don't expect to get rich looking for gold, but you can easily collect some color for your home–collection and maybe even a bragging nugget or two.

You may have heard the story about the man in Africa who went off looking for diamonds only to return home after many years to find a large diamond in his own backyard. My wife kept telling me to check out the creek behind the house for gold, but I kept looking in the gold fields more to the north, and even tried to find some out west. My best success was from buying dirt from a mine in Dahlonega which resulted in paying about what the gold was worth after panning it out.

Most of the gold in Georgia can be found along a line from Clayton, in the northeast, to Buchanan, near the Alabama line. Along this line is Dahlonega, Canton, Allatoona, and Acworth. The gold belt is not well defined and is spread out in places. We live just north of Marietta along a ridge that divides the waters of the Chattahoochee and the Etowah rivers. I like to think of it as our little continental divide. Behind our home we have a stream that flows toward the Etowah. The rock formations here are turned up on edge, and at about midpoint along the back of our lot is a quartz vein that is being cut away by the stream.

I started panning for gold on the corner of the lot at the downstream end of Lost Creek and planned to work my way up the stream and clean out all the gold I could find. On one of our trips to Colorado for a caving convention, my friend and I left a week early to pan for gold and bought a small 2–inch dredge. I set up the dredge in the creek and worked the sand all the way down to bedrock. The gold was very rough and beautiful. Nothing large, just small pickers and flakes. I did fill a small locket with gold for a necklace that my wife wears and a small amount for a display case.

I have not yet worked the creek up to the quartz vein where I suspect the gold is coming from. It has not moved far in the water or the edges would be more rounded off. I guess I am saving the rest of the creek for the future.

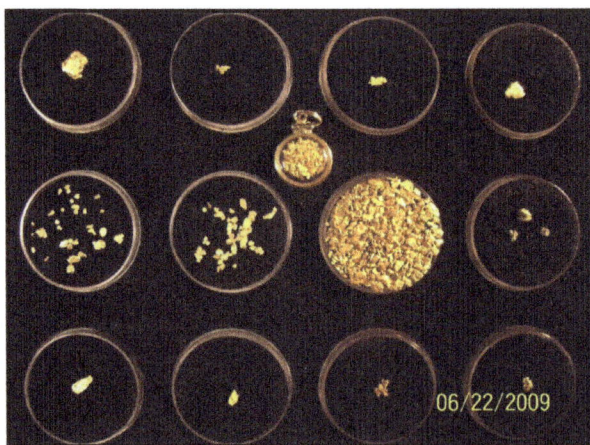

Georgia gold and a locket of gold from my back yard

We used to have gold panning parties when family or out–of–town friends would visit. They could not believe they could find real gold right there in our own backyard.

Subdivisions have taken over some of the old mines in the area. Sixes Mine, in south Cherokee County, produced $200,000 worth of gold in 1849 and now is part of Lake Allatoona and a large subdivision. The Hadaway Mine near Acworth is also believed to have produced a sizeable amount. Ore samples from the Kemp property showed $2.50 to $7.50 worth of gold per ton of ore.

I will never get rich from panning gold, but it is nice to know that you can find gold in your own backyard. So when I get bored again I will drag out the dredge and dredge up sand for a few hours, adding a few more specks of gold to my collection.

Our hawk friend!

Lost Creek

You cut through the earth.
When was your birth?
Make wide your steep rocky banks,
for your beauty, thanks.
Hawks fly and nest above you,
owls roost there, too.
Fish swim in your clear pool,
your water stays cool.

You cut through the rock,
released from your lock.
Bring out your fine bright gold,
from times of old.
Children play in your waters,
fathers look for daughters.
Rocks break up in your floods,
making waterfalls with suds.

You're lost no more,
homes line you shore.
Your gold is secure,
hidden now for sure.

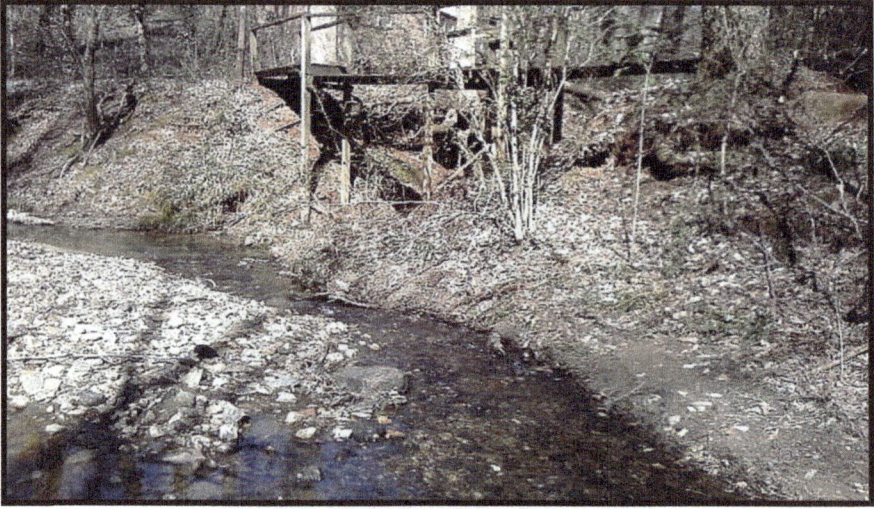

Lost Creek running behind our home

One weekend in July 2002, Buddy Davis and I set out for a weekend of gold panning in North Carolina. Our local club was having a common dig where each person that signs up gets a share of the gold from the dig.

Thermal City Gold Mine is a very interesting place. They have cabins for rent and campsites. We choose to tent camp along the river that ran through the mine. Besides working the common dig, we also bought a front end loader full of dirt and had them place it in the stream just below our camp site. We planned to use the small high banker that I owned to work the dirt for gold.

The high banker doubles as a 2 1/2 inch dredge or a high banker. It has a small gas pump that sprays water over the dirt and washes it down the sluice where the gold is trapped along with the black sand. When the black sand starts to back up or the pump runs out of gas, we wash out the sand into a 5–gallon bucket. We then take a break and divide the sand, panning out the gold. Panning is the fun part. You wash the dirt and sand off the top until you have only a small amount in the corner of the pan. Then you swirl the water around in a clockwise motion until the black sand is slowly moved and the gold shines through. That is truly a lovely sight. You continue this motion until the gold is free of the sand, then you take your dry finger and touch the gold. It will stick to the end of your finger until you touch the water in a small bottle. The gold will then drop very quickly to the bottom of the bottle.

We worked all day Saturday on the common dig and our private dirt pile until dark and retired to our tent. This sure was living. You could hear the stream just below the tent, and the summer night was nice and cool in the mountains. We had just dozed off when we heard a train approaching.

We had been there all day and had not noticed any trains or tracks. The approaching train got louder and louder until we were sure that it was going to run over our tent. I have never been so close to a passing train in my life. We looked out of the tent, and just across the stream and up on the side of the bank where you could not see the tracks was a freight train starting its long pull up the side of the mountain.

We had a good laugh and dozed back off to sleep. Shortly we heard the screeching of train brakes that got so loud that you could hardly stand it. A freight train was coming down the mountain and applying the brakes all the way. That is the way it went all night long, a train would go up the mountain and then another would come down the mountain. After a while it was not so funny. The next day it was all quiet again. They must run that route only at night.

It may have been payback time for me. Many years ago we were on a church retreat in a cabin in the north Georgia mountains, and I took a tape player and a tape with the sound of an approaching train. That night I played the tape on the porch of the cabin. The train sounded like it went right through the cabin. Everyone got a good laugh about the joke, and now the joke was on me.

That Sunday evening we gathered for the drawing for the Gold Nuggets. the first person would get the largest, and it was a nice one, weighing over an ounce. I kept waiting for my name, and then Buddy got his name called and received a small picker. At last I heard my name, I was last on the list. However, they had a special surprise for the last person. It was a couple of crystallized nuggets, or I should say small pickers. However they were unusual, and I was pleased.

Buddy and I did recover a fair amount of gold from our load of dirt, and we enjoyed the weekend, except for the sleepless night with the trains.

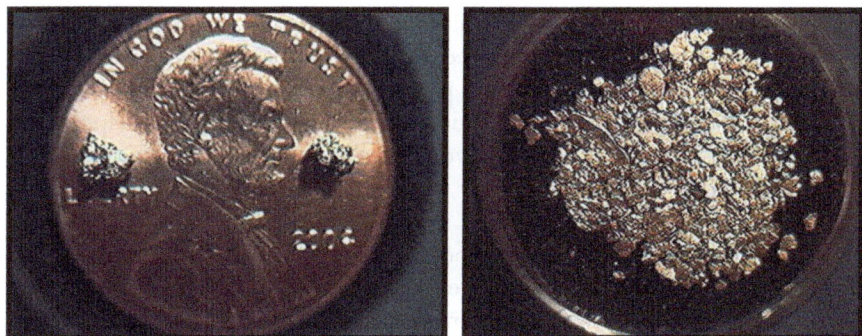

Crystal nuggets from drawing.   Not as yellow as the bright gold of Georgia

The Peat Farm

"Without a dream we have nothing. What is life but a dream and being able to put a little bit of it to work." Hubert H. Crowell.

When Dad left the coal mines, he took up commercial fishing and alligator hunting. He always had a love for the land.

In 1972 Dad purchased the Lake Bonnet Peat Farm, twenty acres of land on the south side of Lake Bonnet Road for $20,000.00. This land starts at the road as sand and then is covered with peat until at the back it is about 20 feet deep. The property came with a dragline that was used to dig up the peat that was sold locally. Dad purchased a bobcat and continued to dig and bag the peat. He enjoyed building equipment to grind it up and showing everyone who stopped by how fast things would grow in the soil mix he created. As the peat was removed, the ponds were filled back in with a mixture of dirt, peat and cuttings from the tree trimmers in the area. Sue Loftin, my cousin, along with her husband, Lvurn "Doc," worked with Dad and helped him on the peat farm for several years.

Dad was seventy when he became a Republican. Ronald Reagan had sent him a letter to join a task force. He liked Reagan because he mentioned the Lord in every speech he made. In 1990 Dad made a trip to Washington, where he met with George and Barbara Bush. "Me and Barbara were talking, and I put my arm around her shoulder and shook hands with her. And I said, 'Forget about George; think about me!' Only in America can a dirt farmer get his picture taken with the president and his wife."

At age seventy-nine he told a newspaper reporter, "It took me 20 years to dig out half this land. I'm going to spend the next 20 filling it up, then I'm going to dig it out again. I'll be but 120 by that time."

In 1982 Dad gave me the peat farm with the understanding that he would continue to work the farm as long as he liked. During the next 14 years the west pond was almost filled, and another small pond was dug on the east side and combined with the previously dug pond on that side.

Dad died in 1996, and I continued the operation with the help of Joe Solis, our only employee. We were very careful over the years to only allow limbs, stumps and sand to replace the peat so that we or someone else could dream and dig again!

We continued to operate the peat farm and began to make a small profit over the salary and expenses of the operation. When you start making money, there is always someone who will get jealous and cause trouble. A fellow with a similar operation on the other side of town was having trouble with the county and told them to check out our operation. County inspectors had visited the farm many times, and Dad would sometimes run them off if they tried to run his business. After Dad passed away, Joe would talk with them and try to comply with all the rules the county brought up about the operation. But as time went on the DEP, Department of Environmental Protection, was in the process of shutting down, what they described as the mom and pop operations in the state of Florida.

Recession of '82

During the recession of 1981-1982, my job was done away with, and technical support for my product line was moved to Rochester, NY. I was offered a teaching position in Rochester with no promise of work for more than a year. To be fair with the rest of the personnel affected, I was not allowed to interview for the job. I did, however, have a scheduled training class to attend in Rochester and was able to sneak in a interview. I did not like the odds and turned down the teaching job. I went back to my old supervisor, Jim Turner, in the Atlanta office to see if he needed anyone to take service calls. He was more than happy to find a lower paying job for me, and I got a company car to replace my reduction in pay.

HUBERT C. CROWELL
Regional Service Engineer
Customer Equipment Services

EASTMAN KODAK COMPANY
Four Concourse Pkwy, Suite 300
Atlanta, Georgia 30328

404 392-2823

During the recession of 1974, I received my largest pay increase when I was promoted to Regional Specialist for Microfilm Equipment. Now the Lord was getting ready to intervene on my behalf again. After a few months, and before my pay cuts took effect, Bob Morthorp had his heart attack. Pete Olsen, the Regional Manager for the southeast region, and one of the investors in Antillies Petroleum, asked if I would come back and take on the Photo Finishing product line that was left vacant by Bob. Rochester did not have anyone at the time to take over the workload.

Pete was the person that introduced us to the deal with Antilles Petroleum. I don't know how much he lost on that venture, but I know that he must have felt bad about getting so many others involved in the bad investment. I often wondered if that may have had a bearing on his wanting to help out. I returned to a new job as Regional Service Engineer and back to my old office, giving up the company car! Well not quite, since I bought it from the company and Kathy loved it.

Jack Ingram, my previous boss, retired, and I was assigned to work for Robert Rosborough, who worked in the Rochester office. I now had to make a great many more trips to Rochester for meetings and conducting classes on the equipment in my new product line. Bob's shoes were not easy to fill!

Each year our group of engineers from each region would meet in one of the regions for a week. We spent a week in Las Vegas one year, and in St. Pete, FL on the beach, which was in my region.

The second time it was my turn, they all came to Georgia, and I took them to North Georgia to pan for gold. They were very excited and enjoyed the day. James Parker, my NY counterpart was now hooked on looking for gold!

In 1991 our office on Concourse Parkway was closed, and I was forced to work from my home for my last year with Kodak. I carried a pager and had my office in our corner bedroom, now Mom's living room.

Retired from Kodak

In 1991 Kodak offered an early retirement program to reduce their overhead. Up till that time you could retire from Kodak if your age and employment time added up to eighty years. The new offer was seventy-five years.

The plan was offered for two years. I did not qualify the first year, but I did qualify at the end of the second year with only one month to spare! I was fifty and would have twenty-four years with Kodak. On my fifty-first birthday in August and with the deadline for the plan ending in September, the same month I was hired, I could retire. It was a very good offer. Those that qualified the first year got an extra one years' pay, those that qualified the second year did not, however they would give us a bridge gap on Social Security added to our retirement.

So with fourteen years of pre–Social Security added to my retirement I could not turn it down. We had a choice of taking a lump sum and rolling it over into an IRA or wait for the normal payout at age sixty-five. The advisors recommended taking the lump sum and showed us a loophole that would allow us to take an equal amount each year from our IRA and not pay a penalty. However we could not vary the amount to be taken by even a penny until age fifty-nine and half or we would have to pay extra taxes and penalties on the total amount!

I was able to take $23,550 each year, and with income from a small computer business and the peat farm, we could make it until I could find another job.

Ecotek LSI

I met Doug Dewitt and Rob Morgan during a December 19, 1992 mapping trip in Pettyjohn Cave. We caved together for about a year, then Doug said that they had an opening at Ecotek, I started working there

January, 1994. This was a testing lab on the south side of Atlanta that checked soil and water samples from nuclear storage and power plants. There was a lot of radioactive material in the lab, so I only visited there once. Rob Morgan and Twyla Morgan worked for Doug in the lab. My job was compiling test results in the computer and generating the necessary reports.

There was one other person working in the same room with me, a lady about my age, and she was always munching on snacks while she worked. One day I saw her grab her throat and started to make strange sounds. I knew right away that she was choking. I turned her around and locked my hands together below her chest, and gave a quick jerk. It worked! I had never used the Heimlich Maneuver before, but she sure was thankful.

Ecotek closed down in July of 1994, and Doug found work up north and would occasionally drive down to Tennessee to go caving in Pumphouse Cave.

Government Records Services

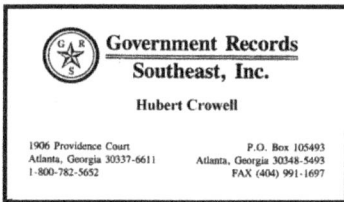

> **Government Records Southeast, Inc.**
>
> Hubert Crowell
>
> 1906 Providence Court
> Atlanta, Georgia 30337-6611
> 1-800-782-5652
>
> P.O. Box 105493
> Atlanta, Georgia 30348-5493
> FAX (404) 991-1697

The same month that Ecotek closed I found work with Joe Williams, who owned a microfilm service company. I worked for him for about 6 months, traveling around the southeast, staying weeks at a time in small towns, microfilming court house records. I hated having to tear out 100–year–old pages from record books to microfilm them, then I would tie them up to be stored in a warehouse as the microfilm quickly replaced the large bulky books.

I had a horn that I loved to play, and during my breaks I would take my van off to some quiet place and get in the back were I would play my heart out. Evenings were the hardest, being alone and away from the family. I would often ride around exploring the countryside. I was microfilming records in Toccoa, Georgia and exploring all the backroads, when I followed an interesting dirt road up a mountain. The road got very narrow with no place to turn around, so I kept on going. When the road started down the other side of the mountain, I really became concerned. There was a huge washout in the center that I was able to straddle with the wheels. One slip and I would be stuck, and no one knew where I was! When I reached the bottom and saw a paved road with only a small stream to cross, I was relieved.

One Thursday in November, 1995 I got a call from Chris who ran the processing equipment at the office. He told me that Joe had sold the company, and there was no need to report to work the next day! Joe and I are still good friends, I just think that he was made an offer he could not refuse.

I signed up for unemployment for the third time in my career and started the application process all over again.

BARCO Display Products

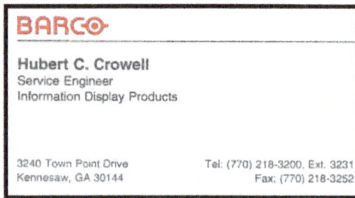

BARCO

Hubert C. Crowell
Service Engineer
Information Display Products

3240 Town Point Drive
Kennesaw, GA 30144

Tel: (770) 218-3200. Ext. 3231
Fax: (770) 218-3252

I would go to the employment office each week and check on any job openings. Almost every job I have had in the Atlanta Metro area has always been on the far side of town, or close to it. I decided that I would not settle for anything that required a long drive. There just had to be plenty of jobs in Marietta where we lived.

One application I filled out was for a technician to work for company in west Marietta, but they could not provide me with the name of the company. The application was returned without explanation. I asked if I could send them a letter, and they tried to talk me out of it, saying it would not help and that it was not common practice. I drafted the letter anyway and explained how I wanted to work for them in this area. The next week the surprised employment office worker told me that I had an interview scheduled!

When God is on your side, I have found out that He somehow makes a way when there is no other way. The interview went smoothly, and I was asked if I wanted to come on as a temporary employee. The company could not get authorization to hire anyone at the time. I started work on May 6, 1996, and I was hired as a permanent employee. I starting working on monitors with Chuck Agna and David Richardson. They were very patient with me. I was having to learn about component level repair of high end monitors.

Dad passed away, on May 22, 1996, only two weeks after I started my new job. They were very understanding and gave me time off. Dad died in the Tampa, Florida, VA hospital, We flew him to Kentucky, where he was buried in the Pleasant Valley Cemetery on the grounds of the church where Mom and Dad were married.

BARCO stood for Belgium American Radio Corporation and was formed right after World War II. With the home office and factory in Belgium, I had to get a passport and traveled with Chuck to Belgium for training.

We went through a move from a temporary location in west Marietta to a larger and better building in Kennesaw, still a close drive from home.

After about two years I was given a new job as Technical Support Specialist, Projection Systems. Back to training again, this time on video projectors, the company's main product line at the time.

I was back at the telephones doing what I knew best, helping others with problems.

BARCO had a reputation of being a high turnover place, and I watched as many came and went, including the people I worked for, one of which was Ray Jackson. Ray was from a small town in Tennessee that I once lived in as a boy. Little did I know that ten years later I would again be working with the same group in a new company.

Peat Farm and DEP Problems

It started with a certified letter on November 17, 1998, from the State of Florida, Department of Environmental Protection, stating that there may be violations in our operations at the peat farm. We were ordered to discontinue accepting any further trash and/or debris at this location until such time that we were granted the required special exception and other required state permits. Dad was aware of changes in the county codes, but he was always told that the operation was grandfathered in as the operation was ongoing long before any of the codes were written.

Now that Dad was gone and we were beginning to make a little profit, though still not much, we were said to be taking income away from the local county–owned landfill. I was called to appear at a meeting in Fort Myers, Florida. From a list of attorneys given to me by the county, I found one that would represent me in this case and hired him.

I scheduled time off from work and we drove to Florida, a bit uneasy to say the least. Thomas Nunnallee joined me, and we drove from Sebring to Fort Myers for the meeting with the DEP.

Our meeting started with a strange comment from the DEP, "Why did you bring a lawyer with you?" Later in the meeting another comment was just as strange, "I thought that we had all you mom and pop operations shut down!" This was followed by a comment, " I don't see anything that you are doing wrong, it is just against the law!" We were told that there would be fines and that we may have to remove the years of fill and pay to have it hauled to a landfill. Test wells would have to be dug on each end of the property and tests run on the water from the wells. The only thing left unsaid was jail time! Who would think that I would not need an attorney!

After a long meeting, we were told to visit a local tree cutting processing plant to see how it should be done. The cuttings had to be turned over every few months and no more than 10% could remain on the property.

I had worked hard to pay off our home and get out of debt. Dad had also given me 2.5 acres of land located in the Fakahatchee Strand State Preserve in Collier County, Florida. He purchased it from a friend in Kentucky for hunting and fishing rights. This was a land development that went under and was restricted due to the black panthers in the area. Each year I would get a letter from the state wanting me to donate the land to Florida, but I would continue to pay the taxes and wait. Now was the time. I offered the land to the DEP in exchange for the fine. They said that they would look into it and let me know. At one point I even offered to give them the peat farm, but they said no, it would just be a liability and they did not want it.

Months of negotiations went on between Tom Nunnallee and the DEP as we began to close down the operation that was now losing money. We still owed money on the new bob cat, so I offered it to Joe, if he could take over the payments. He agreed, saying he may be able to get some work using it or sell it. By the end of the year I had to let him go. In order to get the permits for a class III landfill I would need to hire an engineer firm for $10,000 and pay for a permit, another $10,000. But I knew that they had no intention of letting me continue the operation.

The estimate for removal of enough limbs to show that we have even done something would run about $6,000. To remove all visible limbs and logs that were above the ground would be about $15,000. Add to that the wells and tests, I estimated well over $20,000. I took out a home equity loan to start paying the attorney and expected test and cleanup operations.

On May 19, 1999, I received a final copy of the Consent Order to resolve violations noted in the complaint.

The main violation was of a rule not to dispose or store solid waste in any natural or artificial body of water, including groundwater.

It was agreed upon and I was ordered within thirty days to transfer all visible yard trash from the property to a department–approved solid waste management facility.

Within ninity days we had to install monitor wells and perform sampling to determine groundwater quality. We were able to use one existing well at the front of the property, and would have to drill another one well at the back of the property.

I was required to pay a civil penalty of $3,900.00 for alleged violations. The DEP accepted the swamp land, and determined the value of the Collier county property to be $1,149.50. I would have to pay the balance of $2,750.50 to the DEP. I would also have to pay expenses to the DEP of $300.00 for investigation of the donated property!

We appealed the removal of the waste material and the order was changed to read: "All remaining yard trash left exposed on top of the disposal area shall be compacted to grade and covered with at least six (6) inches of soil." This one change may have saved us well over one hundred thousand dollars that I did not have!

The water test results came back with one test that was above the allowed limit. I was very concerned about the test due to the orange grove across the road, and the drainage of chemicals used on the groves came across the peat farm to the lake. Having worked for a testing lab, I knew that mistakes were possible, and against the advice of everyone, I insisted the test be redone.

The final outcome was that all seventy of the chemicals tested fell within acceptable limits!

The total cost of closing down the Lake Bonnet Peat Farm was $26,767.50 plus two acres of Florida swamp land. The case was closed in May of 2000. Five years later I placed the land up for sale.

On January 24, 2006, just before the Florida real estate bust, we closed on the peat farm for $164,571.43. The home equity loan of $40,211.55 was paid off and $18,000 was given to our church. Praise the Lord!

CHAPTER 12 ELLIJAY

On June 1, 1998 we closed on the purchase of a log cabin on the Coosawattee River near Ellijay, Georgia. Close friends of ours, Bob and Bobbie Dees, owned a home overlooking the Coosawatte River, and they were encouraging us to buy in the area. They called one day late in May and said they knew of a cabin that was getting ready to be placed on the market and would we like to check it out. We drove up and looked it over. The owner was going to ask $81,000 for it and I wanted to offer him less, however Kathy fell in love with it at first sight and told me not to let it slip away. I met the owner the following day along I–575 and made a earnest deposit. At the closing the bank advised that we had just made a $10,000 profit on our investment as the appraisal came in at $91,000!

The cabin was ideal for a second home, since it was only one hour away from our home in Marietta. We decided on owning the cabin instead of moving up to a larger primary home, and it has worked out well over the years. It was small, with only three rooms and a bath on the main floor. The upstairs had two bedrooms and a small bath that extended out toward the back. The roofline came down to three feet on each side of both bedrooms. There was a brick fireplace and a low crawl space under the house for the heating and air. The front porch was covered to within six feet of each side, and there was a deck on the driveway side that was not quite even with the rest of the porch. When I later removed the deck to correct the level, I found that it only had two nails holding it to the side of the cabin! I also extended the covered porch to the full length of the cabin and rebuilt the front stairs and hand rails.

We were flooded during hurricane Ivan in 2004, the water covered the porch but did not get into the house. The heating unit and duct work under the house had to be replaced. The lawnmower under the porch and the outside air condition unit survived, and were only covered in mud. I replaced the oil and gas from the riding lawnmower and it ran fine.

The logs had been stained red, and the locals referred to it as the Red Cabin on the river! We stained it brown and covered the red brick with imitation stone for a nice cozy getaway. We look forward to many more years of spending weekends at our cabin on the Coosawattee River.

Our cabin in the mountains

Trail of Tears

In the 1830's Cherokee Indians welcomed white settlers to their village, and the town was possibly named after Chief Dreadful Water "Ellijay." During the Cherokee land lottery of 1832, Martin Scalf acquired the 160 acres that the town now occupies. Ellijay was incorporated on December 29, 1834.

During the American Revolution on July 26, 1782 at the Battle of Ellijay, Col. John Sevier burned the entire town to the ground. The Treaty of Hopewell was signed in 1785 by the chief of Ellijay (also spelled Allajoy). [14]

Fort Hetzel near Ellijay was erected in 1838 to house the Cherokee Indians for the march to Oklahoma. Chief Whitepath died along with many others and was buried near my hometown in Kentucky.

Just down river from our cabin is the site of an Indian village and the remains of a fish trap across the river that they built.

The Trail of Tears passed near many of the towns in Tennessee and Kentucky were I lived as a boy, and somehow I have a strange attachment to this tragic event in our history that may have started with that clay Indian pipe that my grandfather gave to me.

New cabin fireplace

Retirement Again

I retired from BARCO in August 2003. They were cutting back, and if I stayed with them it would involve a drive across Atlanta again to Norcross. I did not want that! We had started attending a small church just around the corner from were I was working, and Kathy and I had become very involved in helping out there. I decided that I would give the Lord at least three years for the thirty some years that He had provided for us. I went to work for the church in accounting and doing whatever else needed to be done for $1.00 a year. I never collected the dollar but did enjoy the work. I worked almost every day until the end of 2007, about a year and half longer than planned. It was all just a joke about how long I would work anyway.

February 6, 2005 was a Sunday like any other. Kathy and Deanna were helping me at the church when I felt a slight shoulder ache, and then my left arm went numb. I had experienced the shoulder ache a few days before and did not think anything about it. But as soon as I noticed my arm going numb, I knew that it was a heart attack. Kathy drove me to the emergency room, and after a lot of attention, they rushed me down to Atlanta's Emory Crawford Long Hospital. Where I had two stints implanted on Sunday night, and one more, a difficult one, on Monday morning. I was awake through the whole thing and heard the doctor tell the nurse to get ready for surgery if he could not get the stint into the correct position. God was watching over me, and I was back at work the following week.

The recession of 2008 had started, and my retirement funds were dropping fast, down about 2/3 from their high. I had to cut back on my withdrawals or lose it all. Corwin Hamm, who I last worked for at BARCO, called and said that Ray Jackson was looking for someone to help out at DVIGear, a company nearby, only ten minutes from home.

Everyone at DVIGear had previously worked at BARCO and other people they hired later were also from BARCO. They only needed someone part time and to fill in during trade shows, when the owners and Ray would be gone.

Steven Barlow took over the business a few years earlier and had turned it around with the help of Ray. Steven's wife Alice joined us shortly after I started and I considered her my primary boss, although I take direction from all three. I think it is great having three bosses, the more bosses you have to take problems to the better. I currently work three days a week and only five hours each day from noon till five, except when they are out of town. The pay is good, and they are a great group to work for. My younger sister Cathy even worked for them a few years after she retired from the state of Florida.

This is my form of retirement, having worked most of my life, I would not know what to do if did not work at something.

When I worked for Kodak I had a friend Roy Mozingo, who was a millionaire. He still worked at Kodak, and I asked him one day why he was still working. He replied, "I need a reason to get up in the morning!" I guess that is what it boils down to, a reason to get out of bed and stay vertical!

Challenges

I now have to find challenges to keep my mind and body working. Alzheimer's disease runs in our family, and about seven years back I noticed that I was having trouble working out some programming with my cave mapping software and a few other things. I had my doctor test me, and I failed the short term memory test. He started me on 5 mg of Aricept a day, and I started looking for things to exercise my mind. I saw a big improvement and have remained on the drug for over seven years at the time of this writing. I also started working puzzles, and took up writing short stories and poems. I took an online poetry class and have written about 200 so far and put them in eight small books. This will be my first full length book. I try to challenge myself in other ways also, like taking up the fiddle. I take music lessons once a week and try to practice an hour a day. The music seems to help a lot and uses a different part of the brain, I think!

Caving is a big challenge, but I will not go as often now. I noticed that I become disoriented sometimes and my balance is off. My doctor thinks that it may be the progressive lens in my glasses that give me a problem, and soon I will be getting new ones and may change back to normal bifocals. I made Kathy a promise that I would outlive her, however her mother just turned 96 and may outlive us both!

Rusty, our dog, tries his best to keep me active as I chase him around the house and outside three or four times a day. Kathy had me try on some of my old clothes today, and I am going to be challenged to loose some weight or throw some of them out!

Life has and still is good to me. God has blessed me with so many experiences. We never know what He has in store for us here on this earth, and that is a good thing.

Unexplained Things

I know that I have a just God who watched over us, and I also know that He answers prayers, sometime in ways that we do not expect. I thought long and hard before telling this story. When I hear someone like a preacher make a statement that is hard to believe, I go to extremes to check it out.

A preacher that I know well told this story one Sunday from the pulpit. He was working in the 80's for a well known company in Atlanta, and there was a lady that was making advances toward him. The preacher's wife started praying that God would remove this problem from his work place. Well the situation continued to worsen until they heard the following news.

On August 5, 1982, an unidentified Chicago woman was seen to burst into flames for no apparent reason as she was walking down a street. An eyewitness was quoted as saying they "saw her burning and then she fell."

Chicago, Ill. –UPI– "Firefighters were called to extinguish a fire and found the incinerated remains of an unidentified woman who was seen walking across a street one moment and reportedly bursting into flames the next." [15]

Later reports said that she was dead before being set on fire and that gasoline was probably used. The preacher said that this was the same woman from his office!

Now the most interesting person that I have read about in modern times is Ron Wyatt! From 1978 until his death in 1999 he amazed the world with his stories of confirming Bible stories with archaeology discoveries. Most of them have been proven to be untrue. However the stories are very interesting nonetheless. [16]

I have read most of Ron's claims and the most interesting was his last, the discovery of the ark of the covenant! Ron wears an Indiana Jones hat like I do, so I have to give him a lot of leeway. Richard Rives checked out Ron and here is what he said about the man, "I guess you could say that Ron Wyatt was about the nicest, kindest, most stubborn and ornery person that you could ever want to meet. What better friend could anybody ever want. I loved him; and I miss him." [17]

I won't tell the whole story, only that he was allowed to dig in the area known as the Garden Tomb in Jerusalem until his last dig in the summer of 1991. His claims of finding the Ark are very convincing, and like a lot of Christians, I would like to believe them. I think that anyone interested should read about it and keep an open mind. Time will tell, and the truth will come out someday. I will say that because of the caving involved in the discovery, I enjoyed the adventure even the more.

God sometimes heals us in unexplained ways. Many years ago we attended a small Church in Marietta, Austin Ave Church of God. Pastor Richard Russell was our pastor there, and both Kathy and I worked in the church. It was volunteer work with the Sunday School Department. At the time I was diagnosed with a hiatal hernia and suffered for years with pain and discomfort due to the reflux of acid from the stomach. The doctor described is as a weakening of the diaphragm and the only cure was to operate. One Sunday morning it was bothering me, so I went down for prayer and the laying on of hands by the elders. I was relieved of all discomfort at once. I told the doctor about it, and he scheduled another set of tests for me. The tests showed that there was no change in the hernia, and they could not explain the loss of discomfort. That was more than thirty years ago and I have not had a moment of discomfort or that pushing up in my esophagus. My esophagus may have twisted to relieve the pressure, but whatever the cure, I accept it!

CHAPTER 13 MAPPING OF PETTYJOHN CAVE

Forty some years of caving in one of North Georgia's most popular caves, and I have still not seen all of it. When someone takes you to a cave and leads you through it, you feel like, well I've seen this cave, where is the next cave? Pettyjohn Cave in Walker County, Georgia was a different experience for me. Even though most of its passages had been explored by Richard Schreiber and others, we ventured in not knowing where to go. We heard about places and names of rooms, but did not know exactly how to get to them. As we explored, pushing just a little farther on each trip, we began to make the connections. This turned out to be half the fun of caving, not knowing what was just around the next bend or crawlway. As we discovered shortcuts and the best route, we were able to make better time getting to the more extreme parts of the cave. Of course we always accepted help from fellow cavers we ran into in the cave, like the time I met Gerald Moni exiting the cave. He was excited about a new discovery he and Richard Schreiber, who was still in the cave, had just found. "We have broke out under the mountain!" This was the Outer Limits section of Pettyjohn Cave.

John Wallace introduced us to Pettyjohn Cave in July 1972 when we took a group of thirteen scouts to the cave. The road was full of mud holes, and it crossed the dry streambed near the cave. We would often park along the road where it was safe and hike the rest of the way. Snakes were a common sight on the way to the entrance. That day we explored the Signature Room, and afterward I was drawn back to this great cave over and over for the next forty years.

On one of the early trips before the new road was built, I drove my van into one of those large mud holes, and the muddy water came over the hood of the large Chevy van. Water was sucked into the air intake, and the engine stalled. I tried to start it a few times, then decided to leave it there. We had cleared the mud hole, and it was on the side of the narrow road. We hiked on to the cave and worried about the van later. After caving I got a ride into town and found a station still open. They towed it in and removed all but the two back spark plugs, which were too hard to get to. Mud was dripping off the plugs! After getting it started we drove home. That van ran fine for many years afterward, and I never changed the two back plugs.

The Signature Room, Pettyjohn Cave

My Favorite Cave

I could write many stories about Pettyjohn Cave, however I would like to explain here why this great cave is my favorite. For a horizontal caver like myself, Pettyjohn has plenty to offer. Good climbs, challenging passages, waterfalls, formations, intriguing passages, extremely hard–to–reach places–most of which I have not seen, possibilities for new discoveries and good mud.

Good Climbs - For someone looking for climbing challenges, the entrance room has plenty to offer. This long room is over 500 feet long and averages fifty feet wide and thrity feet high ceilings. It has two easy climbs just to reach the back. Near the entrance there is a good climb up into an upper formation room that connects to the main entrance room at the ceiling level. Most visitors rush pass this area to get to the back of the room or to head off to the main waterfall.

To reach the stream levels there are challenging climbs if you avoid the ropes left there by previous cavers. Some of these ropes have been in place for a long time and should not be used. One especially challenging climb is getting up into the Raccoon Room. This large room in the mid–level of the cave gives access to most of the middle levels of the cave. Pettyjohn Cave is divided up into three levels, the entrance room, which is high and mostly dry, the middle levels, which are dry passages making up about 1/3 of the known cave and reaching under the mountain to the north, and the lower stream passages, which make up the largest portions of the cave. A difficult climb from this northern section is up into the Echo Room, the largest room in the cave. It is a 100–by–200 foot room with high ceilings.

A waterfall climb leads to a second waterfall that is much easer to climb and an upstream passage called Schreiber's Extension that is yet to be completely explored.

Challenging Passages - From the main entrance room there are many ways to go deeper into the cave, and at the start of each of these passages you will have a challenge. The Pancake Squeeze is on the way to the waterfall and has a tight squeeze. For harder climbs, go through the Volcano Room and Mason–Dixon passage to the waterfall. Each route from the Main Room is like a cave of its own. If you like mazes, try The Labyrinth in the southeast lower level of Pettyjohn. If you are looking for real adventure, explore the extreme northwest section called The Outer Limits. And for a good technical climb, explore the rooms above the Double Echo Domes.

Waterfalls - If you like underground waterfalls, you will love Pettyjohn Cave. There are two good sized waterfalls on the way to Schreiber's Extension, a loud waterfall about 4 feet high just beyond the Chute and on the way to the Outer Limits, and another one that you have to climb over to enter the Labyrinth.

Formations - Formations are scattered throughout the cave. The Entrance Room contains the largest in the cave. The Signature Room and the passage to it are well worth seeing for the formations. And there is a beautiful formation room just before you get to the Volcano Room. Other nice formations will surprise you along the routes to many sections of the cave.

Intriguing Passages - The Worm Tube is a long 150 feet crawl that is very tight and leads to the Echo Room and beyond. The Z–Bends is an interesting alternative to the Pancake Squeeze when going to the waterfall or the Raccoon Room. There is a downward–sloping squeeze that is a real challenge to climb back up when you visit the East Stream passage and Crowell Domes. The small hole leading from the Bridge Room to the Mason–Dixon Passage is neat. And the stream canyon passage on the way to the waterfall is fun.

Extreme Places - The extreme places are for the hard core cavers that like fourteen–hour trips and want to be pushed to their limits. Pettyjohn Cave offers four such areas: The Labyrinth, The Discovery Room, The Outer Limits, and Schreiber's Extension.

The Labyrinth, which I have only visited the start of, is very complex and care should be taken to keep from getting lost.

The Discovery Room above the Emerald Pool requires that you use the old existing rope or do a hard technical climb. An extension pole was first used to reach this area. I understand that there is much to be discovered beyond the Emerald Pool.

The Outer Limits is an extremely difficult place to reach. I have explored the stream passage to tight muddy squeezes that finally turned me back, and high dry passages where loose rock discouraged me. These were ten-hour trips, and I still have not found the Outer Limits. I met Richard Schreiber once when I was leaving the cave, and he was excited about getting back under the mountain. I believe that he was referring to the Outer Limits. I have a copy of most of his survey notes, but I think that I am missing one that describes how to get there.

Schreiber's Extension is a long stream passage with many leads and places to climb up into along the way. The end is a low stream passage which has been dug out and pushed to a second low room blocked by another low stream crawl. This passage continues around the edge of the mountain and takes in water from along the mountainside. The cave is still lower than the valley but under the edge of the mountain.

Possibilities for New Discoveries - The most promising area that I feel could be developed is to the east. There are many sinkholes along the mountain east of the entrance, and Crowell Domes is the most eastern portion of the cave, with the exception of the Labyrinth and Screech Owl Cave. There is a possible lead from the Echo Room that I would like to push some day, but it would require some rock removal. There is also a large sinkhole on the top of the mountain east of Pettyjohn that the water has I believe been traced to the sump below the Entrance Room in Pettyjohn. Pettyjohn provides drainage for most of this side of Pigeon Mountain until you get to Ellison's Cave, which drains the north end of the mountain. Recent discoveries have been made in Schreiber's Extension, Discovery Room, and the Anamatosis Room. I have 37,693 feet of level survey plotted, which is over seven miles (7.139 miles).

Good Mud - Pettyjohn Cave is known for its mud. There are some places where you will loose your shoes in the sticky stuff, and crawlways where you just slide through in the mud with two slots for your knees from all the traffic. I have seen the lower level flood with the water backing up from the stream canyon passage which is narrow and can restrict the water flow. Always check out the weather forecast before going to the main waterfall.

The Loop in Pettyjohn Cave

When taking someone new to Pettyjohn Cave in north Georgia, I enjoy taking them on the Loop Tour. It is great because the only part of the cave that the route crossed twice is about 250 feet into the cave near the entrance.

The round trip will take about four hours and involve tight squeezes, moderate climbs and some mud, but not the real mud. If the group really wants a challenge, add in the Flat Room and the Z–bends. Side trips can also be made to the Over 'N Under Room or the Echo Room for an even longer trip.

The Loop route consists of the Pancake Squeeze or Z–Bends. Choose one or split the group up with half going through each. (Smaller cavers take the Z–Bends). Next is the Raccoon Room, The Freeway, and then the Bridge Room. Leaving the Bridge Room, crawl into the Mason–Dixon Passage and on to the Volcano Room, then back to the Main Entrance Room.

As one slides down into the entrance of Pettyjohn, you cannot help but notice the smooth weathered–rock slide that thousands of cavers have slid down before. If it is raining or wet, muddy cavers exited just before your party, the last few feet of the cave can be quite challenging, and it will require most of your climbing skills just to exit the cave. A quick turn to the left and down, then back to the right, and the cave opens up into a huge cavern. Until your eyes adjust to the dark, take care climbing down into the large Entrance Room. The floor may be slippery, so while your eyes adjust, try to take in the large formations on each side of the room. The room is about thirty feet high and twenty feet wide. About 200 feet into the cave is the first junction room and a climb.

Down through the floor in the first junction room is the route to the Signature Room, a good trip for first time cavers, with plenty of good sticky mud. The well–worn path up the rock to the left is difficult to climb, but easy to come down on the way out. There is a sloping rock in the center of the passage that will have a distinct crack for a footstep, followed by another sloping rock with one small worn formation in the center that provides another footstep to the top of the climb. A few more steps and you are looking down a steep climb down with a large overhanging boulder on the right and the vertical wall on the left.

Slowly work your way down along the right side under the overhang to the bottom of the second junction room. This is where we start the Loop route, and it is also the most traveled route to the large waterfall at the lower level. There will be two holes at the bottom of the second junction room. The most obvious one is a drop that I would not recommend. After checking it out, turn back away from the left wall and climb down through the breakdown, feet first, until you are under the hole. You can then see that there are no foot or hand holds to use if you came through the first hole.

Continue to climb down under the left wall of the Entrance Room. the cave will open up sloping steeply away from the Main Entrance Room. This is maybe the most confusing area on our tour. On a recent trip I spent almost an hour here trying to find the way on. I keep forgetting that there is another level to descend before climbing up again into a short water passage that leads to the Pancake Squeeze. Climb down to the right over a steep ledge until you can go no deeper. Then turn back to the left and look up for a hidden passage over a small ledge. If the group chooses to take the Z–Bends, then stay low and continue in the same general direction but more to the right, through a low wide room called the Flat Room. Near the end of this room look for a vertical crack to squeeze into and follow it until it opens up. This is the Z–Bends, the taller you are the harder it will be to get through.

For the group that went up over the ledge, take the first side passage through water about 8 inches deep to the end. Duck under the ledge on the right and crawl into the Pancake Squeeze. The Pancake Squeeze is tricky, try and look ahead for the highest part and stay slightly to the left. If the squeeze starts to get tight, try moving more to the left. You may have to remove your hard hat in order to get through. There is plenty of room on each side, so crawling is not a problem. When you drop off the Pancake Squeeze into standing room you should come into contact with the group that took the Z–Bends. Make sure that everyone is back together before continuing.

The next challenge will be a short drop of about 6 feet. If you are tall, you can just slide over feet first to the rock floor below. A better route is along the left side between a stalactite and the left wall, where you can hold on to the stalactite and lower yourself down to the floor. Continue along the right wall for another fifty feet and the left side will start to fall away. Stay high along the right side of the passage. If you climb down through a muddy hole on the left wall to the stream level, you will be on the tourist route to the waterfall. Above this hole high on the right is the Raccoon Room. This is a dangerous climb. There may be a hand line there, but do not put your trust in it as it has been there for years. Climb up and over the ledge to the right.

Cross the Raccoon Room on the right side to the back of the room. Avoid the deadend crawl and stay to the right crawling over several mud walls until you reach a canyon junction. The large walking passage to the right will deadend after several turns. At the junction there will be a nice stalactite with water dripping into a pool with rim stone dams around the edge of the pool. Follow the canyon to the left and climb up into The Freeway. The Freeway is easy stoop walking passage with mud banks along each side. Cross through three rooms about seventy-five feet each until reaching the Bridge Room.

The Bridge Room is a good place to take a break, hang your legs over the edge and listen for the stream about eighty feet below. You could climb down here and go to the waterfall. By crossing over the bridge, which is a narrow muddy arch over the canyon, and continuing through a long trunk passage access can be had to the back sections of Pettyjohn Cave. To continue the Loop, do not cross the bridge, but follow the narrow mud path along the right wall of the large canyon and stay at the same level near the ceiling.

At the end of the Bridge Room look for a small hole near the ceiling. This is the tight crawl into the Mason–Dixon Passage. If you climb down at this point and duck under a ledge, you can follow the lower stream passage to the sump at the lowest part of the cave, 235 feet below the entrance. Take off all your gear and shove it into the hole ahead of you, then squeeze through. After about twenty feet it will start to open and you can slide up into the passage on the left. This passage will start out about four foot high and then later open up into walking with one more tight crawl about halfway through.

After about 500 feet there will be a large junction room. To the left is the Worm Tube leading to the Echo Room, the largest room in the cave. The Worm Tube is 200 feet of very tight passage, and the climb up into the Echo Room is very tough, but it is well worth the effort to see the large room. To the right in the junction room, and over a rock ledge and through a horizontal crack is a small room on the way to the Volcano Room. One more horizontal crack and then climb out and onto the edge of the Volcano Room.

The Volcano Room is shaped like a large funnel with steep sides, and it leads down to the stream passage and the sump. For years the only way out was to climb up a vertical wall to a small window above the Volcano Room. We usually used a cable ladder when coming the other direction. I have free climbed the wall, but it is very exposed. In the late 80's someone dug a bypass crawl under and around the vertical climb up to the window. To enter this crawl from the Volcano Room side, enter head first, pushing your gear. You work your way upwards, twisting as you go. Try to stay on your back because you will have to bend up at the end, and if you are not on your back you will not be able to bend up or turn over. If you are going the other way, you will want to go feet first and on your back. Going downhill is a little easier.

When getting out of the crawl and waiting for the others, it is worth the view to go up to the window and look out over the Volcano Room. There is not much room in the small vertical passage at the window, so before it fills climb into the larger room above. Climb up into another room with walking passage to the left and a climb up on the right. The left passage dead ends. Then climb up along a narrow ledge, first right, then back to the left and up into a large formation room. At the far side of this room and over a lip is another room going down. Stay to the left and enter a crawlway before the room. The crawlway will have a very sharp turn to the right. The corner of the rock at the turn has been broken off to enable the extraction of a poor caver who fell from the window over the Volcano Room and broke a leg.

The easy crawl continues upward over a large breakdown to a short drop into a small room. When you are in this passage, you can talk to anyone who may be in the Autograph Room above. If they are at the bottom of the Autograph Room, they must be only a few feet from this passage. But no visual contact could be made. As you climb down into the small room, turn to the right and slide feet first into another small opening before going completely into the small room. Continue down this small vertical, dry and dusty crack until it levels out.

If you continue to the end of this passage, there is a climb up so hard that long legs are needed to reach the foot holds. Before you reach the end and shortly after it levels out, there is a hole going up that leads to the passage above. The upper passage is about four foot high and wide. It will lead to the drop off at the end of the passage below. Continue up the passage, through a small window and to what looks like a dead-end. It is possible to climb up through the breakdown and into the Main Entrance Room above, but it is very tight and vertical. At the apparent dead–end, lay down on your side and slide under the wall, it is about twelve inches high, but opens up. Crawl over a rock and into another small junction room.

To the left is a passage to the east stream passage and Crowell Domes. Up and to the right is a twenty foot climb up into the Main Entrance Room. One direction is the Autograph Room and the other direction is the second junction room where we climbed down. Climb down to the bottom of the room and then back up the left side. At the top stay to the right and slide down along the right wall into the first junction room. From here it is an easy walk to the entrance and a slippery climb out of the cave.

Richard Schreiber explored and mapped most of Pettyjohn Cave from 1969-83 Photo from The Atlanta Weekly, July 12,1987

Dreaming Deep and Low

Still and quiet, all I hear is my heart,
I strain to see or hear, could this be art?
A lovely painting of black in my mind,
to clear my thoughts and help unwind.

Mountains rise as water finds the cracks,
to make strange places that have no tracks.
Some are drawn to push below,
exploring where the going is slow.

Older now, I can only dream,
of wading some unknown stream.
Still others explore deep below,
taking pictures for all to show.

Water running, the tick of a clock,
or was it the sound of falling rock?
A glimmer of light, what lies ahead?
I guess its time to get out of bed!

Mile 1 of the Pettyjohn Cave Survey

Pettyjohn Cave was not always as accessible as it is today. There used to be a mountain dirt road that curved around the edge of the hill and crossed the streambed northwest of the entrance. Sometimes we would get stuck in the deep mud holes and end up walking most of the way to the cave.

In an effort to correctly establish the true length of the known cave, I have been going over all the survey notes that I have from Richard Schreiber[18], myself and others, and thought it might be of interest to tell what was surveyed and when.

The first attempt to survey the cave was in 1967 by Foxy Ferguson and Richard Schreiber and was eventually scrapped.

January 31, 1969 - Richard Schreiber and Della McGuffin started a survey at the entrance and continued to the back of the Autograph Room. There were no side shots made during this trip, and they recorded 574.6 feet of True Horizontal Cave (T.H.C.). After entering the raw survey data into my cave mapping program, the distance turned out to be 576.6 feet T.H.C. From this point on I will use the computer calculated distances in place of the ones in the notes.

February 1, 1969 - Richard Schreiber and Della McGuffin returned to mapping at the first junction room, mapping the high passage to the right. They sketched in the low formation room high along the right wall of the main entrance room but did not map it. They then returned to the junction maze and surveyed almost straight down into the passage leading to the Signature Room. They surveyed to the end of the narrow passage at the end of the Signature Room but did not survey two leads going out of this room.

On the way back out they surveyed a parallel passage and the north end of this lower level. Halfway back up the climb they surveyed a passage that continued under the main room. This later became the preferred route to the Signature Room. This survey resulted in 1,040.07 feet T.H.C., not the 1,010.4 feet they listed. I believe that they were being conservative in estimating the True Horizontal Cave survey.

February 22, 1969 - Richard Schreiber, Della McGuffin and Bill Damewood returned for a weekend of mapping starting at the Flat Room and mapping through the Z–Bends. At the exit of the Z–Bends they noted the low passage on the left that later became the Pancake Squeeeze.

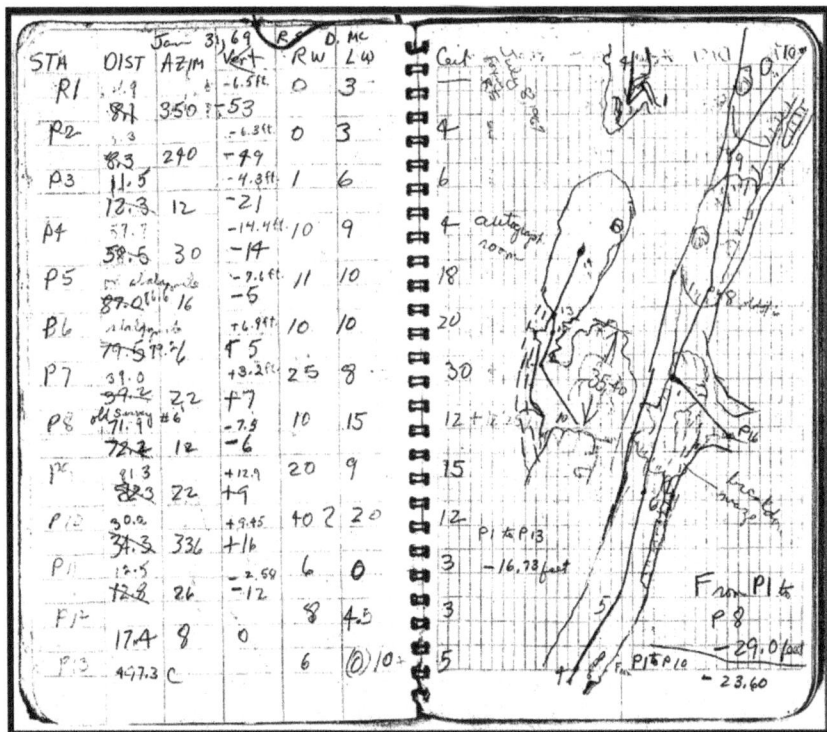

First page of the first survey book

Mapping the passage in a southwestern direction they came to a thirty foot climb down to a stream passage. This stream originates from another cave, Screech Owl Cave, located to the east of the entrance of Pettyjohn Cave. No connection has been made between the two caves.

They surveyed down the narrow stream passage that was later named the Baroody–Holsinger Passage until it intersected the main stream passage in the cave. To the right, one survey shot ended in breakdown with the stream flowing through the rocks. The upstream passage was mapped for 21 more survey stations before stopping for the day at a low crawl and upper tight belle squeeze over a mud slope. This survey resulted in 2,154.33 feet T.H.C. This survey was connected to the main room at the end of the following day with a short survey down from the main entrance room from the second junction.

February 23, 1969 - Richard Schreiber, Della McGuffin, Bill Damewood and Mike Hicks mapped the area that is what I now call the Eastern Maze and the connection to the survey of the previous day. This survey resulted in 788.97 feet T.H.C. The connecting survey station P10 on the original survey notes has a "?" after the station, leading me to believe that there may be some question about the starting point. Later surveys in the Eastern Maze may be of the same passages, at this time I am still trying to sort it out. They did map downstream to a point they referred to as "Hell's Hole."

March 8, 1969 - Richard Schreiber and Della McGuffin mapped more of the area below the 2nd junction in the main room. They mapped a short connection from the Eastern Maze back into the main room to station P9, again with a "?" mark. From station J7 in the Eastern Maze they mapped north again below the east wall of the main room. This survey resulted in 576.80 feet T.H.C.

April 20, 1969 - Marion O. Smith and Richard Schreiber starting mapping toward the Volcano Room from the main entrance room, and after 143.71 feet, station G8 the bottom of a 5.2 foot vertical climb, reached the first mile of the survey. On this same trip they discovered the Worm Tube and the Echo Room.

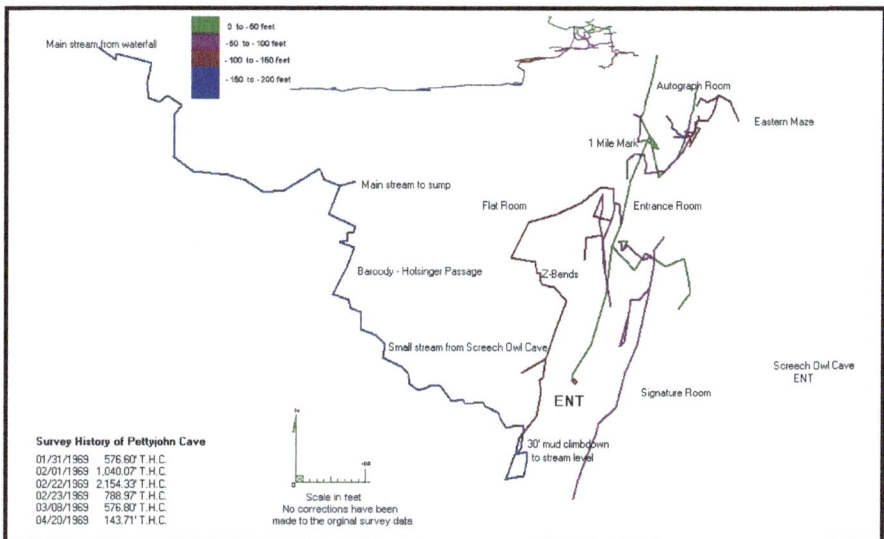

5,280.48 feet of horizontal cave mapped

Mile 2 of the Pettyjohn Cave Survey

About eight feet down you can step into a side passage and continue. The chasm was not mapped. After a short uphill distance, a narrow opening gives access to what I call the Mid–Room because it is about midway between the main entrance room and the Volcano Room. The passage from this room is directly under the Autograph Room, and you can talk easily between the two rooms.

The survey continued through the Formation Room, then down a 14 foot climb at station G31 into another room in the north end that was not mapped. They exited this room at the southwest corner and climbed down to a window overlooking the Volcano Room.

The survey crosses the north side of the Volcano Room and over a hidden ledge. They went down through a low room and through another hidden ledge and then reached the entrance to the Mason–Dixon Passage and the Worm Tube. The survey continued southwest through the Mason–Dixon Passage and stopped before entering the crawlway to the Bridge Room. This survey resulted in 1,100.17 feet T.H.C. (True Horizontal Cave). The total survey length was now 6,380.65 feet.

May 18, 1969 - Richard Schreiber, Della McGuffin, Marion O. Smith, Allen Padgett and Bob Watkins entered the Worm Tube, but Allen and Bob had to exit because Bob became claustrophobic. The Worm Tube is 100 feet of very tight passage, and the climb up into the Echo Room is very tough. The survey continued past the hard climb up into the Echo Room, which was discovered on the return survey trip from the north end. The survey continued north to the Mystery Room. This survey resulted in 1,058.13 feet T.H.C. The total survey was now 7,438.78 feet.

June 10, 1969 - Richard Schreiber, Della McGuffin, Allen Padgett and Marion O. Smith returned to station G70 of the previous survey and explored a hole leading down to a stream level. After surveying around in this lower level, they then found a lead going up and into the Echo Room. The survey was conducted around the perimeter of the room with two side passages, one of which led back to the Worm Tube. The survey notes recorded a total of 630.6 feet surveyed, however when I entered the data it turned out to be 1,134.89 feet T.H.C. The total survey was now 8,573.67 feet.

June 21, 1969 - Richard Schreiber and Della McGuffin surveyed the last shot to the back of the main entrance room and then surveyed down through the breakdown from Station P13 to G12 in the passage to the Volcano Room. They then went to the end of the survey in the Mason–Dixon Passage to continue the survey toward the Bridge Room. After surveying across the Bridge Room, they continued northwest through a group of nice formations and an easy passage to the Over 'N Under Room. They surveyed the lower section of the Over 'N Under Room and then north to Five Points. From there it was a short distance to the Chute or Luge; it goes by both names.

At the bottom of the Luge is a stream passage. They surveyed up stream to Station G193 and then returned to the Luge and surveyed down stream to Station G205. They reported a total of 1,563.8 feet, but it turns out to be 1,738.10 feet T.H.C. Total survey now 10,311.77 feet.

July 12, 1969 - Richard Schreiber and Della McGuffin returned to the upstream passage from the Luge and mapped only 262.74 feet, reaching the 2 mile mark for Pettyjohn Cave.

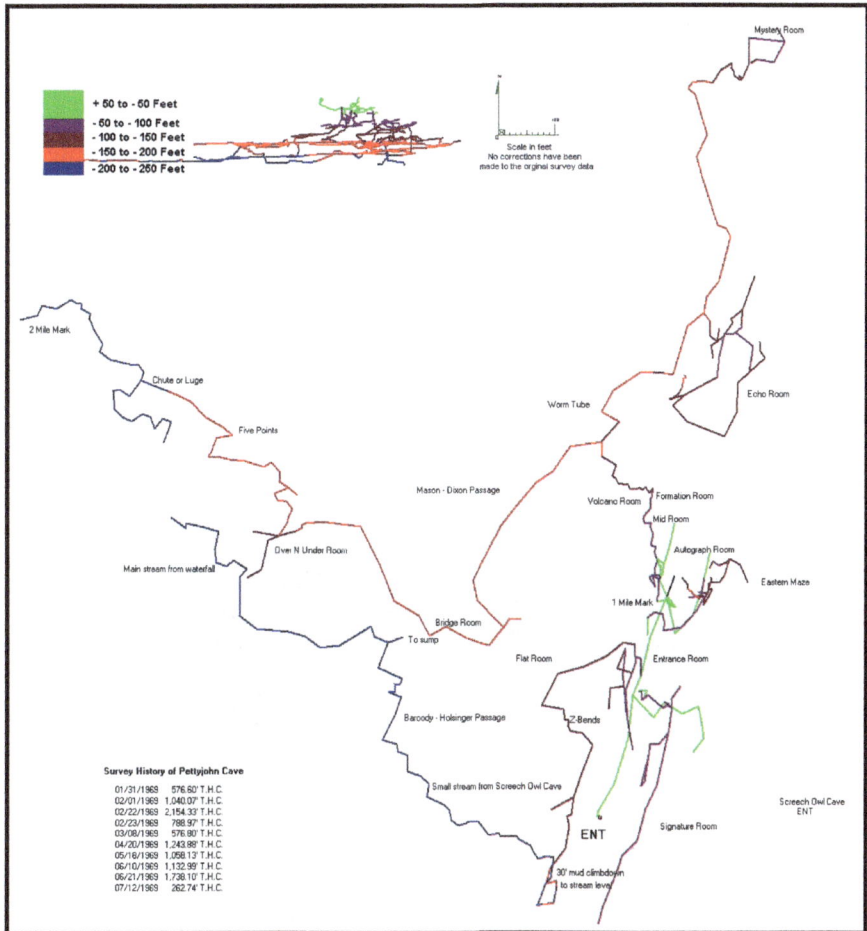

10,574.51 feet of horizontal cave mapped

Mile 3 of the Pettyjohn Cave Survey

The third mile of Pettyjohn Cave resulted in the exploration and mapping of the northwest stream passage, the Waterfall Room and the Freeway, with its connection back to the Raccoon Room. The extensive dryer passages above the main stream near the waterfall were explored and mapped, along with a connection at this level back to the Over 'N Under Room. In the process of reconstructing this historical account, I have entered the original survey data without loop corrections or other changes. When a mile mark is encountered the description may stop in the middle of a survey trip and resume at the start of the description of the next mile.

July 12, 1969 - Richard Schreiber and Della McGuffin returned to the upstream passage from the Luge and mapped the stream passage for 583 feet until they reach a confined 40 foot crawl ending in a collapse. I have been to the start of this crawl, and there is no way I would have entered that muddy tight crawl!

They then returned back downstream to station G193 and surveyed up and out of the stream passage. This must have been a very rough survey as the ceiling heights indicate lots of crawling with one stretch of extremely low passage of over 150 feet with only one spot with a five foot ceiling. The height varied from one and half feet to three feet all the way. The reward was that it connected back to the stream passage and interestingly, at the previous two mile mark. This survey resulted in 1,301.95 feet T.H.C. The total survey length now was 11,613.72 feet.

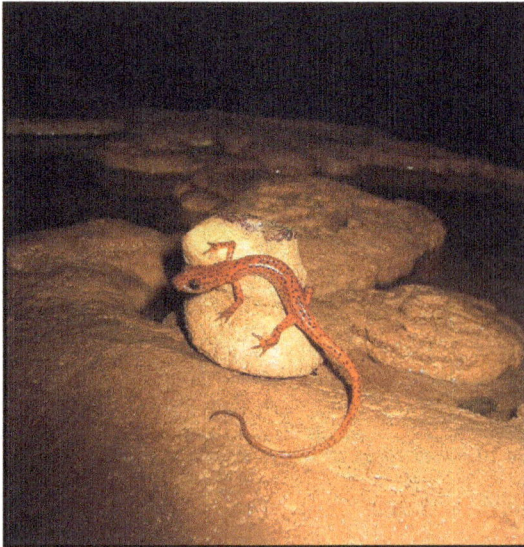

Photo by Tom Moltz 7/19/2003

Leaves, twigs and gravel were found nearby suggesting a connection to the surface.

The survey continued to the Raccoon Room where they found abundant Raccoon tracks, and ended at the climb down to the Baroody–Holsinger Passage. This survey resulted in 835.77 feet T.H.C. The total survey length was now 12,448.49 feet.

August 23, 1969 - Richard Schreiber and Della McGuffin started the "H" survey from station G183, located at the Five Points junction. The survey continued back to the Over 'N Under Room.

They then went back to Five Points and surveyed northeast to station G187 at the top of the Luge, then around the top of the Luge and back down to station G266 and the stream again. At the top of the Luge they also surveyed two shots to the center of a dome.

The survey was started again at the end of the downstream passage and continued downstream until it intersected with a larger stream. They continued the survey now upstream toward the Waterfall Room. The survey stopped for the day at the base of the eleven foot waterfall. This may have been the discovery of the Waterfall Room. There is a large boulder at the base of the waterfall that you can stand on, reach to the top, and pull yourself up and over the top. However you may be in the waterfall as you climb up, depending on the water level. This survey resulted in 1,490.37 feet T.H.C. The total survey length was now 13,938.86 feet.

September 15, 1969 - Allen Padgett and Richard Schreiber started a survey at station G180 near Five Points and surveyed west, discovering Allen's Dome Thing and the Anamatosis Room. They then mapped upper level passages almost to the waterfall area. This survey resulted in 1,125.80 feet T.H.C. The total survey length was now 15,064.66 feet.

September 23,1969 - Richard Schreiber and Della McGuffin made the last survey for the year and completed the first three miles of Pettyjohn Cave. This trip started in the passage that is above the Waterfall Room but not connected. After mapping this area they returned to station H114 and surveyed to the Over 'N Under Room, reaching the 3 mile mark. This passage is easy and has some nice formations. It is also possible to drop down to the stream near the Waterfall Room. You can hear the waterfall when you climb down, however a rope would be required to get back up. This part of the survey resulted in 783.62 feet T.H.C. The total survey length was now 15,848.28 feet.

The first three miles of survey also closed out the first year (1969) of the survey. I would like to congratulate the following for their accomplishment in the exploration and survey of the first three miles in Pettyjohn Cave: Richard Schreiber and Della McGuffin, (Richard was on every trip, and Della accompanied him on almost every trip), Bill Damewood, Mike Hicks, Marion O. Smith, Allen Padgett and Bob Watkins for their help.

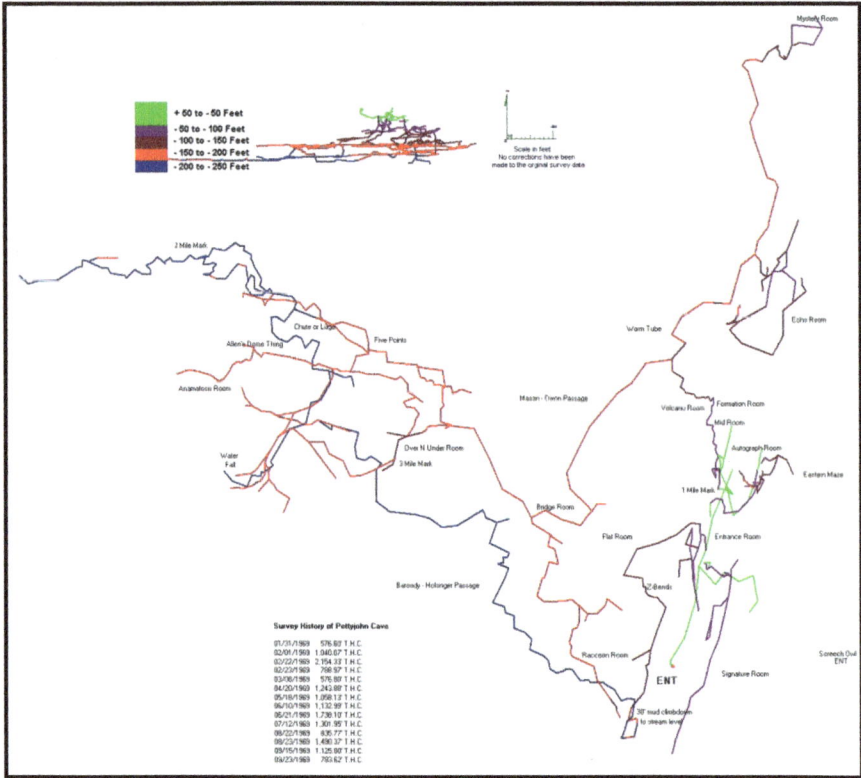

15,848.28 feet of horizontal cave mapped

Mile 4 of the Pettyjohn Cave Survey

Mile four really starts with the passage above the Luge, which led to the discovery of the Pulverizer Squeeze Tobacco Road and the Outer Limits. The lowest point in the cave was also discovered and mapped. All of the streams in the known cave flow to this sump. The discovery of the Emerald Pool pushed the cave to the most northern point, and Tobacco Road pushed the cave to the most western point. With Mile 4 completed you can see just how complex this cave has become. The years 1969 and 1970 were the most active surveying years in Pettyjohn Cave, and all of it was due to the hard caving efforts of Richard Schreiber and those that he could entice into going with him.

September 23, 1969 – After completing three miles, Richard and Della, then picked up the survey above the Luge or Chute at station H40. This is a dry area, and after a twisting passage they climbed up into a fault room with a lot of loose rock. The survey ended with an 80 foot long, two foot high crawl ahead. The survey resulted in 658.45 feet T.H.C. The total survey was now 16,506.73 feet.

April 18, 1970 - Richard Schreiber, John Eastburn, Dick Minert, Allen Padgett and Marion O. Smith climbed down from the bridge room near the squeeze to the Mason–Dixon Passage and mapped downstream under the Volcano Room until stopped by a dropoff.

They then returned to the Bridge Room to map a short connection down from the Bridge Room to the upstream side of the breakdown below the Bridge Room. A short distance upstream there is a side passage that was noted on the February 23, 1969 trip near station P123. The station notes did not give a clear location, and the new survey starts with "D35 – P?" They surveyed the Double Echo Domes and then went up the Baroody–Holsinger passage to map two other leads near station P110 and P99. The one starting at P99 was labeled on the survey notes as M.F. Passage Intestine, with the M.F. scratched through. Both starting points for the surveys are between existing stations, so the closest station was used for the connection. The survey resulted in 1,484.48 feet T.H.C. The total survey was now 17,991.21 feet.

May 13, 1970 - Richard Schreiber, Ted Wilson and Steve Gelfius returned to pick up the survey in the Fault Room that ended on September 23. From the end of the crawl, they found a lead going down. This lead them to the Pulverizer Squeeze, a one foot wide, ten foot high chimney down. If you get stuck in the Pulverizer Squeeze, they may have to leave you there!

The mapping continued west until they discovered Tobacco Road, a long, straight walking passage for over four hundred feet. The survey resulted in 1,048.76 feet T.H.C. The total survey was now 19,039.97 feet.

May 14, 1970 - Richard Schreiber and Ted Wilson returned to discover the start of the Outer Limits, a far reaching passage going north under the mountain. They explored and mapped north for over eight hundred feet before stopping at a stream junction for the day. The survey resulted in 813.20 feet T.H.C. The total survey was now 19,853.17 feet.

July 3, 1970 - Richard Schreiber, John Eastburn, Dick Minert, Rod Price and Chris Morgan (all of the USAF) returned to the lowest part of the cave and mapped down to the sump. The short survey resulted in 95.77 feet T.H.C. The total survey was now 19,948.94 feet.

July 4, 1970 - Richard Schreiber, John Eastburn, Dick Minert, Rod Price and Chris Morgan went through the Worm Tube and started surveying from station G73. They discovered the Emerald Pool, a siphon and an upper passage with air descending. However they did not have the equipment necessary to climb up and check it out. They then returned to station G73 and mapped down the stream to a sump. The survey resulted in 911.34 feet T.H.C. The total survey was now 20,860.28 feet.

August 22, 1970 - Richard Schreiber, Ted Wilson and Steve Wells caved out to the end of Tobacco Road and picked up the survey at station W80A. After mapping about a hundred feet, they went out to the Outer Limits and picked up the survey at station W108. Two feet ahead of station W129 would be the 4 mile mark. The next survey station, W130, intersects a stream flowing from the Outer Limits. The survey continued with the start of mile five.

21,145.10 feet of horizontal cave mapped

Pettyjohn Cave is considered to be Georgia's most muddy and popular cave for non–vertical cavers. There are places where a rope is nice, and one or two places where it may be required, but 98% of the cave can be visited without the use of vertical gear. In recent years, easy access and parking have made the cave a favorite for weekend outing groups. Many have always felt that this cave has many more surprises in store for those willing to put forth the effort and explore the many leads that remain.

Mile 5 of the Pettyjohn Cave Survey

Most of the fifth mile took place in The Labyrinth, a maze of stream passages from the surface water that drains in from Screech Owl Cave and other holes east of the entrance to Pettyjohn Cave. I have been in Screech Owl Cave but not to the end. It is a very small and tight cave. We have also made attempts to dig out other deep holes in the area that possibly also drain into Pettyjohn. Most of the Outer Limits were also mapped in this mile.

August 22, 1970 - Richard Schreiber, Ted Wilson and Steve Wells surveyed up the stream almost to the end of the passage. The survey resulted in 589.87 feet T.H.C. The total survey was now 21,450.15 feet.

September 12, 1970 - Richard Schreiber, John Eastburn and Allen Padgett made a surface survey from the entrance of Pettyjohn Cave to Screech Owl Cave some 325 feet to the east. Screech Owl Cave was probably first found during the spring of 1970 by Ed Renner of the Florida State Cave Club. On September 16, Screech Owl Cave was dug open and the survey begun by Marion O. Smith, Cricket Haygood, Jon Resager and Dan Dougherty Jr.

September 26, 1970 - Richard Schreiber and John Eastburn surveyed the north end of the Outer Limits. While Ted Wilson and Bill Steele surveyed the stream passage from station W112 of the May 14, 1970 survey. The combined surveys resulted in 1,497.29 feet T.H.C. The total survey was now 22,947.47 feet.

October 10, 1970 - George Morris, Allen Padgett, Marion O. Smith and Doug Strait deepened Screech Owl Cave by digging, and then continued the survey.

October 20, 1970 - Richard Schreiber, Marion and Jim Young completed the survey of Screech Owl Cave at 325.9 feet long and 107.1 feet deep. Chuck Horton did the chimney but did not survey because of the lack of room!

October 20, 1970 - Richard Schreiber and Chuck Horton first mapped a short passage just above the stream level near the Chute or Luge. They then went downstream to the main stream and up to the Waterfall, where they mapped the Squirrel Room above the waterfall. Returning to the junction of the two streams, they surveyed downstream to connect to station P135. Next they started a survey up the small stream passage in the direction of Screech Owl Cave. At the bottom of the 30-foot mud climb down they picked up station P77 and started mapping the upper-level stream passage. The survey resulted in 824.96 feet T.H.C. The total survey was now 23,772.43 feet.

November 1, 1970 - Richard Schreiber and Allen Padgett resumed the survey in the upper-level stream passage and surveyed another 259.85 feet T.H.C. The total survey was now 24,032.28 feet.

November 2, 1970 - Richard Schreiber, Allen Padgett, Don Hunter and Barry Prince resumed the survey in the JVC Room. On a rock in the middle of this room is a marker that says, "JVC 1964." I presume that is when this room was discovered. The lower stream passage (Porpoise Passage), was surveyed downstream toward the mud climb down. From the JVC mark they went down three feet under a ledge to enter The Labyrinth. This is a maze section that is south of and below Screech Owl Cave. The survey resulted in 872.72 feet T.H.C. The total survey was now 24,905.00 feet.

June 21,1971 - After nine months of no surveying, Richard Schreiber, Rod Price, John Eastburn and David Teal returned to The Labyrinth for more surveying. The survey resulted in 675.03 feet T.H.C. The total survey now was 25,580.03 feet.

December 7, 1973 - Two years later Richard Schreiber and Allen Padgett returned again to The Labyrinth and mapped 803.77 feet T.H.C. The total survey now was 26,383.80 feet, only 12.89 feet short of the 5 mile mark.

February 22, 1974 - Two months later Richard Schreiber and Allen Padgett surveyed again in The Labyrinth, and on the first survey shot of 32 feet they surpassed the 5 mile mark. However, they were not aware of it due to the calculation errors in the survey books. They continued unaware of the event and surveyed 585.89 feet T.H.C. The total survey was now 26,969.69 feet.

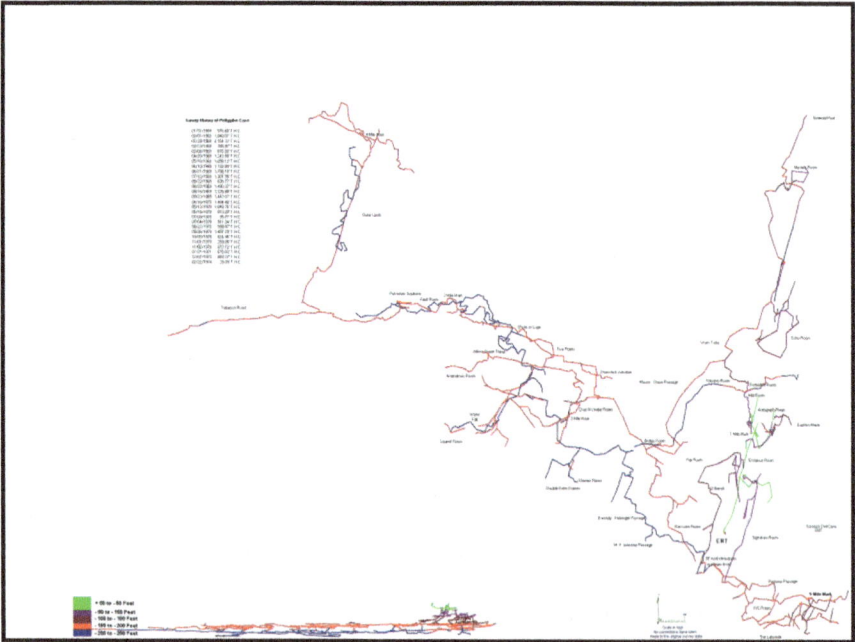

26,412.89 feet of horizontal cave mapped

Survey trips had really started to slow, with three more survey trips in 1974 for a total of only four. There was one more survey in 1981, then four more in 1983, and the last recorded survey by Richard Schreiber in 1985.

After 15 years of caving in Pettyjohn Cave, I started re–mapping the parts that we had visited, unaware of the work done by Schreiber. In 1987 we made our first survey trip and began to record the previous survey station marks and followed these with our own survey when possible.

Mile 6 of the Pettyjohn Cave Survey

Mile six of Pettyjohn Cave is a push to the extreme limits of the cave. The Outer Limits was pushed, then the discovery and survey of the Discovery Room, and next the survey of Schreiber's Extension. The Discovery Room is currently the most northern room in the cave. High above the Emerald Pool and directly under Pigeon Mountain, it is the second largest room in the cave at two hundred and fifty feet long and over forty feet wide in places, with ceiling heights of close to twenty feet. The room ends with a large breakdown.

Schreiber's Extension may have been explored before this survey, and it is the longest stretch of stream passage found so far. Reaching around the edge of the mountain to the west and south, it is the least explored and understood section of the cave.

May 26, 1974 - Richard Schreiber, Rod Price and Ted Wilson picked up the downstream passage out in the Outer Limits and started surveying at station X38. They explored and surveyed almost to the lower end of the Outer Limits, but at the lower stream level. To exit, they had to loop back up the stream to the junction, climb up to the upper level and then cave south again. This is about a six hour round trip from the start of the Outer Limits! The survey resulted in 440.54 feet T.H.C. The total survey was now 27,410.23 feet.

June 8, 1974 - Richard Schreiber and Gerald Moni caved out to the start of Tobacco Road and pushed an upstream passage. Note: There are two stations labeled W151. One is at the far northwestern tip of the Outer Limits, and the other is at the start of Tobacco Road. The June 8 survey was recorded in two different survey books. The correct location was used on a map by Jeff Harris in November 1990, and Richard Schreiber's own survey plot is at the end of the Outer Limits.

From the junction of station W65, at Tobacco Road and Outer Limits, they surveyed down to the stream level and connected to the lower level of the Outer Limits. They then caved up the stream to the northwestern tip of the Outer Limits and pushed this passage another two hundred feet. The survey resulted in 732.90 feet T.H.C. The total survey was now 28,143.13 feet.

November 2, 1974 - Richard Schreiber and Ted Wilson did some mop up surveying in the Outer Limits. They extended the stream from the Outer Limits to a near siphon less than a hundred feet from where it emerges again. The survey resulted in 430.01 feet T.H.C. The total survey was now 28,573.14 feet.

August 10, 1975 - Richard Schreiber, Marion Smith and a group from Massachusetts and Connecticut carried sections of a scaling pole to the Emerald Pool and Warren Heller climbed up, but nothing was gained.

August 23, 1981 - Richard Schreiber, Dwight Drennan, Wesley Sprunger, Pete Uberto and Keith Lynn returned to the Emerald Pool and bolted up the wall or used a rope left from the pole climb. They discovered the Discovery Room after climbing higher and passing through a few tight squeezes. The survey resulted in 409.23 feet T.H.C. The total survey was now 28,982.37 feet.

June 11, 1983 - Richard Schreiber, Wesley Sprunger and Pete Uberto started the survey of Schreiber's Extension from station Z19 in the Squirrel Room. It was discovered by the same group on April 30, 1983. The survey resulted in 1,400.59 feet T.H.C. The total survey was now 30,382.96 feet.

July 9, 1983 - Richard Schreiber, Keith Lynn, Wesley Sprunger and Pete Uberto returned to Schreiber's Extension and continued the survey. On this survey the cave was pushed beyond the most western limits to date as Schreiber's Extension continues around the side of the mountain. The survey resulted in 497.36 feet T.H.C. The total survey was now 30,880.32 feet.

August 13, 1983 - Richard Schreiber, Ed Strausser, Wesley Sprunger and Pete Uberto resumed the survey, breaking the six mile mark at station ZA111.

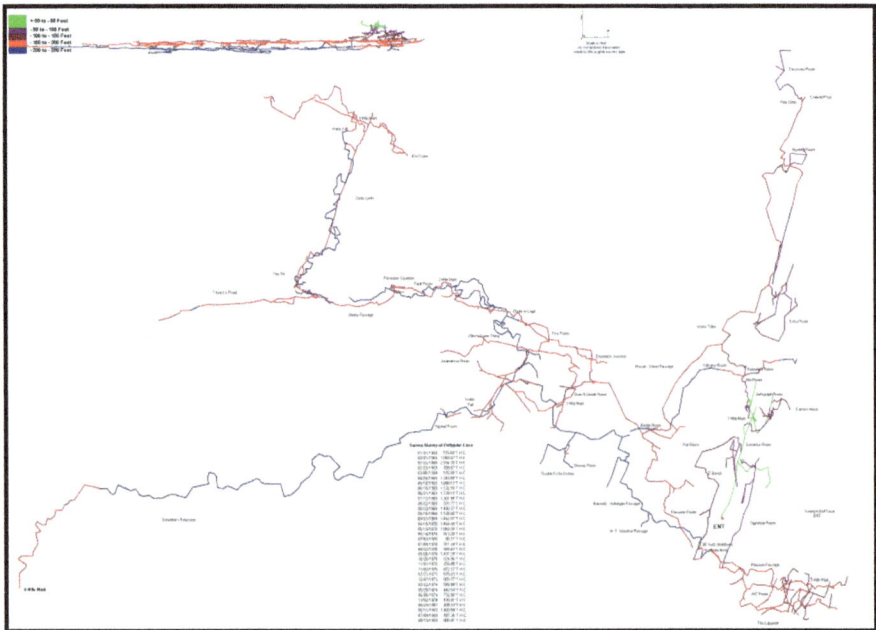

31,686.23 feet of horizontal cave mapped

Mile 7 of the Pettyjohn Cave Survey

Mile seven occurs over the next twenty–six years of caving in Pettyjohn Cave. 1983 brought to a close the most active exploration and survey. Schreiber's Extension is full of leads mostly going up. The survey followed the stream level and there are upper levels to be found just about the full length of the passage with few having been explored or surveyed. Schreiber's notes are full of comments about leads and climbs up into upper levels. The last survey of 1983 has been lost, along with one in 1985. New discoveries have been made in the last few years, and I am sure that there are many more that are just waiting for someone to survey.

August 13, 1983 - Richard Schreiber, Ed Strausser, Wesley Sprunger and Pete Uberto made the longest survey in one day and broke the six mile mark at station ZA111. They stayed with the stream passage all the way, marking leads in their notes for future follow up. At Station ZA122 they stopped the survey and scooped the passage ahead. Then they did a survey out and back to ZA122. They did not go to the end of Schreiber's Extension. I assume that it was completed on August 20, 1983.

The survey resulted in 2,665.53 feet T.H.C. The total survey was now 33,545.85 feet.

August 20, 1983 - Richard Schreiber, Bill Putnam, Wesley Sprunger and Pete Uberto mapped 398.3 feet as recorded by Marion O. Smith in the 1991 GSS Bulletin. This survey book was lost, however I was able to make out some of the station numbers and notes from Schreiber's cave plot at the end of the extension, and I believe that it was from this survey. The data recorded was taken from the plot and a later re–survey. After completing the survey to the sump, they surveyed a stream passage going east off Schreiber's Extension until the passage became too low.

The survey resulted in 441.91 feet T.H.C. The total survey was now 33,987.76 feet.

March 9, 1985 - Richard Schreiber, Pete Uberto, Mike Singleton, Alan Cressler and Melissa Hyde mapped 582.4 feet as recorded by Marion O. Smith in the 1991 GSS Bulletin. This survey book was also lost. I have not been able to find any clue as to where this survey took place in the cave.

Alan provided the following from his notes: "03/09/85 mapping trip with Richard Schreiber, Peter Uberto, Melissa Hyde, Mike Singleton to the upstream section above the waterfall. We mapped about 600 feet with about half of that in virgin cave. Still many leads in that section. Very muddy. 8 hour trip."

March 21, 1987 - Hubert Crowell, Roger Garratt and Mark Gramlich made their first mapping trip in Pettyjohn Cave. This survey covered the entrance to the Autograph Room, which had already been mapped.

However 98.51 feet was gained in the lower part of the Autograph Room that was not previously surveyed. The survey ended with some air flow and evidence of someone digging at the end. This spot is very close to the passage leading to the Volcano Room, so close in fact that you can talk clearly to someone in that passage.

The survey resulted in 441.91 feet T.H.C. of new cave. The total survey was now 34,086.27 feet.

August 22, 1987 - Hubert Crowell, Roger Garratt and Buddy Davis surveyed the Northeast Stream Passage to a string of large high domes. The discovery of Crowell Domes helped to expand the boundary of the cave to the east where there has been very little known cave. Part of this survey was a re–survey. The section that was unavailable from previous survey notes starts with station ES18 dropping 3 feet down to the stream level.

The survey resulted in 511.56 feet T.H.C. of new cave. The total survey was now 34,597.83 feet.

September 26, 1987 - Hubert Crowell, John Wallace, Mark Gramich, Roger Garratt and Buddy Davis explored and surveyed the lower downstream section of the Northeast Stream Passage to a sump. Although this had been previously surveyed, an upper level from the sump was added back over the stream level.

The survey resulted in 118.50 feet T.H.C. of new cave. The total survey was now 34,716.33 feet.

September 23, 1989 - Hubert Crowell, Buddy Davis and Roger Garrett surveyed through the Pancake Squeeze to the stream and then upstream. The only portion of this survey that was not previously surveyed was the short passage through the Pancake Squeeze. This is now the most popular route and avoids the Z–Bends.

The survey resulted in 143.96 feet T.H.C. of new cave. The total survey was now 34,860.29 feet.

November 10, 1991 - Jack Kipp, Buddy Welker and Tom Moltz surveyed High Anxiety, which was re–discovered in August 17, 1991 by Tom. This is located just before Schreiber's Extension turns south. It is an eighty foot climb up from the stream passage, also known as the Lost Hammer Passage. The room is large and reminded Tom of the Echo Room. There were two 3 foot high rock cairns stacked in the middle of the room. These were built by Jeff Dilcher and Laura Campbell prior to August 17. 1991. Jeff had to dig up into the room from the stream level to discover the room. The floor is mostly large breakdown boulders, and the ceiling had a coating of thick calcite.

The survey resulted in 336.70 feet T.H.C. of new cave. The total survey was now 35,196.99 feet.

December 19, 1992 - Hubert Crowell, Gary Beasley, Rob Morgan and Doug Dewitt re–surveyed the Signature Room to obtain vertical data for cross sections. Two small areas that were not on the original survey were gained. A small hole near the entrance to the Signature Room was located on the side of a small depression that you can just fit into. I loved to lead a group of kids into this hole, and as we collect at the back, I tell them to turn their lights out and be real quiet. As each new person packs into the hole the same message is passed on until everyone is packed into the hole.

There is also a small pit at the back of the Signature Room, Doug's Pit. A small lead from the bottom of this pit was later surveyed to almost directly under the entrance of the cave.

The survey resulted in only 80.40 feet T.H.C. of new cave. The total survey was now 35,277.39 feet.

January 16, 1993 - Hubert Crowell, Buddy Davis, Mark Gramich, Rob Morgan and Doug Dewitt re–surveyed from the main entrance room to the Volcano Room trying to resolve a seventy foot vertical error in my survey data. In the process we did map some passages that were new.

The survey resulted in 316.49 feet T.H.C. of new cave. The total survey was now 35,593.88 feet.

August 21, 1993 - Hubert Crowell, Wes Sprunger, Sharon Keener, Gary Beasley and Brad Long surveyed the area above the Double Echo Domes. Nathan Sohn free–climbed the dome in 1992 and discovered Sohn Shine Extension.

The survey resulted in 620.60 feet T.H.C. of new cave. The total survey was now 36,214.48 feet.

March 29, 1999 - Scott Carmine and Tom Moltz surveyed a passage previously discovered by Scott above the Emerald Pool. At the top of the Pole Climb they worked their way through some 3D maze–like breakdown and started to survey toward the southeast. They stopped at the edge of a large breakdown room over fifty feet across and fifteen to thirty feet high. There were more leads than they could explore on this trip. They would return nine years later to complete the survey and map.

The survey resulted in 137.88 feet T.H.C. of new cave. The total survey was now 36,352.36 feet

September 7, 2002 - Scott Carmine, Damon Keys and Tom Moltz surveyed the end of Schreiber's Extension. Scott and Tom dug a trench thirty feet long to drain down the water level at the end of Schreiber's Extension in November of 1998. Scott returned the following weekend with Keith Minor to check on the water level and pushed through a one foot high water passage with six inches of air space to extend the south end of the cave another 464.50 feet T.H.C. The total survey was now 36,816.86 feet.

July 19, 2003 - Scott Carmine and Tom Moltz surveyed a newly discovered passage found by Damon Keys, Scott and his wife, Kristin Carmine, on a previous trip. The Fractured Dome Passage was found in an obscure squeeze down a tiny stream belly crawl at the end of the

Anastomosis Room. The last survey shot for the day was just beyond the Fractured Dome and marks the seventh mile mark plus 4.06 feet.

The survey resulted in 147.20 feet T.H.C. of new cave. The total survey was now 36,964.06 feet.

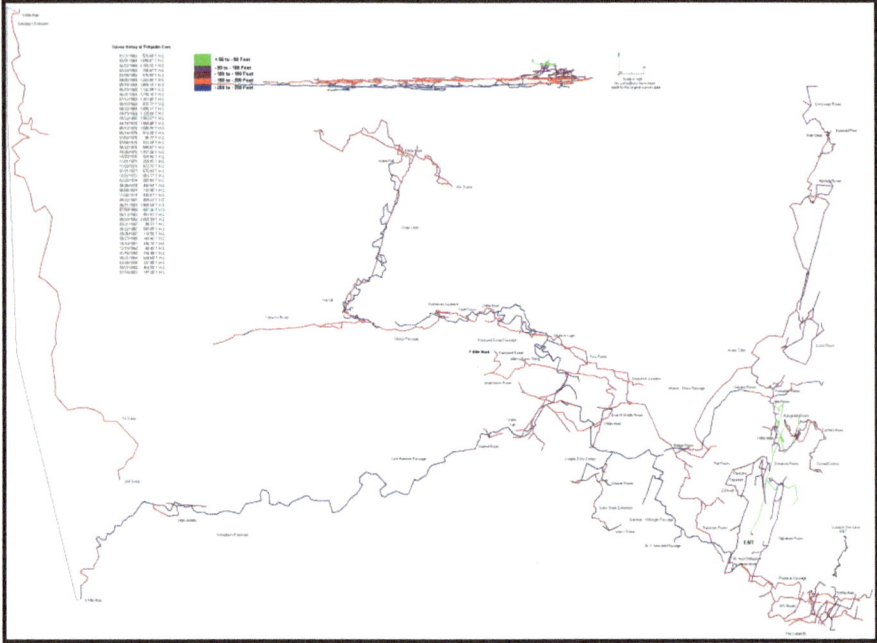

36,964.06 feet of horizontal cave mapped

The surveying of Pettyjohn Cave has been very long and confusing, especially the seventh mile. During the reconstruction of the survey history, parts of the re–surveys were only used when it was certain that the passage had not previously been surveyed. Minor side shots and notes about extended unmapped crawls were not included in the data.

We are missing 582 feet of survey somewhere out in Schreiber's Extension that some day will be re–discovered and re–surveyed. I have also been told that there is two thousand feet of trunk passage out there also waiting to be surveyed.

Mile 8 of the Pettyjohn Cave Survey

After the Fractured Dome Passage was completed by Scott and Tom, there was a five year period of no surveying that I am aware of. I knew of a few small areas that were not on the map and that needed to be surveyed. There still remains all that passage out in Schreiber's Extension that needs to be checked out. I also have a great interest in the northeastern direction.

There must be a lot of cave in that direction because I was once told that the water entering Nash Waterfall Cave was traced to Pettyjohn Cave. Nash Waterfall Cave is north of Atwood Point and Pettyjohn.

Cave locations

October 11, 2003 - Scott Carmine and Tom Moltz continued the survey in Fractured Dome Passage.

The survey resulted in 48.18 feet T.H.C. of new cave. The total survey was now 37,012.24 feet.

March 31, 2007 - Hubert Crowell and Buddy Davis surveyed the lead at the bottom of Doug's Pit located at the end of the Signature Room. This was not on any map and was not well traveled. The passage ended almost 100 feet under the main entrance. There were several nice formations in the 15 by 20 room.

The survey resulted in 97.44 feet T.H.C. of new cave. The total survey was now 37,109.68 feet.

February 2, 2008 - Scott Carmine, Daniel Thomson, Will Urbanski, Kile Klepp and Tom Moltz resumed the survey above the Emerald Pool and name the area "Nervous Breakdown Room," because of the large numbers huge breakdown rocks and the unstable conditions.

Quote from Tom Moltz: "We picked up the survey where Scott and I had left off nine years earlier. We surveyed 277 feet for a THC of 227 feet. A short dig to continue on from our previous survey involved clearing out rocks from a fractured parting. A 31 foot pit connected back to the stream leading to the Emerald Pool. This put the vertical extent at 88 feet. We still had not tied in the survey to the cave."

The survey resulted in 226.93 feet T.H.C. of new cave. The total survey was now 37,336.61 feet.

November 12, 2008 - Scott Carmine, Tom Moltz, Roger Gainer, Jonny Prouty, Kris Fausnight, Kyle Gochenour, Will Urbanski and Ed Pratt completed the survey with a tie in the rest of the cave. Most of the loop surveyed upstream to the Emerald Pool and up at the Pole Climb had already been surveyed. Only the section from the top of the rope to the start of the March 29, 1999 survey was used in the total T.H.C. distance.

The survey resulted in 75.02 feet T.H.C. of new cave. The total survey was now 37,411.63 feet.

February 28, 2009 - Hubert Crowell, Buddy Davis, Gene Ellison, Steven Smith, Jordan Brady, John Brady and Scott Carmine returned to the Eastern Maze in hopes of finding the seventh mile!

Back on September 20, 2008, Buddy and I surveyed 106 feet in what we assumed was un–surveyed passage. This looked very much like the February 23, 1969 "J" survey but was not in the same location. After a closer look at the tie–in of that older survey and re-entering all the data, I did determine that it was the same. On this trip we had not counted the survey of the Nervous Breakdown Room and assumed that we were only 364 feet shy of the seven mile mark. Having now reentered all the data available, I know that we were actually 451.63 feet over the seven mile mark!

The survey did yield some new survey however, and we set the marker. Maybe someday the lost survey book of March 9, 1985 will turn up and that 582.4 feet of survey will give a better location for the seventh mile marker.

The survey resulted in 281.80 feet T.H.C. of new cave. The total survey was now 37,693,43 feet.

Pettyjohn Cave has grown slowly over the years and now offers more of a challenge than ever before for those who are willing to push hard in their search for the unknown. As four of us lay in a small cramped crawlway waiting for the compass and tape readings, I looked at Scott all bent over in the tight crawl we had just slid down into. I asked how he was doing, and he replied, "I'm happy. I'm caving." I guess that sums it up for most cavers. It is something that is hard to explain to people that have not been caving. Poking into unknown places, pushing hard passages, and now and then walking where no one has walked before.

The eighth mile of survey has only started. If you have access to or know of any survey that is not shown or mentioned, please contact me so that it can be included.

37,693.43 feet of horizontal cave mapped

Groundwater Sampling in Pettyjohn Cave

.James Mayer of the Geology Department at State University of West Georgia, wrote about the Groundwater in Pettyjohns Cave in his paper Spatial and temporal variation of groundwater chemistry in Pettyjohns cave, northwest Georgia, USA. Mr. Mayer took many samples, and the reports are very detail.[19]

In 1994, I started working for EcoTek LSI. Doug DeWitt and Rob Morgan who also worked for EcoTek, were caving friends. We also collected water samples and had them analyzed.

The following was provided by Douglas C. DeWitt the supervisor at Metals Laboratory, EcoTek LSI.

The results are in ug/L units, which is equivalent to ppb or parts–per–billion. There were no toxic metals, i.e. arsenic or lead, detected. The levels of other metals detected, aluminum, calcium, magnesium, potassium and sodium, are consistent with the high mineral content one would expect from water in a cave environment.

The samples were taken in the Entrance Room of Pettyjohn Cave, and the from a small room above and before you get to the Volcano Room. Both samples were taken from droplets along joints in the ceiling.

				Trace Metals Analytical Results Cave Samples				

Sample: Bottle 5				Site: Entrance Room			

Analyte	Date Analyzed	Dilution Factor	Result ug/l	Detection Limit ug/l	Note
Aluminum	1/15/93	1	39.1	16.0	
Antimony	1/15/93	1	<12.0	12.0	
Arsenic	1/15/93	1	<14.0	14.0	
Barium	1/15/93	1	19.2	1.0	
Beryllium	1/15/93	1	<1.0	1.0	
Cadmium	1/15/93	1	<3.0	3.0	
Calcium	1/15/93	1	116000	5.0	
Chromium	1/15/93	1	<3.0	3.0	
Cobalt	1/15/93	1	<3.0	3.0	
Copper	1/15/93	1	<2.0	2.0	
Iron	1/15/93	1	9.0	2.0	
Lead	1/15/93	1	<18.0	18.0	
Magnesium	1/15/93	1	3640	22.0	
Manganese	1/15/93	1	<1.0	1.0	
Nickel	1/15/93	1	<4.0	4.0	
Potassium	1/15/93	1	<461	461	
Selenium	1/15/93	1	<30.0	30.0	
Silver	1/15/93	1	<3.0	3.0	
Sodium	1/15/93	1	770	25.0	
Thallium	1/15/93	1	<60.0	60.0	
Vanadium	1/15/93	1	<3.0	3.0	
Zinc	1/15/93	1	<1.0	1.0	

Sample taken from the Entrance Room, Pettyjohn Cave

Trace Metals Analytical Results Cave Samples					
Sample: Bottle 3			Site: Above the Volcano Room		
Analyte	Date Analyzed	Dilution Factor	Result ug/l	Detection Limit ug/l	Note
Aluminum	1/15/93	1	1010	16.0	
Antimony	1/15/93	1	<12.0	12.0	
Arsenic	1/15/93	1	<14.0	14.0	
Barium	1/15/93	1	30.3	1.0	
Beryllium	1/15/93	1	<1.0	1.0	
Cadmium	1/15/93	1	<3.0	3.0	
Calcium	1/15/93	1	56300	5.0	
Chromium	1/15/93	1	3.5	3.0	
Cobalt	1/15/93	1	<3.0	3.0	
Copper	1/15/93	1	11.9	2.0	
Iron	1/15/93	1	452	2.0	
Lead	1/15/93	1	<18.0	18.0	
Magnesium	1/15/93	1	17400	22.0	
Manganese	1/15/93	1	35.6	1.0	
Nickel	1/15/93	1	<4.0	4.0	
Potassium	1/15/93	1	2490	461	
Selenium	1/15/93	1	<30.0	30.0	
Silver	1/15/93	1	<3.0	3.0	
Sodium	1/15/93	1	3640	25.0	
Thallium	1/15/93	1	<60.0	60.0	
Vanadium	1/15/93	1	<3.0	3.0	
Zinc	1/15/93	1	24.3	1.0	

Sample taken near and above the Volcano Room

Three–Hour Underground Adventure

Three hours does not seem like a long time, unless you are climbing, crawling and squeezing through tight places. It was Pete's third caveing trip and he wanted to see more of Pettyjohn Cave, which he had visited on two previous trips. We originally had planned on about five people for the trip, but ended up with just Pete and I going.

Traveling through the cave with just two people is more than likely the best number for a caving trip when there are a lot of tough places to get through. You can double the amount of time for a trip for each additional person as you have to wait for each member of the group to squeeze or climb through a tough place.

We entered the cave on a beautiful November day at 10:00 A.M., careful to avoid all the deer hunters in the area. Deer season had just opened, and this was a popular check–in location. The parking lot was already full, with several large groups entering the cave. We knew that once we entered the cave and left the main room that we would not see anyone until we returned to the main room again.

We planned to visit the Crowell Domes found above a stream passage that flows in from the east.

Buddy Davis and I mapped this section about 15 years ago and have tried to relocate it several times but failed. I am certain where the passage is, but I was much thinner then and braver.

I know that the connection to the domes was small, and in my survey I showed it as a four–foot wide passage. If we didn't find it this time, I would be forced to do a reverse survey to find the passage.

We both wanted to get back early so we planned to check out the stream passage and then head back out.

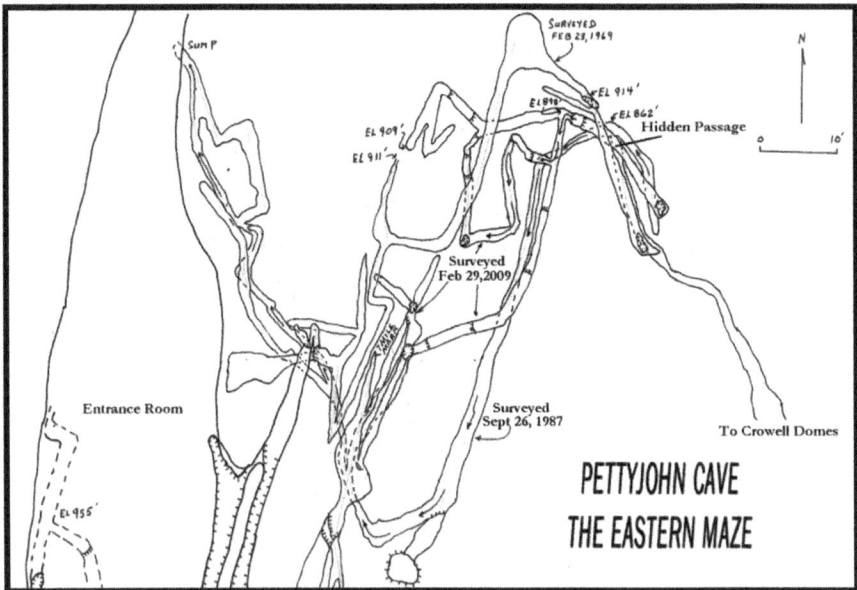

Hidden passage to Crowell Domes

We moved through the entrance room quickly, and passed the first junction room that leads down to the Signature Room. The hand and foot holds are burned into my mind from years of visiting this wonderful cave.

The left side of the main room is a steep slick climb with few hand holds, easy to come down but hard to climb up. Just to the right there is a crack just right for a step, then about halfway up a steep slope there is a small formation of about four inches that makes a perfect step to the top of the first climb.

A young girl was struggling with the harder climb, and I showed her the two steps so she could catch up with her group. They were heading down at the second junction room and headed to the waterfall.

We worked our way down slowly to allow the large group to move on down and out of our way, then we climbed up from the second junction room. The third junction room is another climb down just before reaching the back of the main entrance room. At the bottom our passage turned to the right. Straight ahead and under a low flat bolder is the passage to the Volcano Room.

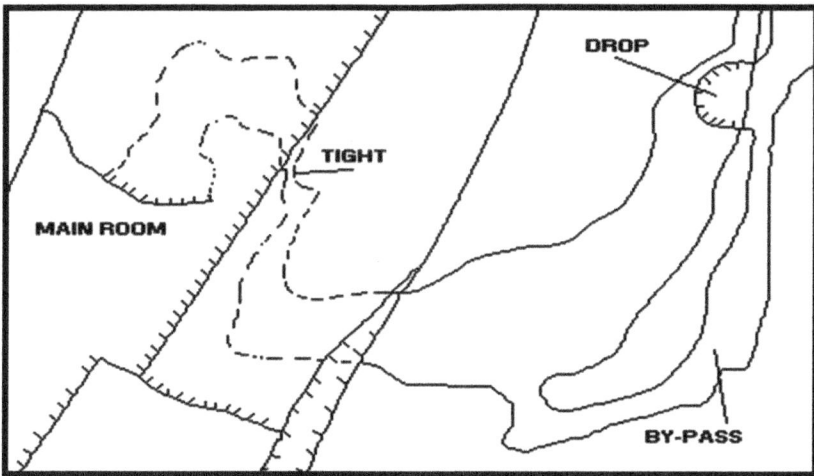

Bypass to avoid drop

After turning right we climbed down another level and looked for the bypass. The bypass is a crawl that takes you around a difficult and exposed climb down along the east side of the main entrance room. The first passage we found I remember as a dead-end. Very close by was another climb down that lead to a crevasse that was two foot wide at the start and narrowed to less than a foot if you tried to stand up in it.

A friend of mine got stuck here by trying to stand up too fast on the way out. You have to drop feet first all the way to the bottom, then hug the back wall until you are laying flat. You can then slide down to where the passage opens up. At the top of this climb on the way out, I slipped and fell about four feet, landing on my back and left elbow. No broken bones, but a few bruises. Being overconfident can get you into trouble sometimes.

Crawling through the bypass we came out on the side of a 20 by 20 room and made the easy climb to the bottom. We continued down through the large boulders to the stream level.

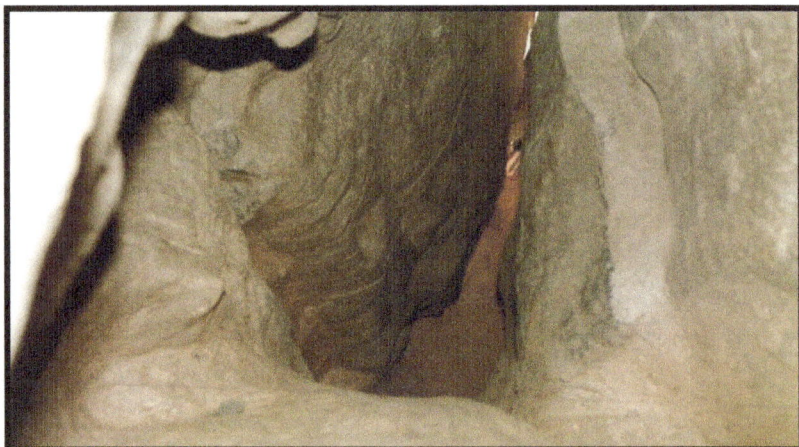

Looking down the tight spot

The Bypass

To avoid the drop, take the Bypass,
a little tight but better than an impasse.
Going down is easy, just let go and slide.
When you reach the bottom, just lay back and glide.

The bottom opens up into a nice low stroll,
now coming back you may feel like a mole.
The upward slope tends to make you rise,
before you reach the spot that is the right size.

Rising up before the end may get difficult,
unable to turn your head or even look up.
To continue on you must relax and subside,
hug the floor until it forces you up the side.

As you become vertical trying for a foothold,
position your arms so they will unfold.
Now you know if you are a little overweight,
wouldn't it be wonderful just to deflate?

If you're in the lead and the slope is dry,
feel blessed—and sorry for the next guy.
If your boots are wet and greasing the floor,
the last person out will curse all the more.

The stream passage contained very little water and was a very easy duck walk up the stream. We found the hidden crawl up the left side of the stream passage and crossed over the stream below, but that was where the search began.

Each time we searched this small area we could not find a way out. There appeared to be only one upper crawl in the direction we wanted to go, but it looked un–traveled and small. I managed to get my whole body length up and into the crawl and pushed as far as I thought possible. I could not see a way on and gave up again. I will have to bring my survey notes back and do a reverse survey to see where I was going wrong.

We had a short lunch and started back out.

The climb up from the stream passage can be made in two ways: you can climb straight up or take the easy route to the side and switch back. At the point where you switch back, you have to watch carefully for the climb up that is directly over your head. If you miss it you will wander around in a breakdown room. I had noted this on one of my maps with a question mark.

It was here that Pete wanted to explore, so we started checking out some of the crawlways. One was just to the right of the point where we climb up and out. The passage went up slightly and then made a sharp turn to the left. I had not been that far and encouraged Pete to go ahead and check it out.

The passage started back down at a slight angle, and as I followed Pete I placed my hand on a large boulder and it moved. I stepped back and let it fall into the passage. I estimate that it was about ninety pounds and about the size of a bag of concrete. You can always tell when a cave is well traveled as there will not be many loose rocks. There was evidence that others had been there, but not a lot of traffic. About fifty feet further the passage split, turning to the right and left.

The right passage really got my interest. It was heavily decorated with formations and two large rim stone dams that were dry but at one time held a large amount of water. There had been people crawling over them, and many of the formations were broken.

I knew that this was not on any known map of the cave and decided to return at a later date to survey the whole area. It was heading toward the top of a small dome that you encounter in the stream passage below. This could also lead to the top of the Crowell Domes.

One of the problems encountered when exploring a well known and heavily traveled cave is that you can never tell what has been explored and documented. Many people just poke into places without a map being drawn, and it remains unknown to the rest of the caving community. So anytime I find a new section of cave, I try to stop and come back with survey gear to map the new or relocated areas.

We named that formation passage "Pete's Grotto" for Peter Zefo.

This was the area that Buddy Davis and I surveyed later on February 28, 2009 and later discovered that it was the same area that was mapped on the February 23, 1969 "J" Survey. I had previously tied the old survey in at the wrong location.

Panic Under the Mountain

Pete, printed out my directions of the Loop in Pettyjohn Cave and made an attempt to complete the loop. The directions were not clear on how to exit the Raccoon room, and they could not find the back exit.

On May 17, 2008, I joined them for a good six hour trip around the loop and a side trip to the area above the waterfall.

This trip took in the Over 'N Under Room as a side trip from the Bridge Room, along with some searching for a connection to the passages above the Double Echo Domes. I was told by a fellow caver that a connection was possible between the two areas. We also reached the area above the Waterfall but did not take the last five–foot plunge to the stream below as we would not have been able to return by the same route and complete the loop.

There were six on the trip counting myself and I will refer to the others by their first names. Pete was the organizer and has been to the cave several times leading groups from his church. Josh, Tony and Pat were on the previous trip that turned around in the Raccoon Room. I believe that John was new to caving, and I have to give him a lot of credit. He has a large upper body and shoulders, and I know that the tight areas were rough. Josh was the most aggressive and wanted to lead, which was fine with me. Each time we made a wrong turn, the rest of us did not have to crawl so far.

After the climb down from the Entrance Room and through the tight crawl in the Pancake Squeeze, we made the dangerous climb up into the Raccoon Room. As you work your way up and around a ledge, there is a point where you have to lean out over the abyss below to get around a rock that prevents you from hugging the wall. If you get down really low, you can just manage to get around the rock without losing your balance. Then there is a five–foot climb with few handholds to get up into the Raccoon Room. There is a hand line here, as well in as many other places in the cave. Although most of these are nylon, they have been in place for many years, and I do not like trusting my life to their safety. Once you place your weight on the hand line, it is difficult to get a good grip on the rock again, which places you at the mercy of the old rope.

In my description of the Loop I had left out the fact that you had to climb down at the back of the Raccoon Room, and cross over several large rocks before reaching two crawls, one lower and one slightly higher. The lower crawl pinches down after a short distance and was tried by the group on the previous trip. The upper crawl was also tried but not pushed, and at this point the group turned around on the previous trip. After a short crawl through the upper crawlway and along a slit in the floor, we reached a junction. To the right it comes to a stop not far from the Flat Room and Pancake Squeeze with no connection. At the junction is a nice formation and the Rim Stone Pools. If you remain in the slit to the left, you can climb up into a nice walking passage leading to the Freeway.

In this walking passage we stopped and waited for Josh to check out a lead down. When he came back up by a different opening, I must have gotten turned around. After about five more minutes of caving Pete stated that we had been there already! Sure enough there was the formation that we had just left. I have no idea how that occurred, but we only went back a short distance. Back on the right trail again, the room suddenly filled with smoke. Someone in the lower passages must have lit up. If it was someone in our group I did not see him. Smoke can fill a cave passage very quickly. I told them that the walking passage was The Freeway, however The Freeway is the tight crawl of about thirty feet at the end of the walking passage. When we reached The Freeway, the smoke had cleared.

I believe that The Freeway was named that because of the two ruts made by your knees as you slide along. It looks like two lanes of a highway, not the easy path that the name implies. The thirty feet of crawlway were made more difficult by the fact that you could not tilt your head to see ahead. There was room for a side pack, and of course the knee ruts enable you to bend your knees to push along, but you were blind to whatever lay ahead.

When you come out of The Freeway and look back, there is a very inviting crawl just above it showing a lot of heavy traffic. No doubt a lot of people take the wrong way, which comes to a dead-end after a short distance.

An easy stroll from The Freeway brings us to the Bridge Room with some nice formations along the way. The Bridge Room is a large open area with about a seventy–foot drop down to the stream level. At one end there is a rock later mud bridge that you can cross over the chasm. Several hundred feet and we reached the Over 'N Under Room with the register. The register has not been maintained for several years. Local grottos used to leave paper and pencils there in a PVC pipe so that visitors could leave their names as a record of their visit. John and Pete remained here while Josh, Tony, Pat and I searched the Over 'N Under Room for a connecting passage to the Double Echo Domes. After about an hour of searching we found our way through a very muddy passage and heard the sound of the Waterfall. Tony and Pat, both experienced in caving, climbed down a couple of levels to get a closer look. In the mean time Josh volunteered to go back and get Pete and John just in case we decided to exit via the stream passage below.

While waiting for us, John drank a power drink loaded with caffeine. Have you ever been in a place that you were not sure that you could get out of? I have, and it is called an anxiety attack. The caffeine triggered a mild case in John, who knew that he was hours from the entrance. He kept it under control, although we were all aware of it by some of the comments he made.

We all got to listen to the sound of the Waterfall, and after a short discussion it was decided that we should stick to the original plan and exit through the Mason–Dixon passage and the Volcano Room. Josh, Pat, Tony and Pete had been to the Volcano Room before, and Josh wondered if the mud man with a hat he built was still there.

From the Bridge Room we eased our way around the drop to the stream level and the entrance of the Mason–Dixon Passage. A small hole near the ceiling, just large enough for an average sized person to squeeze through. I removed my side pack to push along in front as I crawled and suggested that the others do the same. We put our hands in front and could not change position for about twenty feet. Josh charged ahead to lead, laughing as he entered the tightest spot. This became a joke, and when he laughed we knew it was going to be tight. He was enjoying the challenge. The tighter the better. John was next as he was in a hurry to get out. After a short distance you could roll out of the crawl and head straight into a dead-end passage. We had to back up and make a left turn, crawling over a mound of dirt and into a walking passage again.

Entrance crawl to the Mason–Dixon passage

The Mason–Dixon passage is mostly walking, however about three–quarters of the way in there is a twenty–foot crawl just slightly larger than The Freeway and a little shorter. After we all exited the crawlway, John was asking how much further. We were all getting tired. I was getting some leg cramps and was ready to leave also.

When you walk out of the Mason–Dixon passage you tend to go straight for the Worm Tube. We were not up to another long crawl, so we turned back to the right to look for the way to the Volcano Room. It looked like a solid rock wall with no way through until you crawl right up to it, and then the floor drops away and you can see the next room down and under the wall. A short distance to the right and up over a few large rocks, there is another hidden door. You keep climbing toward solid rock knowing there must be a place to get through, when at last there is a small opening between the rocks just large enough to lie down and roll through into the Volcano Room.

We were all admiring Josh's mud man still standing on the edge of the Volcano as I slowly removed my side pack and began to tie the strap around it into a tight bundle. John commented, "Another tight crawl." "Right behind you," I commented back. The climb up out of the Volcano Room is very dangerous, and knowing that someone fell here and broke a leg did not help John feel any better. About ten years ago someone dug out a bypass under the wall to avoid the climb. It is tight and makes a sharp upward twist at the end. You can start in on your stomach, but if you don't roll over on your back before you reach the up part, you are in trouble. Josh went through with his usual laughing, and after he cleared out of the way I followed with much difficulty. John was right behind me, and as I got up, and out of his way I heard him yell, "I'm stuck!" I think I commented that I wished I could help, but I didn't know what I could do. Several minutes later I heard him groaning, saying that he relocated some body parts, or something to that effect. I think that John's climbing skills were improving as he was keeping up now with no trouble, even reaching back to give Pete a hand up on the next rough climb. We only had about fifteen minutes more of hard caving to reach the Entrance Room, and John said that he needed to go on out quick. I advised the others that I was leading John on out and would see them in the parking lot.

Twenty minutes later we were back in daylight after passing several new groups entering the cave. John was half dressed by the time I reached the parking lot, and about fifteen minutes later we were joined by the others. On a previous trip Tony had to take someone out from the Volcano Room. When he tried to return to join the group, he made a wrong turn and spent several hours in the Northeast stream passage until he came across another group in the same area who lead him back out. The rest of the group had come out to find that Tony was still in the cave! All of this brings up the importance of remaining together as a group when caving and watching out for each other. It was however a very good cave trip and we all learned more about the cave and each other.

After studying the map and reviewing where we were above the Waterfall, I noticed a passage with an open lead heading in the direction of the Double Echo Domes. I will have to return and check it out on a future trip. I still have a lot more to learn about Pettyjohn Cave. Now that Pete and his church group have heard the Waterfall, I am sure that the next trip will be through the stream level to the Waterfall and back. Then again, maybe I will make a large loop trip out of it and return via The Chute, Five Points, Over 'N Under Room, Bridge Room, etc.

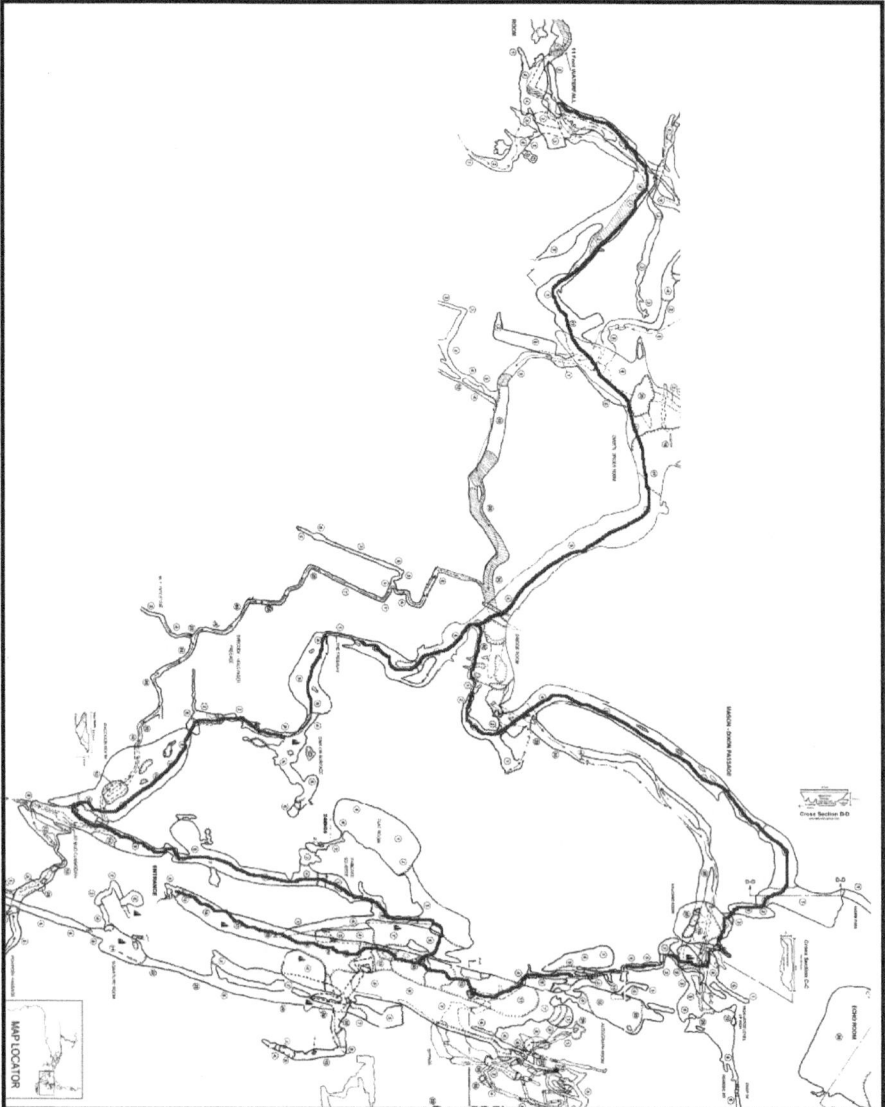

The Loop in Pettyjohn Cave

CHAPTER 14 EXPLORATION OF PUMPHOUSE CAVE

In 1984, while visiting relatives in Tennessee, they told me of their water supply, a pump house at the base of a large hill where they pumped water from a cave lake located below. A previous owner had used cinder blocks to block the entrance to a cave in the side of the hill and built a small dam to back up the stream flowing from the cave. As caving was my hobby, I became very interested and at once wanted to investigate this underground lake. This was too good to pass up. I persuaded one of my relatives, Doc, Lvurn Loftin, to go with me and wait at the entrance while I checked out the cave.

This is my second most favorite cave, after Pettyjohn Cave. Number three is Tumbling Rock Cave.

Pumphouse Cave

With no caving gear and just a flashlight, I thought that I would just see if it amounted to anything. Raising the plywood door at the bottom of the pump house, I entered the cave by wading in ten inches of water for a few feet, and then looked for a way to continue. The ceiling came down to the water, but to the left along the back side of the cinder block wall was a twenty foot long crawl that led to a four foot high room at the edge of the water. After wading through about 100 feet of a low water–filled passage, I was able to stand up in a larger room with the stream flowing along one side. This room had two columns in the middle and several small holes leading off in different directions. I followed the stream for about forty feet and then reentered the stream, which continued in a six foot high by five foot wide passage. The water was now deeper and waist level, and was about fifty–five degrees. I continued to navigate over the rocky bottom around three turns by staying to the sides where the mud and water were not so deep. Alone and with limited light, I called it quits for the day. It would be two years before I could return to push this tantalizing lead.

Caving Alone

Caving alone is not recommended and could be fatal, however I believe that caving is a lone sport, even when you are with a group. Most cavers are quiet and intent on the cave in front of them as their headlight only shows them a small part of the cave at any one time.

I have caved alone on two occasions, once as a small boy and now checking out my cousins' cave. There is a special peace and satisfaction that comes from exploring alone that is hard to explain. Floyd Collins almost always explored alone, and I think that I can understand why. When working your way through a small passage or checking out a lead ahead of the group, you get a chance to really be alone in the total darkness and silence. There is very little life in a cave, and the chance now days of running upon a bear den is rare, however not completely out of the question. For some reason I have never feared the unknown of a cave. I have experienced fear in the woods at night, but not in a cave. It somehow feels safe there. Back in Grassy Cove, Saltpeter Cave, when I had the pleasure of being first to explore that hole that we dug open, it left with me a memory I will never forget, sitting on that ledge and peering off into the blackness, knowing that no one had ever been there before. I did not want it to end, but I knew the others were anxious to hear what I had found. Even when I was stuck in that New York cave, there was a peace about the whole thing, a temptation to just relax in my trapped position and stay there! Floyd must have felt that way many times as he waited alone in that Kentucky cave.

October 25, 1986

About once a month, a small group of friends and I would go caving in well known caves in northeast Alabama, northwest Georgia and east

Tennessee, referred to by the caving society as TAG country. This area is well known for deep pits and long caves. On each trip I would tell them about the cave on my cousins' property, and we would discuss checking it out. We at last set a date and drove up from Marietta, Georgia on a Saturday. There had been a heavy storm the night before, and my cousin said that he had seen the plywood door pushed up and completely open by the water rushing out of the cave after a hard rain.

Roger and Buddy entering under the pump house

Before getting dressed in our caving gear, we walked down to the entrance to check the water level. It was running normal, however it is not unusual for caves to flood hours after a heavy rain. The temptation was too great, so we suited up for caving. Each member of the group carried three sources of light, with one attached to a hard hat with a chin strap. Gloves are required if you plan to take any notes or surveys. In addition to the survey gear, consisting of a Sonic tape measure, electronic Smart level with a laser pointer attached, and a Data Scope compass, each member carried water and a snack. We adopted the map–as–you–go method of exploration. This requires great restraint on the part of each member not to scoop passage. Scooping passage is when a few members would stop the survey and start exploring on their own. This usually results in explored passages not being completely mapped.

Our first mapping party consisted of Buddy Davis, Roger Garratt, John Wallace and myself. We entered the cave and decided to see if it amounted to much before starting to survey, then we would survey our way out. We followed the stream around several turns for about 300 feet, coming out of the water near a T–junction. We followed the main stream through walking passage until it became blocked by breakdown with the stream flowing from under the rocks.

Buddy and John testing the water

At this point, there were no footprints or other signs that anyone had been this far into the cave. We started the survey at the breakdown, working back downstream to the junction. We then took the survey up the side passage, exploring as we mapped. We climbed up about 3 feet with a smaller stream flowing below. We mapped into the bottom of a large pit and then about 50 feet more before the passage became too tight.

Returning to the pit, Buddy and I climbed up and continued the survey while John and Roger retreated back along the passage to check a lead going up at a formation on the left. After mapping a formation room at one level, we climbed to the top of the pit and found large walking passage going in both directions. We explored in one direction for several hundred feet, then returned to the top of the pit, where we were surprised to hear John and Roger coming up the passage from the other direction. They had found a connecting passage around the pit.

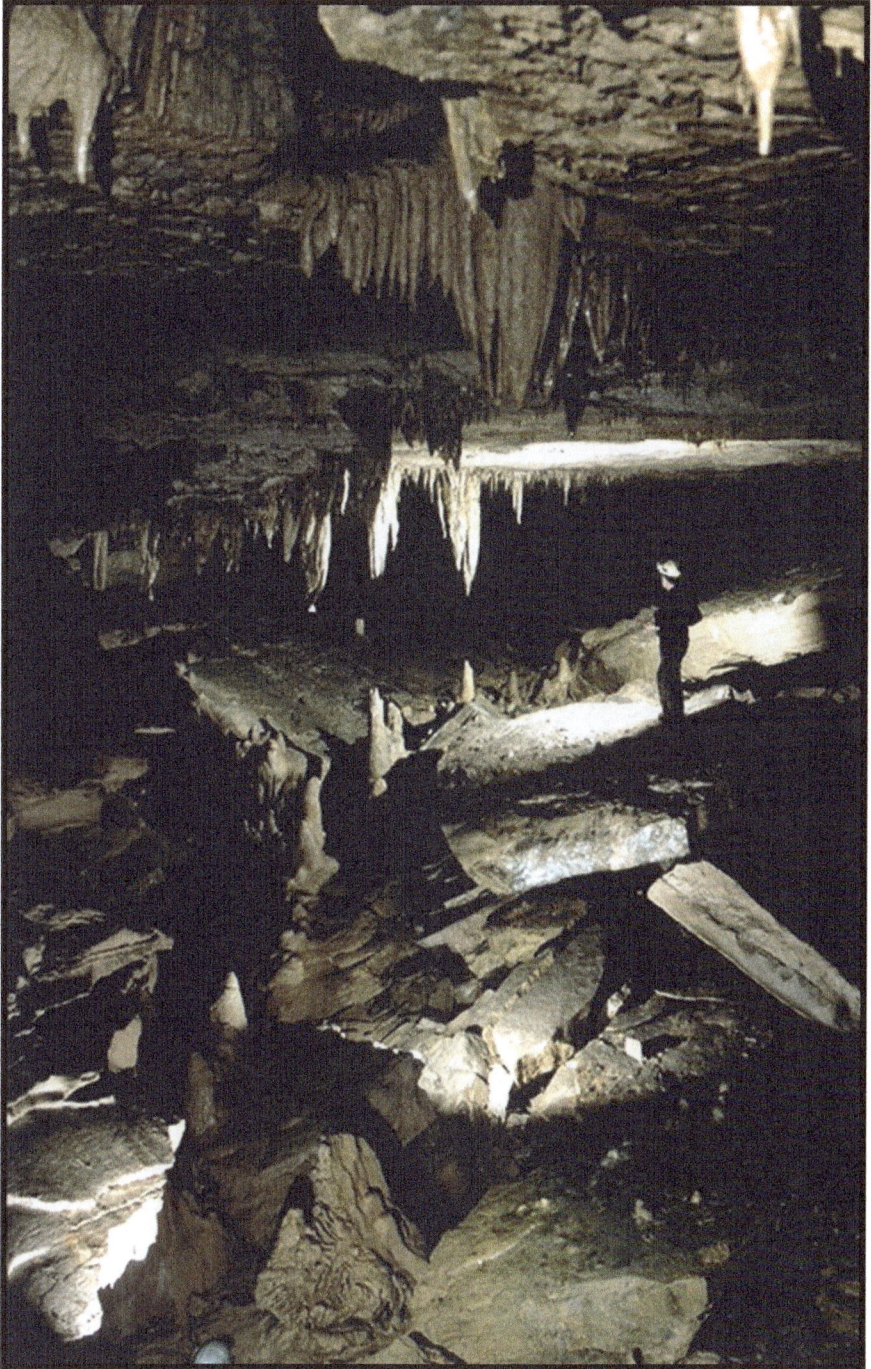

The Hope Room. Photo by Roger Bartholomew

We mapped down the large passage going southeast then turned back to the left to a large breakdown room almost directly over the point where the stream started and where we had first started our survey. Going up and over very loose breakdown, we entered another large passage, which was blocked at the end by a small ten foot pit with a stream flowing across the bottom.

On a later trip Buddy Davis was the first to cross the narrow ledge on the side of the pit, so I have decided to name it Davis Pit. We decided to quit for the day and went back to map the connection John and Roger had found.

Clark Columns

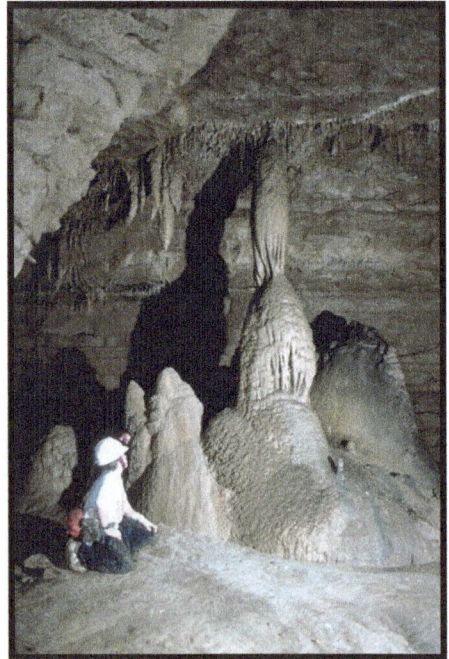

Buddy working his way around Davis Pit

This connection passed two of the largest formations in the cave, which I named Clark Columns, in honor of my first cousins' family name and owner of the property. On a later trip we discovered a large formation room at a higher level. We exited the cave after six hours, having mapped 2,380 feet, all mostly walking passage with many leads to be checked.

January 31, 1987

We added the following to our survey team: John Huggins, Bill Luchring, Jack Pace and Jeffrey Smith.

We started climbing up at the point where Roger and John found the bypass on the last trip. We found that the passage continued to the southeast and up with pits and a large upper room very high in the cave, and we named this The Upper Room. There was a walking lead at the back and one lead going down which was pushed by Jack and Buddy, it would be 1995 before we would map this lead!

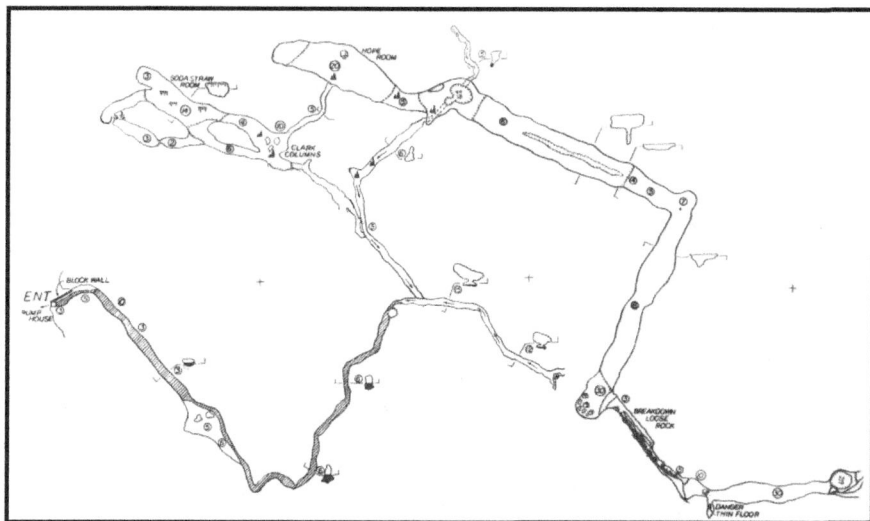

2,380 feet at the end of the first mapping trip

On the way back down, we mapped a high passage going northwest through the best formation room found so far in the cave. A passage behind several large columns continued about 100 feet with soda straws covering the ceiling. The length of the cave was now 3,729 feet long.

A nice treat at the end of each trip to this cave was a catfish dinner just down the road. We would change clothes and just walk the mile to the restaurant! They have large ponds where they raise the catfish. The ponds are fed with water from another cave system.

The room of Soda Straws. Photo by Roger Bartholomew

February 20, 1988

Buddy Davis, Mark Gramlich, Roger Garratt and I returned to push the southeast end of the cave as mapping indicated it as the best possible way for the cave to continue. We brought a rubber raft to try and avoid getting so wet in the entrance stream passage. We waded into the dry area at the first room with the two rock columns and inflated the raft. We could not quite reach both sides of the passage at the same time, so it was difficult to push our way up the stream. Near the end of the deepest section the raft brushed against the sharp rocks and started to leak air. On the return trip out it was useless. we gave up on the raft idea and just decided to tough it out on future trips. You are only in the water for the first and last twenty minutes of each trip, and if you can keep to the sides in the shallow area you only get wet to the crouch. Slip or step in the middle and you're wet to the waist!

On reaching Davis Pit, the pit with the stream, several leads were checked to find a way around. One hole just prior to the pit led to the bottom, and a short upstream passage ended with the stream flowing from under a rock wall. Downstream was blocked at the pit's edge. Finding no easy way around the pit, Buddy edged his way out onto the sloping ledge that went around the right side of the pit, up a steep slope and over a lip. The left passage went down to the stream that was flowing across Davis Pit. This was very dangerous, and on future trips we carried rope to use as a safety line in order to keep from falling down the ten foot pit. This stream was much smaller than the one flowing out of the cave. The passage ended shortly with water dripping form the ceiling. We returned in 1993 to map a 300 foot side passage from this stream passage.

Back at Davis Pit we climbed up to the right into a passage that continued with easy walking about 200 feet and led to the top edge of a large room with rock sliding down to a good sized stream. We decided that we must be back at the main stream level and wondered how much cave we had passed up.

Calling it quits at the top of a large dark void

Off to the left of this room was a large, lower room with crystals on the walls and floor. We named it the Gypsum Room. After a short investigation we decided to save it for another trip. This was turning out to be a major cave with 4,343 feet mapped and many leads waiting to be checked.

March 26, 1988

John Wallace was back with us, as he was unable to make the previous trip. I had been caving with John since the 70's. We met at one of the Dogwood City Grotto meetings in Atlanta. I had contacted the Grotto after a trip to Alabama in which we wasted a half day looking for a cave that I do not think existed. However that stirred up a new interest in caving, and I wanted to see more wild caves. I caved with John about every month for almost twenty years before he was killed in an unfortunate auto accident. John encouraged me to continue my cave map programming. He had a gift, for encouraging everyone he came into contact with to work hard at what they loved to do.

Before climbing down the rock slide, we mapped the large room to the left and found large paw marks on the mud walls in sets of four, as if a large animal had been trapped.

Back of the Gypsum Room

At the back of a side lead off this room, John pushed a crawl with sticks and surface debris. This is named John's Push on the map and could be checked later for a possible connection to a known cave on the side of the hill that we were caving in.

On the way out I was sitting on a small ledge with the rest of the group across the passage from me, when all of a sudden the ledge gave way. As I slid down the almost vertical wall, one leg behind the other, all I could see was large rocks coming up fast. I was not hurt but I was shook up. The extended leg went between two rocks, and the bent leg stopped on top of one. I just crawled out under the ledge the others were sitting on and rested for a good while.

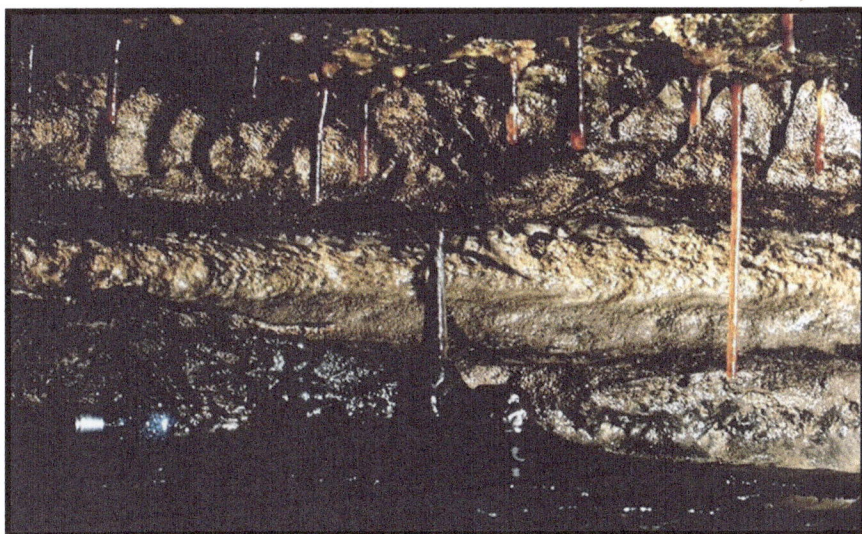

Blood Passage. Photo by Roger Bartholomew

Returning to the rock slide, we mapped down to the stream flowing under a ledge. At the south end of the room was a small pool containing several small fish. They did not appear to be blind, as they would try to hide from the light behind our boots. The passage continued on to the southeast. We took the upper level with the survey, and Roger followed staying in the lower passage.

Blood Passage was named for several red formations about halfway through this long, narrow passage. The lower level turned out to be a walking sized dry stream bed. Again we reached a junction, mapped the left lead to low crawls, and returned to verify that the right lead continued for another trip. The survey totaled 5,910 feet, and the cave was still going! There are some very long caves in the southeast, but most caves are under a mile in length. We were very excited to be exploring over a mile of cave and still going.

On the way out Buddy and I checked a lead going down between the pit and the breakdown. This led to the stream with a possible connection and a good walking lead going upstream.

July 23, 1988

The National Speleological Society (NSS) holds a convention each year, and in 1988 we met in the Black Hills of South Dakota. After returning from the NSS convention, we were all fired up to continue our explorations, so I advised my cousin to save up some drinking water. After each exploration, it took several days for the muddied drinking water to clear.

Roger Hall. Photo by Roger Bartholomew

Buddy, Roger and I were on our best trip so far. We started out pushing the stream level, and by moving several rocks, we were able to continue at water level for about 100 feet, reaching the place where Buddy and I climbed down on the previous trip.

We mapped upstream with wide walking passage and domes, and crossed the stream several times. We named it Roger Hall, after the survey leader. After a low section we came into a large room, studying it for a while, and decided it was the Slide Room. We had connected for a large loop through the cave which would make a good short tour with very little repeat of passage.

Refreshed from our dip in the stream, (I was the only one with a wet suit), we continued to the southeast end of the cave. From the Fish Pond on we have saw no moving water, only pools.

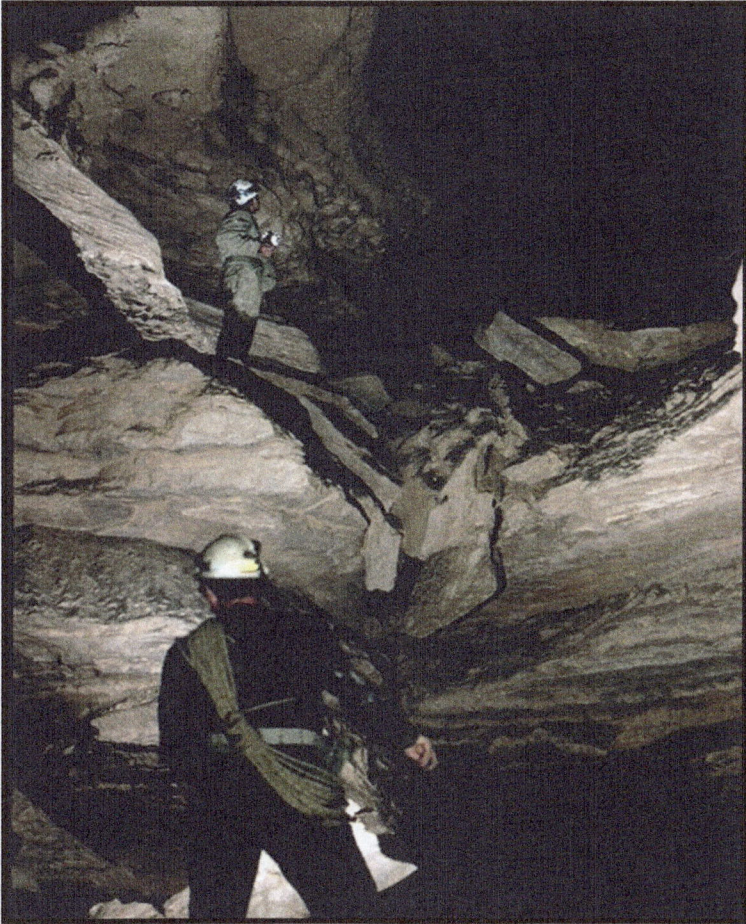

Photo by Roger Bartholomew

Picking up the survey, we began climbing again. About seventy-five feet ahead we crossed over a deep pool of water, the Blue Hole, then we went over a lip into a large room that showed evidence of filling with mud and water. The Catch Basin had filled up, spilling over the lip and creating the Blue Hole. We entered a narrow opening in the far wall, went down into the water and ducked under a ledge. With water to our chests, we climbed another wall and mapped about 150 feet of crawl until it got too tight.

Returning to the Catch Basin, we could see a high lead about twenty feet up a steep mud slope. Digging footholds for fifteen minutes, we found a large oval room overlooking the Catch Basin with another large walking lead continuing to the southeast. We named this room the Oval Office.

The climb up to the Oval Office. Photo by Roger Bartholomew

WE mapped through the Crystal Hall, which was covered with calcite crystals, and the Slab room. The floor was covered with large thin slabs of rock, and we finally met our challenge.

We were at the top of another large room with vertical walls and two deep pools at the bottom. Along the right side was a large rock leaning out over the pools, leaving a narrow passage between it and the wall. However, no way could be found around the room. Our lights could barely make out a dark opening on the far side at our level and about forty feet up a vertical wall. Buddy climbed down to the pools, slid on the mud slide and went in without touching the bottom. He was able to reach a space between the pools where the mud was less than a foot deep, but could not find a way up the far wall.

The mid–level formation room is the first large room we entered from the stream level. We climbed up into the room from the lower left of the large formations through a crack that starts at the bottom of the large white formation. To the right of the picture below you can jump across a five foot drop to climb up into the Mouse Passage.

The Upper Level Formation Room is up and behind this picture, which was taken on the way to the formation room. Straight ahead the large passage leads up to the Upper Room. Just out of view in this picture is the Lost Column, with lower passages down and to the right. To the left is the climb down under the overhanging rock to the passages that lead to the back of the cave. The bat guano in this room is several inches thick on the floor, but is old and not active. I have not seen any bats in the cave, probably due to the fact that the previous farmer had sealed off the entrance for the pump house years ago.

Mid–level formation room

Buddy at the top of Buddy's Plunge. Photo by Roger Bartholomew

The topographical map shows a sink on top of Eddy Hill that is about 400 to 500 feet from Buddy's Plunge. The cave length was now 7,698 feet, but there is more cave left for future explorations. An account of the exploration to this point was written up by me and published in the July 1989 issue of the NSS News.

August 27, 1988

Roger Garratt, John Wallace, Mark Gramlich, Roy Dunn, Phil Larkin, Mark Pegin and I made a five hour trip to try and scale the wall from

Buddy's Plunge. This was mostly a sight–seeing trip with one goal. To climb the wall on the far side of the twin pools. It took us about 2 hours to reach the known southeast end of the cave. After climbing down to the pools with the aid of a rope, we explored the far wall in detail and found that the bolts that I had brought for scaling the wall were not needed. A narrow opening was found on the right side, and we could chimney up to the passage above.

The walking passage continued for several hundred feet before being blocked with loose rocks. Climbing over the loose rocks, the cave ended in a small dome where the ceiling had collapsed, blocking any continuing of the cave to the southeast. The length of the cave was now 7,918 feet.

The collapsed cave. Photo by Roger Bartholomew

August 2, 1989

The NSS Convention of 1989 was held in Sewanee, Tennessee, high on Mounteagle at the University of the South. It was only a short drive from there to the cave, so I led a group of eleven people from the convention on a caving trip. Larry Clauser, Scott Jones, Ken Law, Mark McCandless, Kevin Regan, Paul Donis, Jim Steet, Danny Gillespie, Kathy Welling, Andy Franklin and myself, Hubert Crowell.

Although this was the largest group to enter the cave at one time and only a 4 1/2 hour trip, two major discoveries were made. When the group reached the first breakdown, where the tight water passage starts, several members climbed up through an opening in the right side which led to the upper rooms of the cave. This saved about 30 minutes of caving to reach that level and was used on almost every trip that followed.

After exploring the large upper rooms, someone asked about a lead down through the breakdown on the north side of the room When I looked down I saw a very familiar rock, one we discussed each time we crawled under it. It was fastened to the wall by flow stone, and the floor had dropped away, leaving it extending about 3 feet from the wall at a right angle.

A scary passage under loose rock!

Climbing down this newest connection provided easy access to the back part of the cave. I led the group down two climbs from this point to where the stream picks up again, and we finished up with a round trip through Roger Hall, the Slide Room and back out.

February 17, 1990

Survey team Hubert Crowell, John Wallace, Mark Gramlich, and Roger Garratt explored for about 5 hours. After taking the new easy route to the large upper rooms, John found a passage leading down and south near the first large pit in the big room. Before climbing down into this new section, we stopped for a good view of the Lost Column. At one time there was a large column here which was cut away by the water and formed a pit. There is a nice window that you can stand in and look down at the pit, the edges of the old column forming the sides of the window.

Our new survey started here and went down and to the south. We mapped through a large walking passage with large deposits of bat guano and several leads going down. After several levels and a tight vertical squeeze, we returned to walking passage for about 50 feet. The passage split, and then both leads ended with about 350 feet mapped. We named this John's Grotto.

We then went to the stream level and mapped a short upstream lead. We now had a total of 8,366 feet of passage mapped.

June 23, 1990

Buddy Davis and I returned to check out the latest discovery at the south end of the cave and to check or more leads.

Returning to John's Grotto, we pushed one of the lower leads to a low lead with a mud cobble stone–like floor and named it Cobble Stone Alley. Several leads were checked, and one smelled like gas. It was in this area that we found a strange side passage with the strong smell of sulfur. We were not able to remain in the area for too long due to the odor. After another short walking passage the south end of the cave ended with loose rock. I believe that we were very close to the south side of the hill. All of the cave is above the valley floor and contained in one long narrow hill.

After mapping about 610 feet of new passage with more leads remaining, we exited the cave. Neil Philpott wanted to see the cave and said that he had gone a short distance into it when he was a kid. We took him back to the area we had just explored, where he pushed a new lead and discovered a small room. This was the first cave trip for Neil. He is the son of Bonnie and Billy Philpott, who own the cave. We named the cave after the owners and the pump house, Philpotts' Pumphouse Cave.

January 26, 1991

On the second trip into the cave we noticed that the west end of the large upper room was a question mark as our light would not reach the distant wall. However there was a ravine to cross before we could explore that end of the cave, so it was left for another time.

John Wallace, Mark Gramlich, Frank Dalton and I explored and mapped for a short three and one half hour trip. We mapped along the stream and up through the new connection to the waiting lead. I was able to jump the five foot gap and set a hand line.

Mouse Passage

We mapped up the Mouse Passage, named for the small field mouse seen in the passage, which curved up and around with nice formations.

John Wallace at the end of Mouse Passage

The passage ended with a nice grotto of formations and roots hanging from the roof. The roots had formations growing from them, leading us to believe that formation growth can be very fast under the right conditions. they were about three to four inches in length and were not connected to rock except by the roots.

The length of the level survey was now 8,859 feet with many leads remaining to be pushed.

June 19, 1993

A 6 hour trip by John Hickman, Annette Oeser Ken Oeser, Doug Dewitt, Rob Morgan and I. Doug discovered Doug's Shortcut, another shortcut from the middle cave to the lower stream level. This was in an area just prior to Davis Pit, a side lead to the right that looked very dangerous. Just as you entered the side passage the floor had a hole, and the edges looked like very thin rock with a large opening below. We marked the map with a note, "Danger thin floor."

After carefully walking around the thin area, Doug climbed up to a small opening near the ceiling and found that there was a passage continuing down with several short drops, the last drop being about an eight foot drop into the stream passage below.

6/19/93
BY: KEN OESER

Annette Oeser in the mid-level formation room

Ken was on a photo trip and took some great pictures of the large main room, one level up from the stream passage.

After crossing Davis Pit, we went back down to the north stream that we explored in 1988 to check out the side passage running north. We mapped about 300 feet and stopped with the crawl containing rim stone dams. To continue on would have destroyed the formations. The passage was named after Ken (Oeser Passage). The total cave length was now 9,444 feet of level survey. There are two lengths used in measuring a cave, the total survey length and the total level survey. The level survey is the most common way to refer to the length of a horizontal cave, and total survey when discussing vertical caves.

October 1, 1994

This was a family gathering as well as a caving trip, and we hoped it would turn into a yearly event.

Roger Bartholomew, Buddy Davis, Doug Dewitt, Rob Morgan, Jerry Zeiger, Stacy Story and I returned to show Roger and Jerry the cave. Roger flew in from upstate New York, and Jerry, my first cousin, drove down from Kentucky. This was his first cave trip and he loved it. We took the original trail in, wading through the water and then climbing up and to the left at the first junction. At the first formation we climbed up to the left through the passage that John and Roger discovered on our first mapping trip. We then climbed up into the Clark Column room. These are two large columns named after our grandfather Luther Clark. Bonnie Philpott was a Clark, and Jerry and my mothers were Clarks.

Roger took pictures throughout the cave while Buddy took Doug and Rob off to explore a passage he looked at on the first trip into the cave. After several hours we all met at the Clark Columns, where we discovered a strange formation around the base of the column.

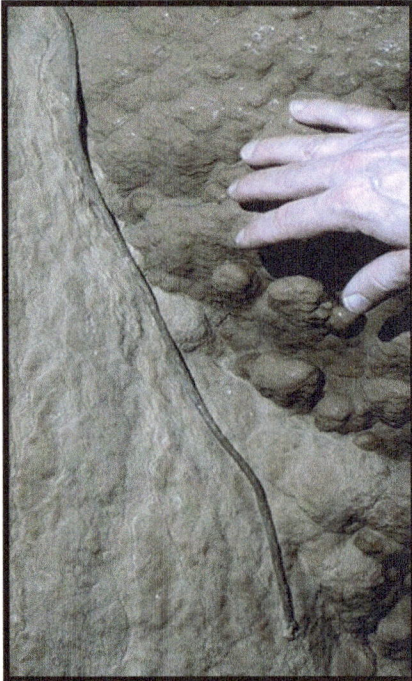

About a year after the cave was discovered, Bonnie allowed a teacher from the local high school to bring his class into the cave. We had cleaned up most of the trash left by the students, but one of them had draped a shoe string on the side of one of the Clark Columns. When I first spotted the string it had already started to crust over with calcite and had become part of the formation. I left it there as a test to see how fast the formation was growing. On this trip I was surprised to find that it had almost disappeared with a 1/32 inch coating of stone in only 8 years with no water flow, only the moisture of the cave! I do not think that you would be able to find it now.

Shoe String! Photo by Roger Bartholomew

Leaving the Clark Columns, we continued through a nice clean crawl, then over some raccoon bones and up into the Hope Room. We named this room in the hope that we had found the main trunk passage of the cave on that first mapping trip. However the large passage ended a short distance to the northwest, and to the southeast became a lower passage, after climbing around the pit that I climbed in 1986

Left to right, Buddy Davis, Jerry Zeiger, Hubert Crowell in the Hope Room. Photo by: Roger Bartholomew

This passage continues for about 200, feet then makes a sharp right turn for about another 100 feet of break down. The end of this passage is directly over the main entrance stream where it flows from under the break down. A short distance to the left and up brings you to a very noticeable rock of about 500 pounds stuck to the left wall. Minerals had glued the rock to the side of the cave, and the floor settled away, leaving the rock exposed. You do not spend much time under this rock! It did however make a good marker for the spot to climb up into the main room just north of the Lost Column. The fastest route to the back of the cave would be to climb up from the stream passage and over to the Lost Column, and then down at the overhanging rock. We then continued over the break down crawl. (This would be to the right if you were climbing down from the main room. After a short distance you reach the hard climb up from the stream.) At this point half of the group was tired and decided to exit the cave. Roger, Buddy and I continued taking pictures along the way. We took this easy route, climbing down, where is hard to climb back up, and plan to return via the slide room and Davis pit. After reaching the stream and strolling down Roger Hall, we turned back to the left and waded bent over to the slide room.

Crossing the Fish Pond we entered Blood Passage. From the Slide Room, when you look at the Blood Passage, you can see three levels of passages. We had explored two of them but had not found the way to the third upper level passage. We followed the lower Blood Passage as it was all walking and arrived at the large junction room. Just prior to the Junction Room, I climbed up to the middle level and then found that I could inch my way up the slope to the third level. With the passage heading back toward the Slide Room, we decided to save it for a future survey trip.

We then climbed up through the right passage from the Junction Room, across the Blue Hole and down into the Catch Basin. Up the mud footholds that were dug on a previous trip, through the Oval Office, Crystal Hall, Slab Room and at last to Buddy's Plunge where we planned to take some pictures.

Roger brought a bright flash unit and took some great pictures. He seemed surprised and said that we sure had a great cave here.

September 29, 1995

Doug Dewitt drove down from West Virginia for two days of caving, spending the night at my cousins'. The two of us returned to the Upper Room to explore and map the side lead that Jack and Buddy checked out in 1987 and that Buddy, Doug and Rob looked for on the previous trip.

We climbed down about 30 feet to some white soda straws and formations, and then the passage split with one lead going straight down and another going along the side of the wall to the left. We mapped about 50 feet to the end and then returned to the down climb. This downward passage continued down to a tight duck under. I pushed under and down. Doug called me "LOOPY" and the name was given to the passage.

Loopy Passage reached a small drop to a lower level passage but was blocked with two large rocks. Doug managed to dislodge them and let them fall into the passage below. The passage looked very familiar, and after finding footprints I realized it was the Cobble Stone Alley. We completed the map from the Upper Room down to the Cobble Stone Alley. I was thankful that I did not have to climb back up that passage. We have never repeated that route. We exited the cave through John's Grotto.

September 30, 1995

The next day Doug Dewitt, Stacy Daniel and I mapped Stacy Passage (64 feet) going north from the Fish Pond. We then mapped the Blood Passage lower level (410 feet), checked out the left passage at the Junction Room, and discovered Crystal Crawl. Doug got very excited about the crystals on the ledge near the end, so Stacy and I climbed up to check them out. The crystals were large, up to four inches in length and 1/2 inch across. Doug continued up the passage to the end of the previous survey and named the passage Crystal Crawl. This was a low crawl that Doug pushed through with some difficulty. He started digging and moving rocks to the side, after twelve feet he found Doug's Room and the Root Cellar (150 feet).

The Root Cellar reminded me of the bottom of a cellar or septic tank. There was water dripping everywhere, with roots hanging down about twenty feet with water running down them. The ends of the roots were about four feet from the floor. I was not too sure about the place as I knew that there was a house located on the surface nearby on this side of the hill. While Doug was setting a survey station at the end of the Root Cellar, Stacy found a low crawl at the base of the pit with loose gravel that lead to another dome about eight by ten. We did not dig into it but left it for Stacy and another day. On this trip we reached 10,292 feet of cave passage mapped, which is 1.9 miles.

January 25, 1996

Buddy Davis, Jan Poler, Doug Dewitt, Donna Oliverson, Stacy Danniel, Jason Johnson and I returned to the junction room just after Blood Passage and climbed up to the third level of Blood Passage. We discovered Jason's Attic and Jason Squeeze.

Jason's Attic, the third level above the Blood Passage

April 20, 1996

During the Clark family reunion at the Dubose conference center at Monteagle, Tennessee, Gene Zeigler, Jon Zeigler, Stacy Daniel, Jason Johnson and I took a four hour sight seeing tour to show Gene, Jerry's brother, the cave.

We made a large loop through the front section of the cave visiting, Clark Columns, the Soda Straw Room, Hope Room, Upper Room, and then went down through Loopy Passage to the Cobble Stone Alley and out.

At Clark Columns, Gene explored a grotto that went up, near the Soda Straw room, and found a long root about the size of your small finger. We named the room the Rope Root Room. The Soda Straw room was mapped on the first trip. This almost makes a loop. After going about 100 feet through a room full of soda straws, hollow water filled formations hanging from the ceiling, the passage drops down to a walking passage for about 50 feet. Near the end you can climb up through a hole and across a nice pool into a 3 foot high room about 50 feet long. At the end there is a small opening where you can shake hands with someone who has gone down a side passage to the left of the columns.

After leaving Hope Room and at the edge of the large pit, Jon Zeigler explored a new formation room for about 20 feet with very nice red and white formations. We named it Zeigler's Grotto.

Zeigler's Grotto

Although we did not survey, we have some new areas to map later, and we did pick up some old survey markers left on the last trip.

August 2, 1998

Upper Formation Room

T. John and I, after the 1998 NSS convention, which was again held in Sewanee, Tennessee, stopped by for a photo trip to the upper formation room. T. John is his real name, just the letter T.

T John in the crawl way to the Upper Formation Room

Upper Formation Room

April 28, 2001

Buddy Davis , Jason Johnson, and I mapped the upper level, which is the third level, over Blood Passage (427.18 feet). The level survey was now 10,856.93 feet, and the total survey length is 11,296.52 feet. We have passed the 2 mile mark!

Our thanks to Billy and Bonnie Philpott for letting us explore their cave.

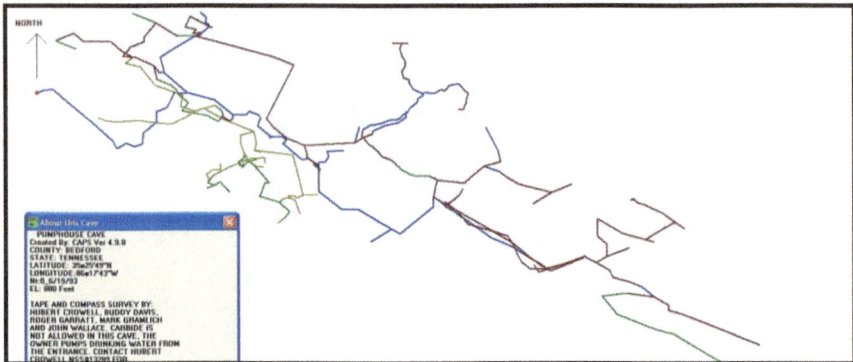

Survey line map, level cave 10,867 feet, 2.05 miles

Just above the Blue Hole. Photo by Roger Bartholomew

ABOUT THE AUTHOR

Hubert Crowell 1941- Born in Kentucky, currently writes, explores caves, plays the fiddle and works three days a week. He has in the past panned for gold, served in the army, and repaired TV's, microfilm equipment, video projectors and other electronic devices. He has taught classes at a vocational school, Eastman Kodak and at church. He has worked at Lockheed, Kodak, BARCO and RCA, to mention only a few. He studied at Southeastern University and Chattahoochee Technical College. Hubert's articles, poems and music can be found at:
 http://www.hubertcrowell.name

Other Books by Hubert Crowell

Available at: http://www.amazon.com/-/e/B0058A2NUC

Blue Skies of August

Chapbook, poems are about childhood, outdoors, exploring caves and other life experiences. Contains color pictures. This is a paperback thirty-eight pages, twenty-seven poems and three fiddle tunes. Rated safe for family reading.

Challenges of Life

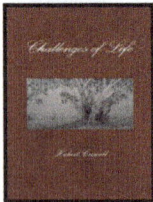

Chapbook, poems are about life in the Southeast and some of the challenges that life brings. Contains color pictures. This is a paperback thirty-three pages and twenty-seven poems. Rated safe for family reading.

Drawn to Darkness

Drawn to Darkness is a short fiction, drawn however from experiences as a child growing up in the 50's and living in the mountains. The cave along the Piney River is real and I explored it as I played there alone. The cave in the book is totally fictitious, but so much like the many caves found in the mountains of Tennessee. This book is about exploration and adventure, about young people having fun and getting to know each other. I have always heard that true stories are stranger than fiction. The fiction in this book is biased on parts of true stories put

244

together for Jimmy, the main character and his friends, John, Clair, and Joann. Centers around teenagers in a small Tennessee mountain town, growing up in an age of uncertainty and threat of nuclear war. But free to explore the world around them. This is a paperback sixty-five pages. Rated safe for family reading.

Pushing The Limit

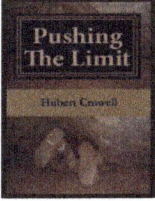

Chapbook, poems are about caving, exploration, panic, humor and self improvement. If you would like to motivate yourself and get out of your comfort zone, then this collection of poems may be for you. Pushing The Limit is about exploring the last frontier and more. Pushing the underground world of wonder and mystery was one of the author's greatest physical challenges. Life throws a lot at us, making experience a great teacher. The author shares some of his experiences so that others might try to get just a little more out of life. We only have one shot at life, so why not push the limit in everything that you do. You will feel much better and get more enjoyment out of all the challenges that life has to offer. Contains color pictures. This is a paperback thirty-nine pages and thirty poems. Rated safe for family reading.

Slight Interruptions

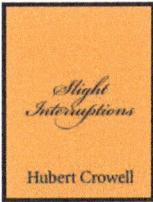

Chapbook, poems are about life in Georgia, some of the trials, interruptions that come in life and healing that follows. Contains color pictures. This is a paperback book of thirty-two pages and twenty-seven poems, glossy photo paper cover. Great for gifts. Rated safe for family reading.

Trees, Bees and Weeds

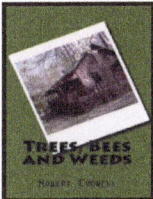

Chapbook, poems are about nature, people, and other life experiences. This is a paperback book of forty-four pages, twenty-six poems, and seven fiddle tunes, glossy photo paper cover. Great for gifts. Rated safe for family reading.

Winter in Georgia

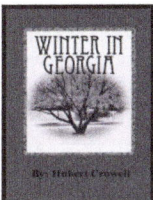

Chapbook, poems are about life in Georgia during the winter of 2011, storms, humor, blessings and experiences. Contains color pictures. This is a paperback thirty-two pages and twenty-eight poems. Rated safe for family reading.

Time to Pause

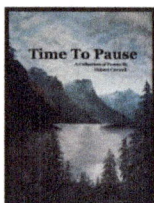

Chapbook, poems are about animals we live around, nature and its affects on us and other things to pause and think about. Contains color pictures. This is a paperback with thirty-six pages, twenty-eight poems, with a glossy photo paper cover. Rated safe for family reading.

FOOTNOTES

---

[1] BIOGRAPHY OF Hubert Hunter Crowell, 1913-1996, written by my dad on May 11, 1989 in Sebring, Florida.

I am currently a retired coal miner and disabled World War II veteran, who was born January 24, 1913 in Providence, Kentucky. I left school in the eighth grade to work with my father, James A. Crowell, in the coal mine. I was buried under a rock fall at age 14, resulting in a broken ankle. When I was 16, in 1929, I went to work at South East Coal Company at Seco, Kentucky until the Great Depression forced me out of a job and back to West Kentucky, where I went back into the eighth grade at the age of 18, in 1931.

I graduated from Providence High School in 1936, was class president and played 25 football games without being substituted. Following graduation in 1936 I married Ola Clark, also of Providence, Kentucky, and later moved to Pontiac, Michigan, where I spent a year doing odd jobs and where our first daughter, Patricia, was born. I returned to coal mining in Providence until 1939, where I helped carry some 20 miners out of Ruckman's Mine, all killed in an explosion. Then we moved to Seco, Kentucky, where I worked in the mines and attended mining school for a 20 night course. I received my First Class Mining Certificate at Lexington, Ky., on June 4, 1941, and our son, Hubert Clark was born in August. I remained in Seco, working as Section Foreman until 1943, when I moved my family back to Providence and worked in a shipyard in Evansville, Ind., until April 1943.

During the winter of 1943 I operated a small independent coal mine until receiving my draft notice in 1944 because I had changed jobs. Sixteen weeks of basic training followed at Camp Fannin, Texas.

On September 10, 1944, I left Boston Harbor on the U.S.S. Mt. Washington for a seven day trip to England, then 12 hours across England by train to Southampton, where I spent the night on a boat in the English Channel. From Omaha Beach I traveled by Red Ball Express train (box cars for 40 men or 8 horses) across France to Heerlen, Holland, a five day trip, to the replacement camp.

In October, 1944, I was sent to the 30th Division Company G, 119th 2nd Platoon, which was made up mostly of replacements as the whole platoon had been captured in Coalshied, Germany. During November we trained with tanks in Guapin, Holland, and I was injured in my right eye during a football game. The injury sent me to a hospital in France for three weeks, then I rejoined the replacements in Coalshied.

On December 16, 1944, our troops were trucked to the Rorer River to start crossing, but the operation was cancelled, and we were returned to Coalshied the same day. That night was spent in confusion on blacked out trucks headed to stop the German breakthrough. The night of December 18th, was spent in Stavlot, Belgium and on the 19th we moved to Stoumount, Belgium. There I saw my first dead German soldier, but not the last.

On December 21, we were sent behind German lines to block the main road between Stoumount and LeGlaze. I dug a foxhole (which is still there), from where I watched Major McGowan pass by and be captured. A German halftrack stopped 50 feet from us and emptied a full belt of 50 caliber machine gun ammo at our hole. My buddy, Dyer, killed the German as he ran from the halftrack. Our platoon held off the Germans as the battalion retreated. We had three wounded, including Davis, a 200 pound man who we had to carry.

December 22nd I was sent in a six man patrol to find the German army which had left the Castle of Froidgour 15 minutes before us. While searching houses in Stoumount on December 23, I found 250 citizens sheltering in the basement of St. Edouard's Preventorium. We attacked the Germans at LeGlaze on December 24th, coming in through the woods. I shot a half track twice with my Bazooka, three Germans were nearby. I used my last round to shoot a King Tiger tank. This is still there and is now part of the museum at LeGlaze. The same day I walked to Tri Points to guard the bridge there.

Christmas day we were bombed and strafed and four men were wounded. M Company lost four men and a 50 caliber machine gun; no trace of them could be found after a direct hit by a 500 pound bomb. I received injury to my right knee but stayed on outpost. Lt. Ammat begged me to stay. We were relieved by the 117th during the counter attack. We marched in to Malmedy on January 13, 1945. My leg was better, I could walk but my knee was stiff. We were pinned down by machine gun fire most of the day and spent most of the night on patrol. On January 14th we followed the Amerleve River. There was some machine gun fire and planes dropping bombs. During the late afternoon we reached Borneau, where Sgt. Weiss was killed and several were wounded. Most of the night was spent in taking the town (this is another long story).

January 15, 1945 was the attack on Ligneuville. The squad sargent asked me to take his place as he said he knew that he would be killed that day. I was the first to get shot, in the right chest, and Sgt. McGennis was killed soon after. I ate snow and talked to the Lord about my injury. He assured me that I would be OK, and I felt no more pain. I was about to doze off when Platoon Sgt. Jay Akens took me by the shoulder to turn me over. He cried, and I begged him to get out of the line of fire. He moved on and was also wounded that day. Scotty, our medic, finally reached me, cut off my gear, and helped me to walk about a quarter mile to get out of the line of fire. He limped from a bullet through his foot, but he stayed until the battle was over.

At the field hospital my right lung was sewn up and pushed back into the hole where the bullet came out in my back. I was sent by train to Paris, France and 14 days later to the 140th General Hospital near South Hampton, England. While in the 140th my mail caught up with me. I had not heard from my wife and two children since I left the states in September. Then it was April. The war injuries improved, but then I had Hepatitis and received a medical discharge on July 12, 1945.

I returned home, cashed in savings bonds and bought a small coal mine. From 1945 till 1948 I operated three small mines, which closed because of no market.

Next I had a job with Nashville Coal Company, where I made seven underground openings in the strip pit. In 1952 I opened a mine near Union Town, Ky. for Nashville Coal. We produced 5,000 tons daily, which was belted from the mine to the Ohio River. That mine is still being operated as Ohio Number 11.

(Note: Dad left out the years of mining in Tennessee.)

I left the coal mines in 1959 with black lung and moved to Florida where I fished and hunted alligators for 10 years, getting plenty of fresh air and sunshine. Arthritis prompted me to move from the lake to higher ground in Sebring, Florida, in 1969. I bought a peat bog in 1972 and have been playing in the dirt ever since. My wife, Ola, oil painted while I fished. She is now in a nursing home, having had Alzheimer's disease since 1976. Our three children are all married with families.

At age 76 I try to stay active. I believe in the Bible and teach Sunday School in a small Baptist Church. The Lord sent me to the battlefield in Europe to draw me closer to him. It was an experience I will never forget.

I am a life member of the 30th Division Association. I went on battlefield tour with them in 1984 and visited the tank I had shot. I am also a life member of VBOB and toured with them in 1988, and made a life member of DAV.

I have had a good life. Enough bad to make me appreciate the good. Print what you like. Thank you.

Hubert H. Crowell

P.S. I am proud to be a part of the 30th Div.

2

SUCCESSFUL USE OF WOODEN ROOF BOLTS IN STONY POINT MINE, STONY POINT COAL CO., HOPKINS COUNTY, KY.

BY L. W. KELLY

*   *   *   *   *   *   *   *   *   Information Circular 7637

UNITED STATES DEPARTMENT OF THE INTERIOR
Oscar L. Chapman, Secretary
BUREAU OF MINES
J. J. Forbes, Director

Work on manuscript completed February 1952. The Bureau of Mines will welcome reprinting of this paper, provided the following footnote acknowledgment is made: "Reprinted from Bureau of Mines Information Circular 7637."

June 1952

SUCCESSFUL USE OF WOODEN ROOF BOLTS IN STONY POINT MINE, STONY POINT COAL CO., HOPKINS COUNTY, KY.

by

L. W. Kelly[1]

CONTENTS

TABLE

ILLUSTRATIONS

1/ Mining engineer, Accident Prevention and Health Division, Region VIII, Bureau of Mines, Vincennes, Ind.

Information Circular 7637

SUMMARY

The purpose of this circular is to show that, under the conditions prevailing in the Stony Point mine, wooden bolts were just as satisfactory as steel bolts or conventional timbering, with a reduction of approximately 80 percent in cost of material. This one fact alone is enough to justify an experiment with wood. This circular will show that production records have remained constant with both wooden and steel roof bolts.

INTRODUCTION

The successful use of steel roof bolts is now an accomplished fact in the coal industry, but the use of wooden bolts in place of steel is a rarity. The first experiment with wooden roof bolts was made in 1949 in the Rio Verde mine, Norton Coal Corp., Nortonville, Ky.[2] This experiment was successful; the company obtained excellent results, but operations in the mine were suspended before enough time had elapsed to prove the value of wooden roof bolts conclusively. It is obvious that, if wooden roof bolts could be used in place of steel bolts or conventional timbering methods, every mine operator would use wood, as the cost is only a fraction of the other two methods. The Stony Point experience has proved conclusively that, under certain conditions and with a certain type of roof, wooden roof bolts can be used successfully.

ACKNOWLEDGMENT

This circular was made possible by the generous and willing cooperation of E. E. Steff, general superintendent, and Hubert Crowell, superintendent, Stony Point Coal Co. The information and time generously given are gratefully acknowledged.

GENERAL INFORMATION

The Stony Point mine is in Hopkins County, Ky., approximately 6 miles southwest of Providence, Webster County, Ky. The mine was opened in 1949, and the use of roof bolts was begun a few months thereafter. It was opened by three drifts in the Kentucky No. 9 coal bed, which averages 60 inches in thickness. The maximum cover is about 120 feet. The fan is operated blowing; one drift is the intake airway, and the other two are returns. One return airway is used as the main belt entry and the other for transporting supplies into the mine and as a manway. The mine is trackless, and the coal is transported by shuttle cars and belt conveyors. All of the coal is undercut to a depth of 7 feet, loaded mechanically, and blasted with permissible

[2] Sterling S. Lanier, Jr., Wooden Pins for Mine Roof Control: Am. Min. Cong., Coal-Mine Modernization Year Book, 1950.

4826

- 1 -

explosives. The room-and-pillar method of mining is followed, and the pillars are not extracted. The entries are driven in sets of five, 14 feet wide on 45-foot centers. The rooms are driven 24 feet wide on 42-foot centers. In all, 129 men are employed; of this number, 118 work underground. The average daily production is 3,000 tons of coal.

CHARACTER OF ROOF AND TIMBERING METHODS

The roof in this mine changes radically from area to area, but a representative section is as follows: Immediately over the coal is a stratum of laminated, hard, black shale, which ranges from 8 to 36 inches in thickness. Above this is a stratum of sandy shale, which averages 6 inches in thickness; this is overlain by 60 inches or more of soft, gray, conglomerate shale known locally as the "kidney bed." As a general rule, the shale falls to the kidney bed, which in this mine forms the main roof (fig. 1).

When the mine was first opened, conventional timbering was used, consisting of 6-inch wooden crossbars or posts set on 5-foot centers. This method of timbering was used for a comparatively short time only.

HISTORY OF ROOF BOLTING

The Stony Point mine was opened late in 1949, and at first the roof was supported by means of conventional timbering - 6-inch wooden crossbars set on 4-foot centers in the entries and three rows of posts set on 5-foot centers in the rooms. In May 1950 it was decided to experiment with roof bolts, and the initial installation consisted of 1-inch, steel, wedge-type bolts in sets of three every 4 feet along the entry. The bolts were 3 feet long and spaced 2-5-5-2. Each bolt was secured by means of a steel plate 6 inches square by 3/8 inch thick. Meanwhile, the roof had changed, and the thickness of the shale lying on the coal ranged from 8 to 36 inches. Above this was about 6 inches of sandy shale and 60 inches of soft, gray shale known locally as the "kidney bed" (fig. 1). The original experiment was successful, and the use of timbers was gradually discontinued. In May 1951, approximately 100,000 steel roof bolts had been used, with no failures. There had been no accidents of any kind from falls of roof in the roof-bolted places, and about 40 tons of coal a shift was mined for each face man. A 12-man crew mined about 500 tons per shift.

In May 1951 studies were made of the material cost of roof bolting, with steel and with wooden bolts. A steel-bolt assembly, which included a 3-foot, 1-inch, wedge-type bolt, a 6-inch-square by 3/8-inch steel plate, and a hexagonal nut, cost approximately $1.00, while it was calculated that a 3-foot wooden bolt with two wooden wedges would cost about $0.20. As a result of the cost differential, it was decided to experiment with wooden bolts. The experimental period lasted about 1 month and was successful. As a result of the knowledge gained thereby, it was decided to use wooden roof bolts in rooms exclusively but to continue using steel bolts in the entries until the wooden bolts had received an extensive trial. This decision was made because the rooms

4826   - 2 -

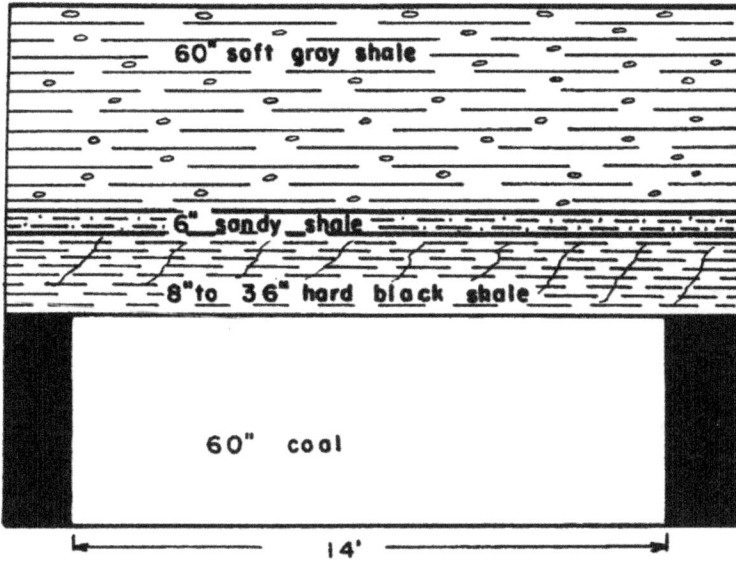

Figure 1. - Representative roof section, Stony Point mine.

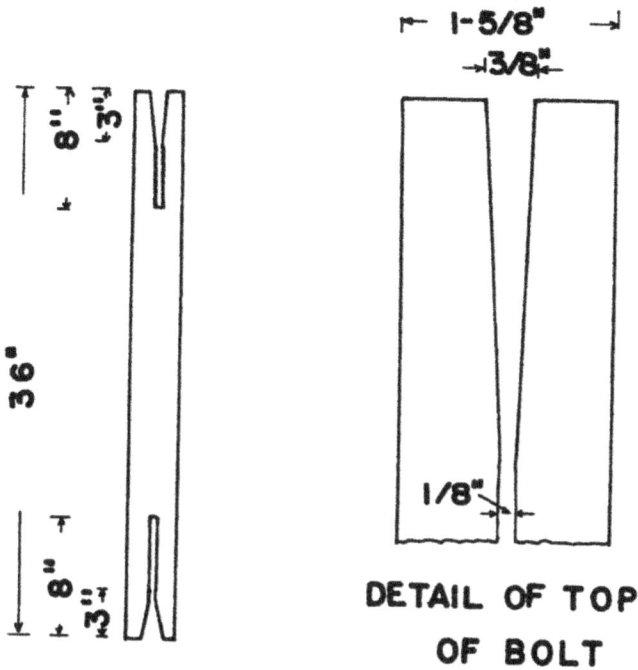

DETAIL OF TOP
OF BOLT

Figure 2. - Sketch of roof bolts used at Stony Point mine.

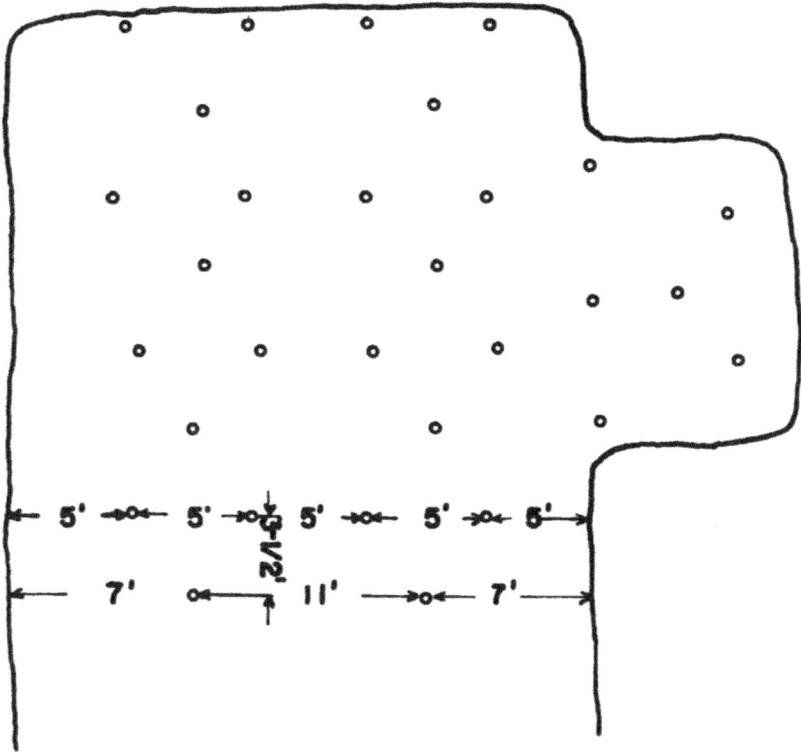

Figure 3. - Roof-bolt pattern at Stony Point mine.
Scale: 1 inch =6 feet.

were worked out in approximately 12 days, whereas the life of the entries might be several years.

EQUIPMENT

The bolts are made at the mine with a home-made doweling machine and a cut-off saw. The doweling machine consists of one rotating blade and rollers, set so that it will receive a piece of 2-inch-square wood 12 feet long and turn it down to 1-5/8 inches round. The 12-foot length is then cut to 3-foot lengths and a 1/8-inch slot, 8 inches long is cut in each end of the bolt with a cut-off saw. For 3 inches on each end of the bolt the 1/8-inch slot is cut out into a wedge shape which is 3/8 inch wide at the top (fig. 2). The material used is green hickory received at the mine in 2-inch-square by 12-foot lengths. One man can make 500 bolts complete in one shift. Two wedges, made of green hickory wood, 1 inch thick at the butt, 1-1/2 inches wide, and 8 inches long, are used with each bolt. The entire cost of a bolt, including labor and material, is less than $0.20.

To facilitate drilling for the roof bolts and also the face holes for blasting coal, a mobile, rubber-tired truck was constructed on which two drills were mounted. A Jeffrey coal drill is mounted on a post for drilling the horizontal coal holes in the face. A home-made hydraulic drill, raised or lowered by means of a small hydraulic jack, is also mounted on the truck for drilling the vertical roof-bolt holes. This drill has been equipped with the necessary fittings, so that it can be mounted on the cutter bar of a 10-RU mining machine in an emergency. Firthite, 1-3/4-inch, carbide, diamond-shaped bit, is used in conjunction with an auger. After experiments with other kinds and shapes of bits, these have proved most satisfactory.

A 10-horsepower motor drives the truck at an approximate speed of 2 miles an hour. Three hundred feet of No. 2 twin parallel trailing cable is used to supply power to the drive motor.

METHOD OF INSTALLATION

Ordinarily a flexible pattern of seven bolts for each 7-foot cut is used, whereby one four-bolt set is followed at an interval of 3-1/2 feet by a three-bolt set and so on, progressively (fig. 3). This pattern is followed when normal roof conditions prevail; but, if the roof becomes weaker additional bolts are used, and if it gets better than normal a three-bolt, then a two-bolt set is used. If the roof becomes exceptionally bad, posts are used in conjunction with the bolts.

The roof bolts are installed immediately after the loading machine leaves the face and before the mining machine enters. The three-bolt set is installed 3-1/2 feet in advance of the last four-bolt set, and the new four-bolt set is installed at the face of the room. In the crosscuts, which are short and narrow, a total of about six bolts is generally used. As a rule, a crew of two men does the drilling and installs the bolts for both the roof bolts and for blasting in the coal face; sometimes when the bolting and face drilling lags behind the mining

4826   - 3 -

cycle crew is increased to three men. The 1-3/4-inch roof holes are drilled first and the bolts installed; then the coal holes, which are also 1-3/4 inches in diameter, are drilled. Ordinarily all of the holes are drilled (seven roof bolts and five coal holes), and bolts are installed in a working place in 15 minutes. As a rule, about 100 roof bolts are installed in a shift. Inasmuch as the mine is operated in three shifts, approximately 300 bolts are installed daily.

The bolts are driven into the holes by sledge hammers. The procedure is as follows: The bolt, with the wedge in place in the upper end, is inserted into the hole and pounded in as far as possible, then the wedge in the outer end is driven home. No plates or blocks have been used with the bolts.

Although the primary responsibility for locating and installing the roof bolts is delegated to the drillers, it is the duty of the foreman of the section to inspect the roof and the bolts between each of the operations in the mining cycle.

In all, 33,910 wooden bolts have been installed; except for two failures, all have been successful.

To show the details of the results of using wooden roof bolts, table 1 is presented.

TABLE 1. - <u>Number of rooms and crosscuts, linear and square feet of roof supported, and number of wooden roof bolts used in Stony Point mine</u>

	No. of rooms and crosscuts	Length, ft.	No. of bolts	Linear ft. of roof supported	Square ft. of roof supported
	18	700	13,200	12,600	302,400
	10	500	4,700	5,000	120,000
	18	300	5,500	5,400	129,600
	12	600	7,400	7,400	177,600
	520	18	3,110	3,110	37,320
Total	58 rooms 520 crosscuts		33,910	39,560	766,920

RESULTS

Since the use of wooden roof bolts has been adopted in the Stony Point mine, 39,560 linear feet and 766,920 square feet of roof in rooms have been supported. There have been two failures in 9 months. The tonnage per face man has been approximately 40 tons a shift, the same as when steel roof bolts were used. When the difference in cost between wooden and steel bolts is considered, a saving of $27,128.00 in 9-months is indicated by the use of wooden roof bolts.

CONCLUSIONS

In view of the facts that this company has achieved virtually the same success with conventional timbering, steel roof bolts, and wooden roof bolts under the same roof conditions, and that this roof will not stand without some form of roof support, it may be desirable for operating people to make controlled studies of this method of support in localities where roof conditions appear to be similar. The fact that the cost of material is so much less than for other forms of roof support should make such experiments with wooden roof bolts attractive.

4826   - 4 -   Int. - Bu. of Mines, Pgh., Pa.

[3] National Reporting, 1941-1986: From Labor Conflicts to the Challenger Disaster, by Erika J. Fischer.

[4] A young goose

[5] Constructed 1905-1913, demolished in 1968 due to leakage problems.

[6] Wikipedia, History of Rhea County, Tennessee

[7] Cincinnati Southern Railway Website
http://cincinnatisouthernrailway.org/index.php

[8] Caves of Tennessee, by Thomas C. Bar Jr.

[9] Details of the accident are from the Interstate Commerce Commission Report No. 3547

[10] Wikipedia; Geology of Grassy Cove, Tennessee

[11] Obituary By Hubert Crowell NSS 13289

John Wallace NSS 6786, 1924-1994

John was a very giving person. He gave of his time, his thoughts and his experiences to all those with whom he came in contact. He was fair and thoughtful. When accepting others' share of travel expenses, John's favorite saying was, "I don't want to lose my amateur status," and would not accept a penny more than an equal share for gas. Even when flying his private plane to cave locations, he would only accept gas money. He was always willing to help escort scout and church groups we took caving.

John knew how to listen to others and encourage others to do more. We talked at length about cave mapping with the computer, and his encouragement helped to develop my cave mapping software. He invented an electronic lamp control that would allow caving for long periods, and published the details in the *NSS NEWS*. He enjoyed living and taught me how to take in more when traveling. We often took side trips to investigate points of interest along the way. Caving, wind sailing, trail hiking, flying, music, amateur radio, canoeing, motorcycle riding and hang gliding were but a few of John's interests.

Being tall has its advantage in caving. We traveled to many NSS Conventions together, and during one of our first, in Bloomington, Indiana in 1973, we decided to exit the spring entrance of Sullivan Cave. There was a drop of about three feet from a crawlway to the water level, and John, being the shortest in the group, was quite surprised when he went completely under the water and had to swim a short distance before he could stand. The rest of us were able to keep our heads dry.

John was a true explorer. In 1972 he discovered air blowing from behind a rock in Grassy Cove Saltpeter Cave and proceeded to dig open an unexplored passage to a large extension. Later discoveries led to what Gerald Moni, a well–known Tennessee caver, described as probably the best formation cave in the eastern United States. John also helped in the exploration of more than two miles of cave in Pumphouse Cave, Tennessee.

Dave Hughes tells the following story about John that shows his true nature. On returning to the vehicles after a wet caving trip, John was approached by a young college student who had participated in the adventure. In the hustle of loading the vehicles and leaving the area, this individual had become separated from his ride home, from his change of clothes and from his wallet. John took the novice under his wing, loaned him some dry clothes and began to drive him home. Along the way, John bought the student a good dinner and delivered him right to the doorstep of his dormitory. When the student asked John what could be done to pay him back for his kindness, John replied, "You've already paid me back. It's good to visit with a new and enthusiastic caver!"

I knew John for 23 years, and he will be remembered each time I go caving or plan a cave trip. His phone calls always began with, "Hubert, are you ready to go caving?" or, "Have you had too much sunlight?" My favorite picture of John is the one of him sitting in a crawlway in his usual relaxed position, legs crossed, hat back, just taking in the cave. Caving, for me, will never quite be the same without John.

NSS News, October 1994

[12] Tumbling Rock Cave is now owned and managed by the Southeastern Cave Conservancy. The cave is open for visitation primarily on weekends, from Saturday morning until Sunday Afternoon. Visit their website for information on access. http://www.scci.org/preserves/tumblingrock/tumblingrock.html

[13] From the article, "Where is Blowing Cave , Georgia?" by Thomas Lera www.speleophilately.com

[14] Gilmer County's Colorful History [Part 2] By Leslie Thomas, President, Gilmer County Historical Society and Vice–President, Trail of Tears Association, GA Chapter.

[15] The Milwaukee Journal – Aug 5, 1982

---

[16] CovenantKeepers.co.uk have one of the better sites about Ron Wyatt's claimed discovery of the Ark of the Covenant http://www.wyattarchaeology.com/ark.htm

[17] http://www.wyattmuseum.com/ron-wyatt.htm by Richard Rives.

[18] I started caving in 1971 and made my first trip into this great cave on July 23, 1972 with a Boy Scout Troop to the Signature Room. Mapping of the cave was well under way at that time and we occasionally ran into some of the mapping groups exiting the cave after a mapping trip. I started mapping and re–mapping parts of the cave in 1987 without access to the previously obtained survey data. When Marion Smith learned of my efforts, he provided me with copies of the old survey books. My thanks to Marion O. Smith for sharing Richard Schreiber's survey notes with me and some of the history of the early exploration of Pettyjohn Cave.

[19] James Mayer – Spatial and Temporal Variation of Groundwater Chemistry in Pettyjohns Cave, Northwest Georgia, USA. *Journal of Cave and Karst Studies 1999 issue.*

CPSIA information can be obtained at www.ICGtesting.com
Printed in the USA
LVOW02*0711230713

344136LV00001B/1/P